These words are dedicated to my daughter Michelle and step children Evelyn and Arnold and to my wife Patricia, who had to put up with me when things didn't go well, but never the less encouraged me every step of the way. To my brothers John and Tony and half-sister Pat. But above all to my sister Evelyn Smallwood without whose knowledge and love I would never have attempted this narrative, and last but by no means least, my brother Michael who was sent to Australia by my father and has not been heard of since.

Preface

Kingsley Fairbridge was born in 1885 in Grahamstown the son of a surveyor employed by the Cape government to survey routes between the towns and gold mining sites in what became Rhodesia. The family moved there in the early 1900's and settled in the Eastern highlands in a small town called Umtali.

During the years that followed, Kingsley accompanied his father on many trips throughout this primitive land. It was on one such journey, when exhausted from the summer heat he sought shelter beneath a tree on the side of a footpath. As he rested, he became aware of the vast emptiness around him that prompted a vision, which was to remain with him for the rest of his life. In his minds eye he visualised a transformed countryside inhabited by families of English farmers keen to tame the vast wilderness and bring order and stability to the population of warring tribesmen and at the same time become a means to counter the black population.

In 1903 Kingsley visited England for the first time His vision grew stronger at the sight of orphanages and workhouses filled to capacity with an estimated 60,000 young lives with no future..

Six years later, on the 19th of October he returned again to England and sought to address a meeting of the Colonial Club. Eloquently and with emotion he put forward his plans for child migration. He began his speech with the following words;

'The colonies have above all things, a superfluity of land for the landless men of Britain. Britain has a superfluity of men for the land less land, but whereas it is good land, then men Britain can spare are not always good men. The best immigrant farmers have been the aristocracy of English yeomen such as England can ill afford to lose. The Colonies should take something that England does not need.'

As a result of his appeal the Fairbridge Trust was formed and prior to the First World War, a small consignment of children pulled from homes around the country were sent to Australia, where with their labour they built rudimentary houses for themselves and were taught basic farming skills to prepare them for employment on Australian farms.

The Great War brought a halt to migration, but in the depression that followed the number of orphaned and homeless increased substantially resulting in a steady stream of children being dispatched to the Colonies again, mostly to Australia, since young colonies such as Rhodesia were considered far too primitive.

Meanwhile Kingsley and his wife continued working tirelessly in the search for funds to fulfill his dream, but sickened by reoccurring bouts of malaria, he died at the age of thirty nine. But his vision lived on and by 1939 over a thousand children had been re-located to the Fairbridge Farm School in Australia.

Child migration was brought to a halt yet again with the out break of the 2nd World war and when it was over, the occupancy of government and religious institutions had increased a hundred fold, despite the evacuation process in which thousands of children had been evacuated to the parts of the country largely unaffected by the bombing. These evacuees were, it could be argued the lucky ones, if one discounts the trauma of separation, for they would not be, as happened in many cases, the unwitting victims of forced migration.

With the end of the war child migration resumed at pace. The Catholic and Anglican churches, Barnados homes and other government bodies led by the Child Welfare department became involved and under pressure to fill the berths of ships bound for the colonies, the authorities in many cases dispensed with laws governing child migration; often in the confusion, without a parent's knowledge, siblings were separated in the drive to fill the migrant quotas and as a result many parents and off-spring were sentenced to a life of searching.

I was one such child that, like a swallow, left for warmer climes. It was a long migration that lasted more than thirty years, before with the help of others, bruised and battered and weary from a head wind that constantly threatened to drive me off course, I triumphed, and I returned to the land of my birth and discovered a family that hitherto had never been more than an infant dream.

The use of embellishments to help fill in the gaps in my memory has been constant. I do not often know what is memory or what was invention in the trivial detail of my narrative, therefore the things which appear logical and un-dramatic may well be fiction. But those which are violent and exciting and may well seem improbable and uninhibited fiction, I vouch are fact; in the interest of reality I have had to use words that are now considered improper even slanderous, for this I ask forgiveness.

Out of respect for the readers that look back with nostalgia on 'Gods own country', I have stuck with the colonial geographic names and places as I knew them before Rhodesia became Zimbabwe.

To avoid any embarrassment to the families of the characters that have helped shape my life I have concealed identities by using first names. While writing, my thoughts have never strayed far from the estimated 150,000 fellow migrant children who, through the dreams of humanitarians, were sent to populate the Empire.

Chapter One

Mighell Street 1942

On New Year's Day in 1939, God created heaven and earth—and me. I wasn't born in a stable though but in a hospital in Brighton, where my earliest memory is not of my mother and father, but of my Granddad, on whose shoulders I am sitting watching a long line of soldiers marching past in boots that beat a tattoo in my head and on the tar ahead of a stream of clattering rumbling tanks.

Granddad gripped my knees when I let go of his forehead to wave both hands at the procession as it passed the gate to his house, the same house as I recall where I sat on Grandma's lap beside a bay window watching cloud shadows float across the Downs. They were so close, and I can still remember the balmy scent of new-mown hay wafting in through the open window.

From my vantage point on her broad lap, I remember looking down on a child playing with the buckles on her shoes, and the warmth of her arms that held me so tight. I could feel the bones of her corset pressing against my back like the bars of a birdcage and remember her hands covered in swollen blue veins.

Father was conscripted in 1939 to a bomb disposal squad stationed locally, but he chose to make his visits home infrequent. When he did, it appeared it was to fulfil his conjugal rights by impregnating Mother. Those visits could be plotted by the births of myself, John, and Michael and corresponded to the Army service card that Rose, his third and last wife had in her possession.

After Father left for service to the Far East in early 1942,

Mother sold our house that my Dad had built to cover her debts. So we left Haywards Heath to live in a Council house on Mighell Street in the poor part of Brighton. It was a house that stood in the perpetual shadows of other tenement houses, on a street where sunlight seldom warmed the cobbled streets. My elder sister Evelyn remembers the grey-green moss that grew thick in the crevasses of slimy walls that towered above pavements littered with garbage thrown from the windows higher up, windows with panes that no longer reflected the passing clouds. The same moss grew greener in recessed doorways and beneath windowsills, and grew greener still in gutters where it flourished on sea mist and the stench of decay.

A few doors down from our house stood a Public House, complete with a swinging sign that only swung when the wind howled and blew down the street with such force that it broke the latch on our window that somebody fixed with a piece of wire. Further down, almost on the corner at the bottom of the street, was a greengrocer shop with boxes of sad-looking vegetables stacked outside. Inside the shop was a counter with jars of rationed sweets. Behind there were half-empty shelves and the shopkeeper who wore the same expression day after day.

The house we lived in was small, suitable for a young couple with no plans for a family. It consisted of one square-shaped room with a single entrance off the street. Behind the entrance door stood a small cupboard that Mother used to store a tea set and paraffin stove that was seldom lit.

It was the bed that filled the room, a large brass one with big shiny balls on the legs. This bed accommodated the entire family and at night we took turns sleeping next to Mother, three at the top and two at the bottom. When we met years later, my sister refuted this. She told me I had been 'Mother's pet' and while the rest had stuck to a rotational order I always slept next to Mother. Because she had a very sharp memory and was three years older than me, I believed her.

I remember so well the brass bed reflecting the light of the candle that stood on a little bedside table on the side Mother slept. There was a tall wardrobe against one wall that was always open, displaying Mother's dresses and shoes. Beside that stood a table littered with Mother's face things with a lopsided mirror that, if I stood on tiptoe, allowed me a glimpse of the reflection of a ceiling light hanging from a thread of twisted flex. I never knew that light to shine. Instead, we used the candle that only Mother was allowed to light, with matches with red heads that could be struck on almost anything.

A wooden framework along one wall was the only other piece of furniture. It was covered, most of the time, with drying clothes that were the source of creepy candlelit shadows that stuck to the wall at night. I even remember the hand towel that hung beneath the bedroom basin that stood on brackets beneath the single window with greasy curtains that stank of candle wax. There was no bathroom in the house so Mother laid a towel on the floor and washed us at the basin, except Evelyn who was old enough to wash herself.

We children spent most days begging from passers-by and patrons leaving or entering the public house, or shoppers at the entrance to the greengrocer's, while Mother, Evelyn said, plied her trade in the brass bed. It was a time for growing up, as day by day more and more characters slipped in and out of my world. Strangers that either left their imprints or drifted through my memory like faceless shadows that were without substance. Like the drunks who lurched through the doors of the public house and passed us on the street, spouting their frightening incoherent jargon, while mixing with tramps that begged from the beggars and the crotchety couple who refused to give and drove us instead from their door. Thank God for the prostitutes who lived in the rooms around us, loud, laughing cussing souls, friends of Mother who shared with her what little they had.

Then there was the old lady who wore funny hats with feathers; a figure of fun, a comic benefactor, who limped down the street with the umbrella she used as a walking stick; an animate figure who wore a ruffled blouse, a dead fox around her shoulders, and skirts that brushed the pavement... face wrinkled like screwed-up parchment and eyes that were brown reflective marbles, similar to the fox with the make-believe snarl that displayed snow-white fangs growing from a shiny muzzle that sprouted long polished whiskers and a bright pink tongue that was stuck to its palate.

One time I remember reaching up on tiptoe to touch the eye of the fox before pulling away in alarm at the unfamiliar feel of ice-cold glass. The old lady looked down and smiled, then reached for my hand and placed it on the fur. I ran my hand back and forth feeling the softness, let my hand stray to touch a paw before I pressed the pad to my nose and drew in the scent of perfume and animal.

The old lady's giving followed a pattern. As we watched and waited, firstly she would open her handbag and fish around inside for her purse. It seemed to take forever for her to find it and just as long again to find a coin. I can still hear the clunk of the coins inside the purse as she felt each in turn until satisfied. When she had retrieved the coin, she held it in front of her eyes and perused it for precious seconds. If the coin was the one she had imagined it to be, she would drop it into my sister's hand. If, however, the coin was not the chosen one, she would drop it back into the purse and start the whole process again. We learned to be patient, for often the coin was the difference between us eating or starving.

The war was never far off. Hardly a day or night went by that the sirens didn't sound that awful eerie whine that had us scuttling to the safety of the house and the brass bed. Often, we would be awakened by sirens that whined so loud the noise seemed to come from within the room itself and was a prelude to the drone of aircraft churning the night sky and the screams and shouts of frightened neighbours.

Mother broke the law one night by drawing the black blind aside, ever so slightly but just enough for Evelyn and me to look out upon sweeping beams of light that seemed to change the night to a fairyland. Orange streaks arced and dipped and popped into balls of fire that exploded into echoes of bangs that rattled the window before the explosions of the big guns along the seafront boomed forth a reply that rolled across the ceiling and down the walls to where we crouched. Then as the sounds died down, I remember hearing Mother's comforting voice and the cry of a baby before the sound of war stopped as suddenly as it had started, gurgling with a last bout of sporadic booms that came from far off, then ceased altogether.

The silence that followed each raid was such that every little sound in the room—a rustle of bedcovers, a cough, a whimper, even a breath—was as clear as church bells on a Sunday morning.

Evelyn, late one afternoon in August 1942...

"I was eight years old when Mother sent me to the greengrocer's. It was a day like any other when, with ration book and a sixpence grasped in my hand, I walked down the empty street. I hadn't gone far when out of the clouds swooped a plane, so low I could see the pilot in the cockpit. I waved at him as he passed over, blowing up dirt and stones. Suddenly I was frightened. I froze when I heard Mother screaming. I heard the plane again, loud, screeching. I looked up; it was coming back, twisting and turning. I saw something fall from its belly, there was a bang so loud the world burst into bright sunlight and my ears exploded in a cacophony of screams and shouts. Then silence as a wind blew me into Mother's arms. There were women everywhere around the bed, feeling, touching, kissing. I heard their voices ever so softly."

It came to pass that the pilot of the German plane had been among others on a raid to Hastings and in his haste to escape across the Channel, he had jettisoned a bomb that served to lighten his load thereby giving him more speed and a better chance of getting away. The bomb reduced to rubble a house in a street one away from Mighell Street.

I remember a day when my sister and I were begging among a small crowd that had collected around a dog lying in the gutter, its head on the pavement, mouth pulled back in a snarl. It was my first sight of death, though it didn't look dead because a wind was ruffling its fur, making it look alive. Curiosity drew me closer. I knelt and nervously touched the animal's nose and recoiled at the cold smoothness. That night I had a dream: a large brown rat crawled from a hole in the gutter next to the dog; it sat on its hind legs and began to rub its face with its forepaws; then it stopped rubbing and looked down the street; after a moment it stopped looking down the street and turned to face me, blood-red eyes staring into mine, before it wiped its face once more; suddenly it turned and scuttled away into the darkness. I woke up screaming. Somebody comforted me. I can't remember who.

Chapter Two

Mighell Street 1943

Early one morning—it must have been March 1943 for reasons that shall become apparent—I awoke to the sound of crying. It was so dark in the room I was unable to pinpoint the source of the sound. Was it Evelyn, I wondered, I called out to her, but she didn't answer and the sobbing ceased. I awoke yet again to the sound of a baby's muffled cry that was followed by a whisper that seemed to come from above. This time I kept silent and pretended to sleep as the whisperer struck a match to a candle.

Instantly, my mother was born in a mantle of brilliance! The flickering shadow on the wall endorsed her presence and flooded my senses with a memory that would last forever. I closed one eye and peeped through the other as my mother lifted her baby from the shadows and settled the infant in the crook of her arm and gave it her breast. For what seemed an eternity she was outlined in the candlelight. The forward tilt of her head caused her waves of black hair to fall forward and hide her face and the head of the nursing child.

I watched her lift the edge of the bed sheet and dab at her eyes. The action made me realise it was her I had heard sobbing. I watched her every move as she finished nursing Pat, then laid her down out of sight in the wicker basket beside the bed.

Her shoulders were shaking and she sobbed as she stole quietly from the bed and with her back to me moved to the basin. Candlelight lit up the wall and slipped past her nightgown, and in doing so outlined her figure in my subconscious mind and proved her existence.

In those few precious moments she had been made known to me, was now part of me. It was then she took me by the hand and led me to the basin fixed to the wall. I felt at my back her soft enveloping warmth. I felt her breath on my naked shoulders as she washed my hands and face.

I turned this way and that way in a futile attempt to see her eyes but was blinded by the waves of glimmering hair. I felt her hands on my skin, soft silky-smooth hands that hugged me to her thighs and her tummy's warmth. I breathed in and tasted her mother-smell, stared up at the curve of breast, fleetingly her chin, and the shadowed recesses of her nostrils, her lips, and the taste of tears as she kissed me.

It was as dawn broke that I heard the sound of engines turning into Mighell Street. It seemed like hours ago that Mother had washed and dressed us, prepared us for what was about to happen. We were lined up on the pavement outside the house. I remember clearly Evelyn stooping down and tying my shoelaces, which Mother must have forgotten to do.

Two vans, one white and one black, appeared and drew up on the kerb close to where we were standing. It wasn't long before two men in uniform alighted from the black van and joined up with two women in skirts from the white van. They stood and talked for a minute, then made their way towards us. The two in skirts passed by me and after a few words to my mother one of them removed the bundle from her arms and walked back to the white van. The other took my mother by the arm and led her to the uniformed men, who took her by each arm and steered her in the direction of the leading van. Up to then, the exercise had been carried out efficiently and with cold precision. I had no idea what was happening.

Suddenly, as she reached the van, Mother screamed, stumbled, and fell struggling to the ground. Her screams brought faces to the windows of the houses. Shouts of derision rained down on my mother's captors. I could hear her muffled cries inside the black van as one of the women bundled the four of us into the white van and it sped away.

Funnily enough I can't remember crying on the journey to Warren Farm, yet I can remember vividly an avenue of gnarled trees with petrified branches that reminded me of grasping hands and crooked fingers.

Maybe it was because in those last hours my world had matured at an alarming rate. Feelings of happiness and sadness from whatever source, once so easily absorbed and dissected before being cast into the melting pot of my childhood, had suddenly left me in a state of flux and under the spell of events that were too 'grown up' for me to understand.

Until then the deprivation and the sounds and sights of war had been so much a 'game', without physical pain, and had even carried the edge of excitement that often displaced fear in my heart. But now, what had happened in the past hours was hurting me. I was beginning to feel my mother's grief, missed her presence and the invulnerability of the house on Mighell Street. I was beginning to feel, with my brothers and sister, the fear of the unknown.

What price the future of a family? FOURTEEN POUNDS TWO AND SIXPENCE had been the sum of my mother's guilt. "Monies drawn from welfare for which she was not entitled," toned the accusing words of the prosecutor. War, rationing, and hunger were obviously not mitigating circumstances in the mind of the judge who sentenced her, and in his ignorance sentenced the children to a life apart.

Mother died the records say, of cervical cancer soon after the war ended in 1945. I can only surmise that her cancer was a result of her forced promiscuous lifestyle. In her young life (she was in her early thirties when she died), she had suffered seven pregnancies (the last child being born, and dying all within the last hours of her life). I'm convinced that it was poverty and the degradation of having to prostitute herself to feed and clothe us that were the reasons for her untimely death.

Whatever is said, I know she suffered more than most yet nobody seemed to care. There is nothing to say she even existed other than a mention on a few officious forms and a few lines in the inside pages of the local 'rag' about the trial. No photos, no letters, not even a gravestone to mark an unknown grave. But I remember her even if others don't.

I remember her, every day of my life. She is with me whenever I close my eyes. When I see suffering, I see her, but never mind, I will always love her.

Chapter Three

Warren Farm 1943 – 1945

"Warren Farm school's a jolly nice school, but I don't think it's true.
For once you get inside it, you'll have some work to do.
Up and down the corridors with a dustpan in your hand,
As long as you're in Warren Farm, you'll never be a man.
So beware boys, the matron's coming, she likes to see the dormitory,
Nice and clean, so do I, have a try, how'd you like to be me,
stuck in a bed with three?
A lump of duff and that's enough, carbolic for tea.
Our patients don't get off enough; our patients don't get off enough,
Six o'clock in the morning you'll hear the matron shout.
Get out of bed! Get out of bed! Before you get a clout."

Warren Farm was built in 1853, the brainchild of a Board of Guardians who entertained the idea of erecting an Industrial School at Woodingdean on the outskirts of Brighton in the county of Sussex. It was ostensibly built for the purpose of training children of the poor to the 'habits of industry', thereby relieving them of the bane of 'pauperism'.

The school was completed in 1862 at a cost of approximately £17,750 (Pounds), which included the land and the cost of a road from the village to the school. The school was self-contained with accommodation for 600 boys and girls, classrooms, a sanatorium and infirmary attached to a facility for boarding and treating the mentally handicapped. In August of the same year, the school was opened to 77 boys and 65 girls who marched into the home, led by a village band and a host of dignitaries.

Up to and until the end of the Second World War thousands of children would have passed through her doors and found life daunting, made miserable by the cold unattractive décor, the stone flag floors and the brick paved playground. Most of all those who lived within, and the locals who lived without, will remember the high flintstone walls embedded with shards of glass—a forbidding structure indeed that surrounded the complex and one which no doubt would have left the locals with the question: was it to keep us out or them in?

The archaic Victorian unwritten law regarding siblings in care dictated that siblings should be separated as soon as possible after entering an orphanage. This would ensure the children were manageable and avoid the homesickness that was sure to happen if children of the same family remained together.

And so it was, we were separated on the morning we arrived at the large wooden door in the arched entrance to the home and one by one, we were led inside and taken to different areas in the home. Evelyn was taken to the Girls section, and John and Michael to the Infants dormitories on the ground floor. I was led to the Boys dormitories on the first floor where I was deloused in a huge bath with a white liquid that stung like fire. I screamed and screamed so much that the matron holding me still had to resort to shouting and violence to subdue me.

I clearly remember looking over her shoulder as she knelt in front of me with a towel, at my pile of clothes that Mother had dressed me in that morning. I left the bathroom wearing black knee-length shorts, white shirt, and black hobnailed boots. I now looked no different from the hundreds of other boys that lived in Warren Farm, for we all wore identical clothes, slept in identical beds beneath identical blankets, ate identical food, and likely shared identical thoughts.

With time I grew to forget about my siblings, but at times, especially in winter when the ice-cold sheets crackled with my movement and numbed my dreams, and while the boy in the bed next to me sobbed and pissed frozen piss, I dreamed of Mother while we whispered to each other.

There were two paintings at Warren Farm I remember so well, which portrayed only too well the hypocrisy of life.

One hung in a prominent spot in the dining-room and depicted a man in flowing white robes wearing a crown of thorns standing before a roughly hewn door lit up by the light of a lamp he carried in one hand. With the other hand, he was rapping at the door, his head tilted sideways as if listening to what was going on behind it. The lamplight lit up a deep-red heart painted on one of the door panels and the mans bearded face. Drops of blood seeped from the crown of thorns over his forehead and into his grey side-whiskers. But it was the eyes that stick out in my memory—they looked down on whoever it was that knelt on the floor begging forgiveness for wetting the bed. On the frame, I still remember a brass plaque that bore the artist's name and the title of the picture: Knocking at the Door.

The other picture hung in a prominent spot in the stairwell at the top of the stairs leading to the boys' dormitories. I'm not sure if it was painted by the same artist but it too portrayed the same man but without a crown of thorns. This time he was captured sitting on a rock looking out to sea, pointing to where a flock of seagulls were perched on rocks, while others wheeled in a cloudy sky above. He was surrounded by a group of men and women who appeared to be listening to him and he had his arms around two children who knelt at his side. Above a brass plaque read: Suffer the Children.

It was the playground, which I remember as being the

'hub of life'. It was surrounded on two sides by buildings and on the remaining side by a stretch of railings erected after a section of the surrounding wall had collapsed in a storm. It was a fence with struts that were wide enough, without letting a body through, to allow the inmates an unsurpassed view of the countryside. A view of fields and rolling hills, and a valley that led a path to a wedge of sea that in summer stood out bluer than the sky and in winter disappeared in a grey haze.

There was so much to see in that little stretch of heaven beyond the railings— whether it was grazing sheep with young at foot, gambolling free knee-deep in grass and clover, or flocks of seagulls and plovers wheeling and dipping behind a horse and plough. I was with my friend one time, when we spotted a hawk fall like a feathered stone into the field and rise with something wriggling in its talons before it flew away and disappeared into a cloud shadow floating across the field. Rabbits there were aplenty, and so tame they ignored our presence at the fence as they played hide-'n-go-seek among the clumps of cowslip that grew up against the railings.

Chapter Four

Irene and the Potato Harvest

Irene and I met in the playground. That's where it had to be, because that was the only place where girls and boys came together. Irene was older than me by at least five years that would have made her twelve. She was tall and slim with long black hair like my mother.

Perhaps it was this that attracted me to her, that and her kind gentle nature. I think she must have been assigned to the younger children as a carer, to protect them from playground predators who preyed on anyone who possessed something they wanted. They were seen one day coaxing some poor bugger into the coal shed. (I hated that coal shed because it was dark inside and said to be haunted which made it a scary business when it was my turn to help fill the coalscuttle). Word got around the poor bugger had been 'bum fucked' but nobody said anything. There was no greater sin than 'snitching' in the eyes of the inane minority given more than a measure of ignorant cruelty inherent in the young, growing up in a dog-eat-dog environment they didn't hesitate to exact retribution against the 'saints' among us who had the courage to report such incidents.

And there were amongst us a few who stood out, being 'different' from the rest, the cripples for example, the hare-lipped (of which there were quite a few), even the bed-wetters and those who were either excessively thin or fat—all were fair game to the kids from the 'rough side'.

There was one child who stands out in my memory above all else. Billy Budd was his name. We were told he was the sole survivor after his house was demolished in an air raid on London, the shock of which had left him stunned, speechless and devoid of all hair even to the eyebrows and with an inexplicable hunger. To appease this we, and I shamefully admit this included me, took great delight in feeding the unfortunate lad on an added diet of scraps from the dustbin, an assortment of vegetation and last but not least an assortment of earthworms that could be found aplenty in a garden adjacent to the flintstone wall.

We all had our childish cruel streaks I guess, but then cruelty was after all a way of life at Warren Farm when one considers the cruelty that went with the punishment for bed-wetters. Before washing their sheets, they were forced to stand against a wall with the same sheets draped over their heads as an acknowledgement of their guilt.

As time went by, Irene and I became inseparable. She shared her knowledge of nature with me. She could name any bird that frequented the countryside around Warren Farm, knew the names of the trees too and all the flowers and crops that grew in the fields.

She was a landowner's daughter who on the death of her mother before the war, refused to live with relatives, but chose instead to live with her father.

"He was never the same after the war began," she told me while we were sitting, backs against the flintstone wall seeking the warm rays of the sun. "He would listen to the radio all day and shake his head. One day I went with him to the recruiting offices in Brighton. He seemed to be in there for ages while I sat outside and waited. We did not speak again that day or the day after until the following morning when he told me to pack my suitcase and brought me to Warren Farm."

The farm was left in the care of a manager who posted on her father's letters written from wherever he was at the time. They were kept in a box beneath her bed in the dormitory and every so often she would carry the box, like treasure, clasped to her chest to the playground where we would sit together and sift through her memories.

There were times, strange as it may seem, when Warren Farm was an exciting place to live in. Take for instance the potato harvest, that might have gone unnoticed had it not been for Irene who having witnessed it all before knew all there was to know about it. On the day before the harvest commenced and before the sun went down, she took me by the hand and led me to the railings.

The playground was empty except for a few children playing their last games before supper. They were too engrossed in what they were doing to share with us the sight of a pair of magnificent Clydesdale horses, pulling what Irene pointed out was a 'spinner' with tines raised gleaming in the rays of the setting sun. I watched in wonder as the labourer released the horses from their traces and dodged the huge feathered hooves as the animals milled around, glad to be free.

I looked over my shoulder as we left the playground for a last look at the man bent over the machine, preparing it for daybreak.

We were back that morning, hands frozen and bodies laced to the railings. There were scores of us to watch and cheer the arrival of the horses led by two men. One had a whip wound around his body the butt tucked into his belt, and the other, the younger of the two, carried a bag slung over his shoulder.

While one in-spanned (Afrikaans: term for a yoke or harness) the horses, the other moved around the spinner with rag and spanner, crouched hunchbacked, rubbing and tapping, before straightening his back to light a pipe and lean back against the machine, his face hidden behind a cloud of grey smoke. He was joined by his companion who too pulled out a pipe, lit up and added to the smoke that wafted off in the direction of voices and shrill laughter that soon materialised into the forms of a bevy of girls. They were uniformly dressed in drab trousers and jerkins, gumboots and headscarves and carried an assortment of forks, bundles of sacks and baskets.

As they congregated around the two men, their loud voices were punctuated with peals of laughter. The younger of the two men sought to escape the advances of one of the girls as she chased him round and round, pinning him in the end against the machine. Encouraged by the jokes and ribald laughter she kissed him, an act that brought the crowd behind the railings to life with catcalls and whistles.

A cheer rose up when at long last the driver raised his whip and sent its tip snaking forward to 'tickle' the flanks of the horses. With a jolt the spinner lurched forward, tines flashing, as the driver raised his voice and I heard him calling to the horses in the language of the ploughman.

Before the horses reached the far side of the field, the land girls began filling sacks with potatoes, then stacked them in pairs, leaning them one against the other in long rows. In the wake of the toiling girls, others raked up the withered vines into heaps to dry out the dew.

As the day wore on the men and women stopped now and then and sprawled out in the sun to eat, chat, and smoke. Sometimes the younger man fed the horses from the bag he carried with him. The field was littered by now with row upon row of bags and heaps of vines. A horse-drawn cart arrived with still more girls who loaded the sacks onto the cart, leaving behind the heaps of vines which were then set alight.

It was midday before the field was reaped and the spinner and horses passed close to the railings on the way back from where they had come, leaving the girls still busy filling bags and raking up chaff. It was then that two or three girls broke away from the group and began raking vines into a huge heap close to the railings. This brought a cheer from those amongst us who had witnessed the previous harvest, and a build-up of curious excitement in the breasts of those who like me, were witnessing the event for the first time.

The screams and shouts of excitement drowned out the roar and crackle of the fire as it took hold, spouting out flames that leaped higher than the fence and delivered a blanket of warmth through the railings. The girls piled on more and more chaff until the playground was smothered in smoke and grey figures that danced around in the heat waves and floating ash.

As the flames died down we watched the girls drag a sack to the fire's edge and toss potatoes into the burning embers. Then the feast began. As fast as the girls handed the piping-hot potatoes through the railings, as speedily were they consumed. There wasn't a single child that day who didn't eat its fill of the white, fluffy, chestnutty spuds. Irene and I ate and ate until we could eat no more, then with bellies full we made our way across a playground that was covered in a carpet of slippery black skins to our spot beneath the flintstone wall to digest and discuss what we had witnessed.

Chapter Five

The Madman

The great feast had long gone and rain, sunshine and wind had washed, dried and blown away all signs of the potato harvest. The field had been ploughed so that all that was left were the bare furrows and flocks of birds that Irene and I watched swarm continually in search of anything that moved or lay on the rich brown earth. It was a balmy afternoon considering the time of year and the playground was packed with children, either sitting around in groups chatting, or playing less strenuous games like hopscotch and marbles.

Suddenly the peace was broken by the sound of a siren and the whine of an aircraft, and there it came, over the brow of the hill. "So low," Irene said, "that I could see its shadow on the grass beneath." There was instant pandemonium in the playground as the plane cleared the stone wall and rose sharply in a steep climb, shrieking and blowing up clouds of exhaust and dust.

Children were everywhere, screaming in terror, falling and crawling, not knowing what to do or where to go. "Above the cries" she said, "I could hear the voice of Matron shouting out garbled orders as another plane screamed over a little higher in pursuit of the first.

"I stopped for a second and looked up in time to see it twisting and turning heading for the sea. All around me were the youngest, in shock, wandering around. You were sitting down crying," she said, "so I grabbed your hand and another and another till my hands and arms were filled with children, one so small I had to carry her and I ran dragging you all to the shelter. When I reached the shelter I pushed you all in one by one. You were the last."

I hesitated at the top of the steps. There were others with screaming voices and flailing arms that urged me in. Behind me I felt Irene's hands pushing, before I slipped and fell down the stairs and into the sea of faces... there was a flash of light, pain, then darkness.

I woke up in a bed in a ward in the infirmary. My head from above the eyebrows to the crown was wrapped in a bandage stained with blood. There were four beds in the ward. In the bed opposite mine lay a man. I could tell that he was a man because his head was on the pillow, while his feet reached the bottom of the bedstead.

He was half-sitting in a nest of pillows that raised his shoulders like a pair of wings that cradled in the formed apex what looked like the thrusting bald head of a roosting vulture... feral eyes staring into mine...

I remember wincing against the pain of light, raised a hand to touch the source of pain through the restricting bandage... felt with alarm the unfamiliar roughness and called out again and again.

My cries drew the attention of a nurse who appeared like a ghost dressed in white headgear, a white blouse and light-blue skirt. She leaned over and whispered unintelligible words. At her touch I struggled to sit up but she held me down against the pillows with both hands and called out to another nurse, who arrived carrying pills in a small transparent cup and a flask of water. I swallowed the pills and lay back, quietly enclosed in the arms of the nurse... the last thing I remember then was the eyes of the patient and the light above his head.

I don't know if it was the same day or another that I woke up and a nurse appeared in a circle of light. She sat down on the side of the patient's bed and fed him like a child. She caught his attention with whispers while she dragged a napkin beneath his chin to catch the dribbles of food and spittle, then held the napkin beneath his lips to catch drops of milk that fell from the spout of the cup. When he had finished she wiped his mouth and settled him back amongst the pillows.

Curiously, I watched as she straightened the bed covers and switched on the dull night light above his bed before she glided to a window to lower the blackout blind. I remember following her every move as she leaned over me and switched on the nightlight. I can still hear the rasp of her stockings and the swish of her skirt, the click of the latch as she closed the ward door.

I woke up to a noise, perhaps it was a cough, I'm not sure. It was dark except for the dull arc of light above each bed. At first only the face of the man was visible to me, then as my eyes habituated, the beam of light extended to the bottom of the bed, highlighting the complete form of the body beneath the blankets. For what seemed an eternity in the silence, the patient remained motionless, until without any preordained signal he opened his eyes. Slowly, like a corpse rising from the grave, he lifted himself onto his elbows then slowly pulled the covers aside with one hand, revealing his body clad in a white nightshirt that had risen above his waist, exposing his navel and genitals. There was movement in the shadow made by the light, as he extended his legs over the side of the bed and then eased forward to stand on his feet, the nightshirt falling to cover his exposed loins. He half-turned to face the foot of the bed, stopped moving for a second or two, his eyes focused on me, then shuffled forward. His breathing was loud and erratic. It crackled deep from within as he seemed to breathe simultaneously through nose and mouth. The light above the bed highlighted his features, the gleaming eyes and amber pupils. He moved closer to my bed, leaned over me, then raised his arms, fists clenched...

The sound of his breathing permeated my world... A fist

smashed into my cheek before I was fully awake. I didn't feel the pain of the blow at first. It was more the sound of his breathing that forced the scream from me, a scream that was cut short by another blow that as I turned away caught me on my forehead. Then I felt pain, intense pain as the stitches split... the terrifying taste and smell of blood.

The more I screamed the more the blows rained down like hail. My cries for mercy seemed to have some effect... I became aware, even through the panic and fear, that each time I begged and pleaded rather than screamed the assault seemed to lessen, so I crawled beneath the covers and heard from afar the sounds of the beast. With this blessed relief my bowels and bladder responded by opening unbidden, releasing a wave of shit and piss that bathed my limbs in warmth and seemingly calmed the beast's basic instincts, for almost immediately through the blankets I heard the sound of his breathing gradually recede as he moved away.

I lay under the cover of the blankets and waited. My mind was beginning to clear but terror was partially replaced by the thought of the punishment that awaited me in the morning when it was discovered I had committed the unpardonable sin of messing my bed.

It was this that motivated me to leave the bed and crawl on hands and knees around the foot in the shadows, avoiding the light, to the small cupboard beside my bed. Stealthily I retrieved a picture-book from on top of the cupboard then carefully, so as to avoid drawing the attention of the monster by the sound of tearing paper, I removed the pages. In a frenzy, I scooped up the excrement and filled each page, screwing up each end to avoid spillage, then crawled across to the window and placed each package in a line on the sill. It was a long, forbidding task, fuelled by the terrifying prospect that at any time the beast might awaken... there was still one thing left to do and that was to hide the evidence of my sins. As soundlessly as possible I rolled up my soiled nightshirt and sheets and hid them under the bed to hide the evidence.

It was at this very moment that the enormity of what had transpired left me trembling on the knife-edge of despair... I felt so helpless and wretched that I sank to the floor beside the bed and wept.

How long I sat there I don't know. What thoughts spun through my infantile brain I have been spared of, or even what prompted me to do what I did next. Perhaps it was some survival instinct that encouraged me to crawl across the floor on hands and knees to the door. On reaching it, still on my knees, I reached up for the door handle but it was just out of reach. Ever so slowly I rose to my feet and gripped the handle.

I remember turning the doorknob ever so slowly, trembling and shaking, in fear of waking the beast. I turned to look at him, but I didn't know if the eyes were open or shut because all I could make out were the shadowed sockets.

Holding my breath I turned the knob and pulled but nothing happened. I pushed but still the door remained fast. I pulled and pushed, sobbing in frustration. I was tempted to scream and bang on the door but I was fearful of the beast in the shadows. Thwarted, I sank to my knees and closed my eyes...

I came to know that it was common practice to lock the door of the ward. The infirmary was, I learned, part of the mentally-ill section of Warren Farm and the practice of locking the door was designed to keep mental patients from straying.

Why I was placed in that ward, with what the staff must have known was a deranged patient, nobody will ever know. An oversight perhaps, commensurate with the times? But what took place that terrible night, no one could ever imagine. The actions I took to defend myself against the recriminations of the staff—that I was sure would come about when it was found I had messed my bed—would appear bizarre to anybody that has not had to face the dire consequences and the humiliation of praying for forgiveness for what was considered a crime by the staff at Warren Farm.

Chapter Six

In the Arms of an Angel

I lay on the housemother's bed. The bandage had been removed and a piece of lint and plaster covered the healing gash on my left temple. I was dressed in a snow-white nightshirt and the sheets on the bed carried the faint scent of perfume. My eyes were centred on two dolls seated on top of a wardrobe, either side of a pretty mirror in a pink frame that was tilted down to catch my reflection on its smooth surface.

I waved a skinny arm at my 'twin', at the same time raising my nightgown to my waist inspecting my tiny penis. I was holding the slip of skin between finger and thumb when the door opened. Startled, I dropped the hem of my nightshirt! Unperturbed and smiling, she crossed the floor to my bedside, sat down and took me in her arms. We cuddled for a moment, then she licked her lips and raised my nightshirt and trained her tongue down, pressing her mouth against the pulse at the base of my throat, moved lower and circled my flat little nipples with her tongue, then lower still to my navel. She tickled the tiny indent with the tip of her tongue and mewed like a kitten as she kissed the silky soft skin at my groin.

She was kind and loving and wore her rich red hair in a bun. I loved the way she released her hair, exposing in doing so the lick in her armpit. I was mesmerised by the way her hair fell to her shoulders and sprung forward in red waves to hide her profile each time she leaned across me to tilt the mirror.

She stood beside the bed and turned to face the mirror. I was lying nude, on my side, torso raised on a supporting elbow. From this position I had a clear view of her front in the mirror. The glass reflected her clothed body from her neck to her upper thighs. She turned her head in my direction and smiled while beginning to undress. She stared at me intently as she removed her clothes, one piece after another—buttons undone, hooks unhooked, the dress, the shoes, the underwear, the stockings. Finally naked, she turned her head to the mirror, and I watched her hands fondling her breasts. I took in the sprinkling of freckles running from above her breasts down to the nipples and, lower still, a dusting of mottled spots on her smooth white belly that led down and disappeared into a frighteningly thick red fleece then reappeared, lower still, on the broad expanse of her snow-white thighs.

She turned towards me, pushed me gently on my back and climbed onto the bed to face me. My legs were lost between her thighs. She rose onto her knees and fondled herself through her thick pubic matt. Still fondling her groin, she stooped from the waist and took my penis between her lips. She lost it, searched, found it and took the penis once more between her lips. I was frightened by the sounds she was making, the foreign smells. I pulled back at the pain and pleasure I felt from her manipulating hand that blurred as she worked my penis. I cried out, she smothered the sound with her lips, mothered me with her taste and smell, screamed, then shuddered and fell away to lie beside me. She continued fondling my penis as her trembling receded and her breathing returned to normal.

I lay at her back with my left arm resting on her upper torso, one hand on her breast. My face was burrowed into 'my mother's' red hair. My breathing stirred the red locks on her shoulder. I pursed my lips and blew a lock of hair to one side revealing freckles on her white skin.

The time I spent with her was far too short. I experienced love in all its forms and at a time when affection in any form was sorely missed. Sex didn't enter the equation; she simply made me feel wanted. Perhaps, self-consciously, I was missing my mother and she was taking her place.

Chapter Seven

The End of the War and a New Beginning

1946 – 1947

Away from the throng of laughing, playing bodies I sat in the sunshine with Irene, our backs against the flintstone wall, lungs inhaling from deep in the diaphragm as she had taught me to do, so better to appreciate the subtle scents of pasture and clover borne on a gentle breeze that rose above the wall.

It was so pleasant to close my eyes and picture in my mind's eye what lay beyond. The glorious green canvas that, as Irene pointed out to me, was at the beginning of time encumbered with gently swelling hills raised and leavened by the seasons into smooth green protuberances, and lifted to the heavens by an unseen power to support the weight of a sky littered with rolling clouds that left their shadows on the hills.

Irene was wearing a flowered dress that day, with buttons down the front. She sat with her head bent forward, profile hidden by coils of her coal black hair. In her hands I could see a framed photograph that she handed to me and inched closer, our bodies touching.

The photograph, I will always remember, depicted a seated soldier wearing a tunic buttoned from waist to throat. A beret clung to his head at a steep angle hiding one ear in a fold while leaving the other with a clearly visible tuft of hair sticking out comically from behind it. A splendid badge was pinned to the front of the beret and seemed to glow on the dull matt surface enhancing the subject's smile.

"It's your Dad isn't it?" I asked, handing back the photograph.

"Yes." she replied and thought for a moment." I wonder

what he is doing right now."

"Where is he?" I asked.

"His last letter was posted in Italy."

"Where's that?"

"It must be a long way away. It's a long time since his last letter."

"When do you think he'll be back, Irene?"

"Soon, I hope. There's talk the war may soon be over."

We stopped talking for a while and just sat, looking over to where a group of children were pointing excitedly through the railings at two horses galloping down a hill, manes streaming and clods of earth and grass flying from their hooves. We watched until they disappeared into the valley. I felt Irene, in a show of emotion, take my hand in hers as she turned to face me.

"Where's your dad George?"

"I don't know. He never writes. Maybe he's dead."

"And your Mum?"

"I don't know. Maybe she's dead too."

"Do you remember your Mum and Dad?"

"No."

"Do you have any brothers or sisters?"

"I have a sister called Evelyn with hair the colour of yours."

"Where is she?"

"I don't know," I said, rising to my feet. "We came to Warren Farm together, but I don't see her anymore."

August 1946. It was a year since the war had ended. Much had changed at Warren Farm. At last we were allowed to set foot outside the flintstone walls. There was nothing to stop me now from venturing out into places that I once looked upon as an inaccessible dream world.

Hardly a day went by that Irene and I would not have been seen, baskets in hand, scouring the pastures, hedgerows and woods for blackberries, wild strawberries, crab apples and mushrooms. And to add to the change, I and a handful of boys were chosen to sing with the permanent choir of a small church called St. Wulfrans in the village of Ovingdean. It was a small, quaint church built in the 1600s, and barely a mile away as the crow flies from the home.

The pathway to the church wound its way through fields of crops and pastures that waved and rustled in the wind as if to hide the swaying, dancing faces of poppies that played hide-and-seek with us as we passed by between two green hills that formed Happy Valley. Then on across pastures cropped short by sheep and cows, and on over a style that bridged a stone wall that separated a tilled land swarming with butterflies that fluttered in clumsy flight right up to the lychgate.

It was here we would catch our breaths after a journey that was seldom taken at a walk but more at a skipping run until we reached the gate. From then on, it was at a more solemn pace that we passed under the wooden archway, past the alms box set in stone and on to skirt the gravestones that had leaned over through time, or were bowed under the weight of cherubs and angels, to stand at last before the solid arched door that swung on hinges forged centuries before, the vicar said, in the blacksmith's shop in the village.

How well I remember that beautiful timeless building and the peace and tranquillity that dwelt inside. The stained glass window above the altar shone its light on those who knelt at the feet of the crucifix. Profiled forms caught in the flickering flames of a hundred candles, souls embalmed in the transcendental tone of the ancient organ that stands to this day on the balcony that juts out over the congregation.

Never to be forgotten were the decorations at Christmas; the bitter cold outside, the warmth inside from the breathing of a congregation packed so tightly together that some folk stood or knelt in the aisles. They shared hymn books, head to head with strangers who, like we choirboys resplendent in our red cassocks, sang with such gusto that the old church trembled.

The Harvest Thanksgiving service was no less memorable, a little quieter perhaps, but no less spectacular visually, with sheaves of wheat and other grain crops stacked in corners and against the lectern. Legumes lined up in contrasting shapes and sizes filling the windowsills with colour. There was even a sheep tethered to its owner in the front pew, and here and there were willow cages that contained chickens and ducks. The cages were decorated with flowers and randomly placed where they could be seen but not touched. Everywhere one looked were bunches of flowers that not only added a blaze of colour but filled the old church with scents of the countryside.

Chapter Eight

The Hospital

For years I had walked on the sides of my feet. Nobody had noticed, not even me, until one day someone did notice and I found myself back in the infirmary sitting on the side of the bed I had occupied two years before.

The ward was as I remembered it except the air raid blinds and the bars that had once covered the windows had since been removed making the room appear lighter and brighter, a change that helped suppress but did not entirely eradicate the memories.

I was feeling uncomfortable and was ready to leave when the doctor walked in and put my mind at rest.

Under his watchful eyes I removed my boots and placed my feet in his lap. He stared at my feet for some time, pulled and prodded, got me to walk across the room and back, then he sat me down and retrieved my boots from beside the bed. I watched him press and prod at the areas where my feet and toes had left bulbous swellings in the constricting leather.

He carefully measured the boot soles against the bottom of my feet. He placed my feet once more in his lap and ran his fingers along the hard skin on the outside edges and the sensitive flesh on the soles before he removed my feet from his lap and rose to his feet.

The doctor left the ward with my boots. I could hear his voice in the passage raised in anger and it wasn't long before he returned with a wheelchair.

The following morning I found myself in a bed in a ward in hospital, staring at the ceiling. A ward so different from the one at Warren Farm for it was filled with many beds and was busy with the constant passage of nurses and patients dressed in striped dressing gowns.

It was night time on the same day and the ward was in darkness except for the dull light above the bed of a patient being administered to by the figure of a night nurse. I was awake when there appeared through the door at the end of the ward a bed on wheels and two nurses. One nurse pushed the bed while the other, with torch in hand, steered the bed along the aisle between the rows of beds.

I gave a start and pulled back in alarm against the pillows as I felt the arms of the nurse encircle my shoulders and lift me into a sitting position.

"Where am I going?" I cried out in alarm, at the same time struggling against the arms that held me.

"You are going home," said a voice from the dark.

"Oh thank you," I said in relief as the nurses slid me onto the bed.

The bed bumped through the doors and out into the brightly lit passage. I lay back, head in my hands, contented and secure with the thought that I was on my way home. I even found time to amuse myself by counting the ceiling lights as they appeared above my feet then disappeared behind me. Appeared, then disappeared. Appeared then disappeared, in sync it seemed, with the sound of the bed's wheels kissing the linoleum floor.

All of a sudden, the bed stopped and without warning turned sharply and nosed through a door that swung shut behind me.

I looked up apprehensively at a ceiling dotted with lights surrounded by one huge light that shone down on a bed without covers and at the same time illuminated ghostly white figures without mouths but with eyes that stared out from beneath hairless skulls.

In silence, I was lifted from the bed with wheels and placed on the narrow bed beneath the dazzling light. Apprehension swiftly turned to fear, then to screams when a chrome mask was placed over my mouth and I inhaled and tasted the vile aroma of chloroform.

Twice the mask was withdrawn then replaced. I felt as if I was suffocating. I could hear my voice pleading before the sound of my voice faded into a dream of an azure blue ocean, and a pier that hovered above the sea along which there appeared a never-ending procession of technicolor serpents that wriggled head to tail before disappearing into the sea of blue. It was a sea with a horizon of heat so intense I could feel it through the subliminal passage of a phoney sleep, which was interrupted again and again by a return to consciousness before plunging back into oblivion.

I awoke to the throat-constricting stinging taste of bile, the pervasive odour of hospital and the remains of the stench of chloroform and nose-burning vomit sticking to my sleepwear. Then the face of an angel in white and the caress of a cool wet flannel. Muddled times they were, when night was day and day was night, before the final awakening into a world of drifting white spectres and the brightness of the ward.

It was about a week after the operation that I learned to manoeuvre my body on crutches in such a way as to avoid putting the full weight on feet that were still tender from the stitches and shiny steel pins.

The nurse who taught me to use the crutches was a good teacher and I was a quick learner, so within a short space of time I could traverse the length of the ward without help, which was good because it gave me the opportunity to visit the other patients in the ward.

One patient in particular, for whom I felt a mix of compassion and curiosity was strapped from the waist to the top of his head in bandages with slits in the bandages around the mouth and eyes that enabled him to eat, breathe and see what went on around him. A thin sheet across his body concealed a network of pipes that led to a number of bags hanging from a trapeze above his head. Most of the time he seemed to sleep.

I spoke to him a few times when he wasn't sleeping and I had to pretend to hear what he was saying for his words were always muffled by the bandage and his tongue seemed to get in the way. Nevertheless, he was always glad to see me. I could see it in his eyes and the way he gripped my hand with a hand that was pale and smooth as tissue paper, which made me realise he was much younger than he had appeared wrapped in the bandages.

There were others like him in the ward, silent, inert shapes that never moved yet were still there when I finally left the ward. There were others that didn't appear sick, like the red-faced man who laughed and joked all the time and called me "Laddie." One night I woke up and there were nurses around his bed, but in the morning the bed was empty. What happened to him? I don't know. I only remember the empty bed that was soon filled by another. Death and the finality of it never entered my mind.

Sun streamed in through a window across the ward and I could feel its warmth through the sheet. It was early afternoon, a tranquil time when the activity in the ward was at its lowest, a time when those who felt the restless pain of night could catch up on lost sleep. It was not so much pain that kept me awake at night, but rather the groans and cries of those who suffered real pain, the kind of pain I have since come to understand, that transcends morphine. Pain, just like my friend in bandages felt, and the ones who seldom moved, except at night when pain must have been at its worse and who now slept so soundly.

I have often wondered why, as it was for me, that with daylight pain lessened, only to return with full force after dark? Was it because the night was without the distractions of day when pain was forgotten behind the picture of a life seen, felt and heard? Or was it that pain is more evident in the darkness of night when there is nothing to detract from the introspection of one's agony?

I wanted my dreams. I would daydream, looking through the window opposite me when I imagined the sea waves at Woodingdean crashing on rocks and the hiss of water retreating across a pebbled beach. This was not my home, Warren Farm was my home. I felt homesick and wanted something that was far away. My two mothers, the one with the black hair or the one with the red hair, smooth skin and wet ticklish lips and my friend with the flowered dress behind the flintstone wall.

It was wings I needed and dreamed of, to fly above and away from dreams of serpents and the suffocating smell and the sound of pain. Eyes wide shut… a cough, a cry… the rasp of stocking against stocking… a white faceless figure passing into shadow. I needed sleep. No! It was impossible. There was too much movement… and my memories were gone!

Chapter Nine

The Prosthesis, the Monocle and the Nurse in White Knickers

We met on the way to the exercise ward. He was ahead of me to begin with, wearing pyjamas and odd shoes and walking with the aid of a single crutch, one leg bent and the other as straight as the leg of the crutch, one arm supported and the other swinging in time to a lop-sided gait.

I caught up with him at the door of the exercise room. We both stopped, deciding who should go through first. "After you," he said, as he pushed the door open and nudged me through.

The room was deserted except for a single nurse, who upon seeing us stopped what she was doing, strode across and led us to a bench beside a set of parallel bars. While the nurse adjusted the apparatus to suit my height, I cast a sidelong glance at the man sitting beside me. I looked on in horror as he removed his leg, leaned it against the bench only inches away from my leg, and proceeded to massage the scarred stump. I felt a tingle up and down my spine as I watched him knead the raised flap of skin and stitch marks, then reach for the prosthesis with its mysterious web of straps and the shoe that didn't match the slipper on the good foot.

With the nurse supporting me, I attempted to traverse the bars by gripping both bars while at the same time sliding along with the bars tucked in my armpits. Halfway across she withdrew her support and left me dangling, a move that made it imperative that I use my feet to enable me to support my body. The pain was almost intolerable and I cried out each time my feet came into contact with the floor, but somehow I was able to traverse the length of the bars at lest three or four times before I was allowed to rest.

My place on the bars was taken by the man with the prosthesis who moved along the bars like a monkey, grinning at me each time he made a turn on the apparatus. It was the first of many hours we spent together. He became like an older brother and even persuaded the nurses to move his bed next to mine in the ward.

It was a day of surprises that began mid-morning after my one-legged friend and I had agreed to meet for a turn in the exercise room.

I remember he was late in coming and when he did, he was in the company of a strange looking silver-haired man with a very bad limp, one eye without a pupil and the other hidden behind a monocle attached to his dressing-gown pocket by a long cord.

This strange figure preceded yet another startling scene that lay in store for us when we opened the door to the exercise room. The place was in chaos with a number of hospital staff in the throes of rearranging the room. The apparatus and mats had been moved against the walls leaving the centre of the room bare. In place of the apparatus, the staff were arranging row upon row of benches, strategically placed so as to be facing a bright green mat beneath a window at one end of the room.

We sat down close to the front waiting for the action to subside. When it did there were a few moments of silence before the room began to fill from behind us with patients who drifted in through the door in a steady stream. Some came in wheelchairs, others on crutches, some strolled in on foot. A stretcher case was carried in and placed on a massage table against one wall. There was even the odd bed on wheels pushed into position on the perimeter of the noisy crowd. Who said the sick were silent? My God! This lot made more noise than spectators at a boxing match.

As suddenly as it had started, the bedlam trickled to silence with the entry of a solitary nurse through a side door. You could hear a pin drop as she weaved her way to the green mat in front of the window. She stood for a moment with a grin on her face, legs apart, surveying the patients, a focal point for all who stood, sat, lay or reclined. She was a comely girl with flushed cheeks, ruby red lips and above her grin she wore a nurse's cap pinned at a steep angle to a set of auburn braids. The material of the blouse and skirt I noticed was not of the same type as that worn by the nurses in the ward. It was a lighter material, sheer enough to reveal the white straps and cups of a white brassiere, while the light from the window behind her outlined the division of her thighs.

She began her routine with her legs spread wide and hands on hips as she swayed her body from side to side, each movement causing her blouse to cling to each breast in turn. After a while she changed the movement by bending at the waist and at the same time reaching out with her right hand to touch the toe of her left shoe and vice versa, each movement revealing her shape and the outline of her underwear.

Bored with the proceedings I turned to chat to my friend with the prosthesis who was clearly annoyed at my intrusion. Immediately he changed his position so that I was between him and the nurse. This way he was able to speak over me without taking his eyes off the girl. Unable to capture his attention, I turned around in time to see the girl lie down on the carpet in the shape of a cross, arms outstretched, palms pressing down as she raised her knees and splayed her feet. I heard murmurs and soft chuckles from behind me. Out of the corner of my eye I caught sight of the man with the monocle, mouth open wide, his dead eye staring into space, his monocled good eye fixed on the girl who slowly straightened her knees, lifted both legs from the waist and, with legs suspended, slowly opened and closed them displaying flashes of white above the stockings.

Occasionally the tip of her tongue leaked out the side of her mouth to lick her lips.

She sat up and rested awhile with legs spread wide and without her realising it revealed, in the shadows, a gusset of snow-white knickers.

For a moment or two there was silence broken now and then by a nervous cough, followed by a rush of clapping, cheering and wolf-whistles when she rose to her feet with flashes of white panty and left the room, seemingly unconcerned at the atmosphere she left in her wake.

I looked up questioningly at the one-legged man. He said something that was lost in the flurry and movement of the departing patients. I turned to face the man with the monocle and watched him wipe his brow with the sleeve of his gown and smile before handing me my crutches. I thanked him before the three of us, with me in the middle making me feel quite grown up, joined the queue leaving the room.

As I grew older I realised that I had witnessed my first sex show. A strange time and place in which to become a man. Some time in August 1947, I was discharged from hospital. I shall not forget walking down the ward between the beds saying goodbye to all the patients. It had been two weeks since my operation and my feet, though healed, were still a little painful, due more I suppose to the physiotherapy that now had me walking on the soles rather than on the sides of my feet.

The last person I said goodbye to was the man with the prosthesis. He was sitting on the side of his bed swinging his good leg, his stump hidden inside the leg of his striped pyjamas, the prosthesis with its mysterious web of harness on the bed beside him. We talked for a while... I can't recall what we said, emotions were running high right then you see and I didn't want him to see me cry. Then he slid from the bed and, balancing on one leg, put his arms around me before we shook hands and I left.

Chapter Ten

The Stranger in the Pinstriped Suit

It was in October 1947 that I was called to the headmaster's office.

I was with Irene when the call came via a messenger in the form of a young boy who slept in the same dormitory as me. At first I ignored his shouts as he ran towards us and instead continued to gaze, with Irene, through the railings at a flock of birds that rose and fluttered like whimsical wisps of paper above the field of ripe grain. "The headmaster wants you at his office. Right away," gasped the panting boy and without another word spun on his heels and raced back across the playground.

I left Irene standing at the railings and took off at speed, overtaking the messenger on the way. Thoughts rushed through my mind as I ran. Thoughts that centred on an incident that had happened a long time ago…

The classroom was well lit with several large windows that faced the playground. The desks had attached seats and were set out in rows with a passage between each row, just wide enough for the teacher to walk up and down. The desks were occupied according to age, the youngest at the front. I was seated in the front row slightly to the right of centre, next to a girl who was a complete stranger.

The teacher, a woman with grey hair tied up in a bun, was stooped in front of a blackboard resting on an easel. She had her back to me writing, for I could hear the rasp of chalk and the scrape of her nail that put my teeth on edge.

Beneath the desk I could feel the warmth of the girl's thigh pressed uncomfortably close against mine. She inclined her head towards mine and whispered in my ear, giggled, then took my hand in hers and pressed it to her groin. With the teacher's attention still focused on the blackboard, she giggled again and at the same time slipped my hand beneath her dress. Bewildered, I glanced down at the crotch of her blue knickers and my hand pressed to the softness. Instinctively, I pulled my hand away and looked up into the eyes of the teacher.

I received my first caning that day. Both of us in fact. She went in first. I heard her scream and she came out sobbing. Then it was my turn. God! It was sore. Across the top of my hand, the fingers burning, I flinched and pulled my hand away at the second strike. It only prolonged the agony and in the end, unable to constrain my struggling, he held me down by my neck across the desk and beat my backside instead.

Apprehensively I knocked on the headmaster's door. No response. I could hear voices inside and I knocked again. The door was opened not by the headmaster but by a stranger neatly dressed in a grey suit with faint stripes. He had hair that matched his suit and a moustache that was little more than a short sharp strip, exactly halfway between his nose and top lip. He was neat as a pin down to the grey shoes that shone and reflected every move he made.

I remember well the contrast there was between the stranger and the drab office and lacklustre appearance of the man seated behind the desk—a figure that hadn't changed at all since the time he had held me down across his desk. In fact it could well have been that the clothes he wore now were the same he had worn then. The smell of the office hadn't changed either, that same old musty mixture of old books, dust and pipe smoke.

Does he remember me, I wondered? But I needn't have worried, judging by the lack of interest in his expression and the way he absently rifled through the sheets of paper he held in his hands.

"So you are Master George Bowley," said the stranger, taking my hand and shaking it. "Do you know why you are here?" he asked.

"No, sir," I answered.

He thought for a while, then turned his head and nodded at the headmaster who without a word gathered up his papers and left the room, closing the door behind him. The man in the pinstriped suit sat me down in a leather-backed chair and described at length a country called Rhodesia and the home I was going to. "You, young man," he said, "are going to somewhere where the sun always shines." With these words he stretched across the desk, picked up a brochure and handed it to me. It felt smooth in my hands. I looked at the picture on the front, a beautiful picture that depicted a house surrounded by leafy trees in a green meadow with children playing. "No more hunger," he said, "and no more war." Oh! How wrong he was.

Chapter Eleven

The Meeting and the Leaving 1948

The headmaster's office was exactly as I had last seen it, except for a huge vase that had once stood on a bookcase near the desk but had since been removed and replaced by an ornament that bore no resemblance to anything I could think of. The headmaster too, had lost none of his looks and charm, he still wore the same jacket and trousers, the same expression. The scene still lacked something though. Oh, yes! He wasn't holding a sheaf of paper in his hands, neither was he seated behind his desk, but was standing instead beside a lady who was his exact opposite.

She was introduced to me by the headmaster as Miss Hussey, a member of the Fairbridge Society whose vocation it was to prepare migrant children for the journeys overseas. She was a slim, dainty woman of average height with tightly curled hair fashioned in such a way that the lobes of her ears were hidden except for the tips that peeped from her curls like the ears of a mouse. Her facial features were unusual insofar as the chin and forehead sloped away slightly, making the nose look longer than it was. This aside, she could still be termed attractive, having deep-blue eyes that were enhanced even more by the fine-rimmed glasses that she constantly removed to clean with a dainty handkerchief she kept in a slim handbag slung across her shoulder. Her clothes, too, were neat and feminine. She wore a tweed jacket and matching skirt. Beneath the jacket I could see a pink blouse with cuffs of lace buttoned to the throat. On her thin yet shapely legs she wore tan stockings and on her feet elegant slim shoes.

From the start I felt comfortable in her presence. Perhaps

it was her kind manner and the way she crouched in front of me, took my hands and spoke so softly. Her face was so close I could see my reflection in her glasses and smelt her perfume. "I have a surprise for you," she whispered, as she rose, still holding my hand, "Come with me."

We left the office and walked down a passage that echoed our footsteps, past the stairway that led to the upstairs dormitories and on until we reached a busy room with bodies moving to and fro. The door to the room was not the self-closing type like those to be found throughout the home. This door was kept open by a heavy doorstop that kept it pinned to the wall, allowing the constant passage of bodies carrying all manner of things like pots and pans, linen and crockery.

We were met outside the room by a matron who, after a brief discussion with Miss Hussey, left, returning a short time later with a boy with fair hair and a pink face. Miss Hussey crouched beside me and the boy, took our hands and drew us together.

"George," she whispered, "this is John, your brother." She then stepped away, leaving us facing each other.

I don't remember what followed. For the life of me I can't. I can only imagine how it must have been with the two of us strangers looking at each other. Shy, a little uneasy no doubt, captured by and with the oh-so-familiar gestures befitting two children meeting for the first time—you know, hands behind the back, looking down at the shoes then up at the ceiling approach, followed by the uneasy shuffle and perplexed smile.

John was convinced that it was me who made the first move. Perhaps it was, I don't remember. He also remembers quite clearly, my handing him a penknife—surely the same knife Irene had given to me one Christmas as a gift that had once belonged to her father?

It was early on the day following our coming together that I rose and dressed in my Warren Farm uniform. It was the start of a day to remember, a day that had already begun the previous evening when I was told that my newfound brother and I would be travelling to London to be fitted with our Fairbridge School uniforms.

Miss Hussey met us at sunrise, neat and smiling and wearing a skirt and blouse with a fluffy cardigan around her shoulders. I caught the scent of her perfume as she kissed us both on the cheek and helped us into the van.

Oh! How exciting it was experiencing the world! A frenetic rush. I had never experienced anything the like before. It was warm in the van and I still remember wiping away the annoying mist of my breath on the window, a haze that constantly threatened to obscure the sight of people passing by in a blur. Buildings and trees moved by at a more leisurely pace affording a lucid view of window boxes exploding in colour. No scene stayed the same. There was always something to relieve the sameness of row upon row of houses, with a sudden break into a different world of green pastures dotted with cattle, sheep and horses, hedgerows and comfortable-looking farmhouses with grey smoke drifting from their chimneys.

The excitement died when we entered the streets of London, to be replaced by open-mouthed wonder at the immense congruency of brick, steel, and glass that reflected the sparse green foliage of trees dotting the curbs here and there. Beyond everything the geometric shapes of tall buildings blocked out the sky and enclosed in their shadows the hum of buses, the variegated sounds of hooters and klaxon, tram and taxi and the sting and stench of exhaust fumes. It was a foreign, intoxicating blend of everything that put my brother to sleep but forced me to keep my eyes open. I would have fallen asleep too if my interest hadn't been rekindled after the driver slowed down and pulled to the kerb before a bridge spanning the Thames.

Miss Hussey alighted from the van and motioned to me to follow. We left John sleeping in the care of the driver while the lady led the way to the bridge on which a crowd had gathered.

The river was at low tide, leaving behind wide banks of oily black mud that gave off a stench of decayed seaweed and enveloped in its oily grasp dozens of sad-looking boats swarming with roosting sea birds. But it wasn't this desolate scene the crowd had come to see. Oh no, it was something much worse than that. It was a scene so bizarre and cruel it has remained with me forever.

There were children, not a handful, but ten, twenty, thirty, perhaps even more, both sexes and ages. The majority were my size, some a little bigger, others even smaller. The Mudlarks, as they became known to me, were at the time as much a part of London as the Houses of Parliament. They were beggars displaced by the war and the depression that followed and were kept alive, it would seem, to entertain those who, like me and the crowd, tossed down coins from the bridge and were amused by their antics as they fought in the filth to survive. "Hey mister. Please mister," came the calls from two I saw standing on the periphery of the struggling mass. In response, a few coins were tossed in their direction. I was amazed at the dexterity they showed in catching the coins in the air but even more astonishing was the ease with which they reclaimed the coins that fell in the mud. They were truly amazing, these Mudlarks. Most of them, I understood, had survived the blitz but the odds were still stacked against them, and as is natural with the young, there was no substitute for survival.

I wasn't sorry to leave the bridge. Miss Hussey hadn't said a word so I'm not sure whether she felt the same way. Why on earth, I thought, had she shown me those pitiful scenes? Was it a cunningly subtle way of revealing to me the alternative to the life that had been prepared for me, or was it simply to prove to me that there were others far worse off than I?

Later that day we boys met up with the other seven boys that made up the party and were introduced to Miss Mill, the lady who would accompany us on our journey. She was introduced by the Chairman, General Hawthorne, a dapper ex-army man with a regimental moustache and a penchant for quoting the 'glorious' words and phrases of Kipling; the work carried out by the Fairbridge Society, and what was expected of us; 'the chosen few', in keeping the Union Jack flying in a country with a great future. He ended his stirring speech with a rendition of Kipling's poem *If*.

We sang the Anthem and toasted the King and Queen at a modest luncheon put on for our benefit in the dining room at Rhodesia House. This was followed by a session of photographing, and the issuing to each boy of a uniform. It was a simple and smart outfit consisting of a grey blazer with a fancy 'F' sewn onto the top pocket, two pairs of grey shorts with matching socks, two white short-sleeved shirts, two ties, two hankies, a pair of black shoes, and a grey wide-brimmed felt hat.

Each item of clothing had been tagged with a number that signified the number of migrants in numerical order that had been shipped to Rhodesia thus far. My number was 60, John's was 61.

A small leather suitcase was provided into which was packed my clothes, a toilet bag and any other worldly goods I might have amassed over the past nine years, but they had been lean years so there was nothing to pack except my new clothes and my memories.

> I bought a penny's worth of mouldy cheese,
> And stuck it behind the door,
> And when I got up in the morning,
> It was dancing on the floor,
> Singing Mum, Dad, take me home
> From this paralysed chicken's home.
> I've been here a year or two

> And now I'm coming back to you.
> Goodbye, all you suckers, goodbye Fanny, too,
> Goodbye, all you suckers
> And jolly good luck to you.

I remember nothing of the last day at Warren Farm. I like to believe it was spent with Irene, my dearest friend, the one who had been my guiding light through the ups and downs of five years of institutional care. Or, and it is more probable that having grown up with a dislike for 'goodbyes' I would more likely have sulked or put on a façade of indifference. How John and I felt at the time however, is of little consequence since one thing is for certain, as the records show, we left the home before daybreak on the following morning while Irene and the others were fast asleep.

Chapter Twelve

The Journey

My world had spun so fast then, that I remember nothing of the journey to London that morning or the trip to Chelsea on the Thames. In fact my world only stopped spinning when we stopped that afternoon on the embankment below Blackfriars Bridge where we found ourselves aboard the *Discovery*, the ship that had ferried Scott and Shackleton on their first journey to the Antarctic. We walked the decks where they had stood for many days and nights, on the same ship that was frozen in, immobile, for two long winters in McMurdo Sound. We explored the cabins where the men had lived and slept that night in their bunks, dreaming perhaps, of what they may have dreamed, for we too were explorers in a sense.

I remember rising early the next morning to see skeins of fog rising from the Thames, and peering over the guardrail I looked down on a solitary figure clothed in an overcoat and balaclava with a bag slung over one shoulder. I watched him walk slowly along the embankment then stop and look up at the bowsprit before he retraced his steps, stopped immediately below where I was standing, dropped his bag and lit a cigarette. Who was he? I wondered, a sailor perhaps? Just then, my thoughts were interrupted by voices and the sound of footsteps coming from below. It was Miss Mill and the rest of the party. By this time the fog had shifted and the sun had begun to disentangle itself from a strip of dark cloud on the horizon. It brought with it light and warmth and an opportunity for me to study Miss Mill without her knowing it.

She was stood against the guardrail with her back to me talking to fourteen-year-old Craig, the eldest of us. I had not been aware until then just how short she was. In fact, I can remember how surprised I was to see that Craig was fractionally taller and from where I stood, because of her slim girlish form next to Craig's stocky build, she could easily have passed off as his younger sister.

She was a Scot without the accent, of indeterminate age, undeniably attractive with tight black curls and a tan I have come to learn most girls 'would die for', attributed to having spent most of her life in India.

Despite her lack of height, she made this less obvious by wearing the right clothes to emphasise her svelte figure that included form-hugging evening dresses, sundresses, and blouses with scooped necklines that showed off her tight apple breasts. But there was more to her than her attractiveness, for she possessed other qualities that were unequalled by any of the housemothers I had known or would ever get to know. The ability, for example, to look into a person rather than at them and treat each of us as individuals—and all this despite never having had children herself.

I remember her best, however, as a gifted storyteller. She kept us enthralled for hours with her tales from *The Jungle Book* by Kipling and real-life stories from her years as a serviceman's daughter in India. She was everything a housemother should be. But it was only in my senior years that I learned of her own personal tragedies, which made any I may have suffered seem infinitesimal by comparison and helped me rid myself of much of the self-pity that was a legacy of my own circumstances. There were few amongst us that suffered like she—the loss of a father and fiancé within months of each other—and left me with the feeling that perhaps it was those horrific events that were the root-cause of her affinity with those she cared for.

The Discovery was a hive of activity on the morning of our last day in England. It began with a huge breakfast served up by the *Discovery's* sea-cadet crew who then lined the decks to wave farewell as the coach and its eager passengers left the Thames for the short journey to Portsmouth. As a last treat before leaving England we were taken aboard *HMS Victory*, Nelson's flagship that lay in dry-dock on a sea of concrete.

I remember her as 'gaudy' in comparison to the Discovery with its black hull, single smoke stack and modest rigging that were a far cry, it must be said, from Victory's magnificent opulence and yet both shared the memories of the deaths of Lord Nelson and Sir Robert Falcon Scott.

It was late afternoon when the coach arrived in Southampton but I doubt if any one of us carried the thought that soon we would be leaving England for good. For all eyes and thoughts, like mine, were centred on the *Maklimberg* and her shining handrails, sheet-white bridge and funnel with a broad band of yellow outlined in black from which spiralled a coil of grey smoke.

When the ship's horn sounded for the last time, it seemed much louder than before. A small group of people had gathered on the quayside and had begun to wave. None of us knew who they were, but we waved back anyway at nobody in particular and continued to wave as a tug pulled the ship around to face the open sea. Led by Miss Mill, we moved along the deck to the stern in time to see the land disappear in the darkness. We were still there until the shore lights disappeared into the waves. It was the last I saw of England for more than thirty years.

The cabin John and I shared was small with most of the space taken up by two bunks, one above the other, a toilet and a basin. Being the oldest and the tallest, I chose the top bunk that was level with the porthole. By lying on my back, I was able to touch the ceiling and in the same position my feet were only inches away from the porthole. It opened enough for me to smell the sea air and feel the cold air around my feet.

We had been at sea only a short time before Miss Mill

called us for dinner. It was in the passageway leading to the dining room that we all began to feel the effects of seasickness brought on by the smell of food wafting through from the kitchen. I remember through a haze of nausea, seeing a table decorated with long-stemmed glasses, a ring of faces and again the strong smell of food.

Not one of us according to Miss Mill, ate anything that night. Instead, we returned to our cabins to endure a night of vomiting. There was no escaping the horrible feeling as I lay on my bunk in the darkness, tossing and turning, and trying in vain to neutralize the nauseating effects of the rocking sensation. At last, exhausted from retching, I must have dozed off. I was awakened by the sound of John vomiting in the sink, the sights and sounds of which sent me off once again to reach the state where there was nothing left to bring up but spit and bile.

Miss Mill dropped in once during the night to attend to John who I thought looked terribly ill. He was gasping like a fish out of water, his fair hair stuck to his forehead above eyes that were wide-open and staring right through me. When he tried to stand with her help his legs buckled like those of a crippled marionette.

I awoke next morning with bunged up nostrils, tasting the foul taste of stale vomit, but strangely, the world no longer swayed and everything was as quiet as a graveyard. Instinctively, my eyes focused on daylight and a vertical shadow line through the sweaty glass of the porthole. Curious, I moved on hands and knees to the ring of light and wiped the glass with the sleeve of my shirt. The shadow line turned out to be a jetty support covered in barnacles. Have we reached Africa, I wondered?

The Maklimberg docked that day at the Hook of Holland from where the party boarded a coach for the port of Rotterdam.

Driving through Holland was like travelling through a prism, reflections of a thousand colours in the bright sunlight. Mile after mile of multicoloured tulip fields, emerald green pastures peaceful and alive with grazing sheep and cows and snow-white geese. The coach hummed over picturesque bridges, spanning transparent waters framed with banks of tufted rushes. It went through busy towns that still carried the scars of war, rumbled over cobbled roads that wound through quaint villages of lop-sided houses and towering church steeples, and on beside footpaths that flirted with bicycle riders wearing smiling faces.

We stopped once beside a windmill and climbed to the top where a mammoth stone creaked and ground its way in a never-ending circle, beneath giant vanes that circled so slowly there was time to look out and over a panoramic tapestry of interwoven scenes of heaven and earth.

Under a clear blue sky we stopped for tea at a teahouse beside a placid pond. With the sun warm on our backs, we spent time skimming smooth pebbles on the mirrored surface before sitting down at polished tables with gay tablecloths, waited on by a pretty country girl wearing an embroidered blouse, white bonnet and beautifully patterned clogs that made a fascinating clucking sound on the cobbles., and oh my!—who could forget the delicious cakes piped with frothy fresh cream?

The coach arrived mid-afternoon or thereabouts. The move through Customs was quick and before long we were looking upon the breathtaking sight of the *SS Indrapoera*, built in the 1920s and the pride of a luxury fleet that once ferried wealthy tourists and businessmen around the tropics. At the onset of war, she was stripped of her colours and luxurious trappings and was commissioned instead to ferry Allied troops from one hotspot to another. It was thus as a troop-carrier we found her in her camouflaged coat. The only difference between past and present was her cargo which consisted of hundreds of Dutch, and a handful of English migrants and their chaperone, on what was to be the ship's final two-and-a-half week voyage to Cape Town.

The scene on the dockside was one of organised chaos with passengers and porters carrying loads of baggage, rushing to and fro like egg-carrying ants, up and down the well-worn gangplank.

Our party might have expected something different from the living quarters we had found on the Maklimberg—larger cabins, perhaps with their own bathrooms and tables, chairs and cupboards in which to store luggage.

Imagine our surprise, however, when after descending a spiral metal stairway into the bowels of the ship we were confronted by a heavy metal door that opened up into a single gigantic dormitory, filled with block upon block of metal bunks that almost reached a metal ceiling that was studded with lights.

Each block was numbered with numerals painted yellow on the walls adjacent to each block. How fortunate it was that our allotted bunks, whether by accident or design, were situated on the periphery which meant we didn't have to climb over others to reach them.

There was no privacy. Men, women, girls, boys and babies all shared the same space. There were, however, a few people who, like Miss Mill, sought for and achieved a modicum of privacy by hanging blankets around their bunks. The majority on the other hand were quite content to dress and undress either beneath or above their bed covers.

The ablution blocks were better organised. There were two separate rooms partitioned off into male and female sections, but serviced by a single metal watertight door that slid in grooves in the floor and above on the ceiling. It was so heavy it had to be operated by a huge metal spanner that was slotted into a ratchet that was pulled back and forth to open or close.

Meals were self-served in two dining saloons that were furnished much like the dining rooms in any public school. There was a small lounge for adults with leather easy chairs and a handsome bar. For the younger set, a soft drink of cheap bland raspberry-flavoured water was freely available from huge bottles strapped to companionways and passageways leading to the decks.

But what a change from the Maklimberg, not to sense the pitch and roll of the sea and the nausea that came with it, to look out and see a horizon steady as a rock and a sunny sea breeze warm on my face.

I was in my favourite spot one day, right there in the bows on a platform that overlooked the keel cutting through the waves. I was caught up in the fascination of watching schools of flying fish leap clear of the curving bow-wave to skim the surface like silver bullets.

Was it her presence I sensed at my back, or was it her shadow on the platform? I can't remember, but something made me look over my shoulder to see a beautiful smiling girl with long blonde hair flowing in waves past her shoulders. I think I smiled in return, I'm not sure, and I turned into the wind once more. Then suddenly she was beside me. I felt our arms brush and I stole a glimpse out the corner of my eye. Gosh! She was so pretty and about my age too, perhaps a little older. It didn't matter; I was smitten, so much so that my heart leaped in response to a foolish urge to downplay my feelings. Play hard to get, I thought, by looking away indifferently, pretending to see something that wasn't there, but I reckoned without the lure of her open innocence.

In fact I gave a start when with no warning at all, she shouted words in English, so close I felt her hair against my cheek. Instantly my pretentious resolve crumbled and I joined in her excitement when she grabbed my arm and pointed in the direction of a school of porpoises breaking the surface in front of the bow. "Look! Look!" she shouted, pointing down through the guardrail at their grey sinuous bodies that darted back and forth just below the surface. The ice was broken, the introduction complete, and we were more than just friends when she took advantage by reversing our roles and for days led me around on a leash of euphoric puppy love.

Her name was Amanda. That much I do remember and so did Miss Mill when, years later, in a time of reminiscing she remarked: "And you above all my boys fell in love with the only English-speaking girl on the ship!"

It was hot on the day the Indrapoera docked in Las Palmas, so hot in fact, that at first Miss Mill decided we should stay on board for the four hours and forgo the optional visit to Las Palmas. However, after pressure from us to disembark she consented, a decision she lived to regret.

The trip started off well enough with us stopping to slake our thirst at a roadside café beside an impressive fountain decorated with bare-breasted stone maidens. This became the subject of much ribald comment from us, and we unknowingly sparked the interest of a nearby group of pox-ridden beggar women who promptly surrounded our tables and demanded alms. This upset Miss Mill no end and with parasol swinging she set about the crones who scattered from her fury to all corners followed by a barrage of choice words that I for one had never come across before.

It was the first any of us had seen Miss Mill in a rage! Believe me when I say it was quite frightening until, thank goodness, she was calmed down by a stranger who seemed to appear from nowhere, a dapper-looking gentleman in a white suit and straw hat. He chatted to Miss Mill with a consoling (or should I say cajoling as events would prove) arm around her shoulder, before bowing in gratitude when she erred by giving him a fee in advance for what he described as a whistle-stop tour of the environs that would include a visit to the 'King's palace'.

We walked for what seemed like hours in the blistering heat following in the footsteps of our so-called guide. He led us like the proverbial "three blind mice' along winding streets with washing and folk hanging from shuttered windows, past entrances decorated with gaudy murals. We arrived at a crossroads and stopped with our backs against a wall, to allow the passage of a stampede of dark-skinned children, whose shouts and peals of laughter I could still hear long after their bobbing heads had vanished in the stream of humanity thronging the pavement.

The street converged with others into an open, paved square in front of a cathedral with sculptured spires and a clock that indicated we had one hour to get back to the ship. It was about then that Miss Mill realized she had been conned. The 'guide' simply vanished, leaving us stranded in front of the 'King's palace'.

The return journey was a nightmare that at one stage threatened to end in a poor area amongst squalid houses and dejected-looking people, none of whom could speak English. Then, just as the world seemed to be at an end, salvation arrived. It was a dilapidated taxi driven by a maniac who, urged on by a very angry Miss Mill, ignored all rules of the road and sped along the narrow streets at breakneck speed, nudging through the crowds at intersections before breaking through onto the familiar palm-lined boulevard that led to the docks. We simply flew the last mile or two but we made it just as the Indrapoera was about to weigh anchor.

Miss Mill faced the music from the Purser for having held up the scheduled departure, but all eyes were on our 'accidental heroine' as we learned of the repercussions of the ill-fated tour and of how we had so narrowly escaped the next boat back to England.

That day ended like most others, with a story she told so well. It was Rudyard Kipling's tale of a fearless mongoose named Riki Tiki Tavi and how as a family pet, it saved a baby from the bite of a cobra. I remember her words washing over me, filling my heart with such a sense of kinship for and with those around me. I wondered if, as she pointed out, my feelings were not akin to the soldiers who not so long ago had occupied these very same bunks. Were they like ourselves, she asked, victims of a war headed for an unknown destination?

Chapter Thirteen

Cape Town and the Black Man with the Barrow

April 2nd 1948. There was no great fanfare or waving crowds to meet the Indrapoera and its boatload of unknowns. Instead, she lay deserted and forlorn in Table Bay harbour after what had been her final voyage.

She had, I presumed, meant nothing more than a 'means to an end' to those of the emigrants who never stopped complaining about the cramped quarters, the food and the boredom. But for us it had been a supreme voyage of adventure, a dream it could be said, that in the years that followed was discussed and broken down into the finest detail in Miss Mill's little flat at Fairbridge.

There was a series of camera flashes on the periphery of a bustling crowd beyond the queues in the Arrivals hall. A press photographer was busy with a hidden camera, each flash lighting up the face of Miss Mill in conversation with a reporter. A few words between her and the annoying cameraman saw him turn and shift the lens towards the group of children standing idly by or sitting on the mound of suitcases. A sudden flash picked out the figure of Craig with hands on hips and foot firmly planted on a suitcase like a hunter with his trophy. The camera flashed once more to catch Craig's mischievous smile that appeared the next day in the *Cape Argus*. The camera panned the rest of the group, including me. I was caught unawares in profile, eyes set firmly on a black porter with a barrow stacked with suitcases. In the photograph, only the porter's face was visible, eyes shining like raisins in a fruitcake, smiling down on the boy who stared back mouth agape, obviously thrilled at his first glimpse of a black man.

Having completed her interviews with the press, the chaperone led her brood from the hall to a waiting coach, which drove us to the immigrant holding camp. It was here that a reception was held in our honour.

I remember most of all how hungry we were. We hadn't eaten much all day, and to make matters worse, we had to sit through a speech given by General Hawthorne, a speech Miss Mill was later heard to describe as one similar to that afforded a company of departing troops and which ended with the poem *When* by Rudyard Kipling.

I slept like a dead man that night (speeches have that effect on me), and at daybreak, after a whopping breakfast, we boarded a bus for Cape Town station to begin the final leg of our journey.

Chapter Fourteen

The Last Leg

The waiting room was crowded with passengers and well-wishers seated around tables laden with beer bottles and thick-ribbed railway glasses.

Against the far wall a bar had attracted a rowdy crowd of patrons. They pushed and shoved while demanding orders from two stressed-out bartenders who, between pouring drinks and handing over bottles, snatched at proffered notes before stashing them in a till overflowing with notes and coins.

To one side of the entrance to the waiting-room a group of passengers stood and stared up at a clock, appearing to listen intently to a monotonous female voice that miraculously pierced the hubbub of scraping chairs and the deafening hum of a string of voices, and issued instructions on the arrival and departure times of traffic. After each set of instructions given in English and Afrikaans (language spoken by South African's of Dutch descent), there was a rush for the double-door that led out onto the platforms, leaving the waiting room momentarily half-empty before it was once again filled with the next set of travellers. All this constant movement took place under two ineffectual ceiling fans that struggled in vain to disperse the pall of cigarette smoke and the stench of stale beer.

Miss Mill meanwhile, had laid down her newspaper for the umpteenth time to light another cigarette. The ashtray at her elbow was full of butt ends, each cork-tip smeared with her bright red lipstick. Through a veil of grey smoke, yet again she snatched a glance at the wall-clock and the minute-hand that had advanced barely ten minutes since her last look.

Bored and restless, I left the waiting room and wandered off along the platform, stopping outside an empty telephone booth that had a notice painted above it that read NIE BLANKES in bold black print. The door to the booth was open and the floor inside was littered with pages from a directory, the remains of which hung beside a handset that dangled in space like a spider hanging from a web of tangled wires. To complete the scene of devastation, I saw a coin box that had been ripped from its moorings and lay strewn across the floor.

I continued my stroll, pausing in front of a kiosk that was almost entirely hidden behind magazines and newspapers that hung like Christmas decorations above a small rectangular opening that revealed the head and shoulders of the shopkeeper. He smiled at me and indicated at the same time that I should step aside. I smiled back and made way for what I thought to be two tall soldiers, dressed in smart khaki uniforms with sinister-looking peaked caps pulled low over their eyes. There was something mean and exciting about the shiny leather straps across their chests and the polished gleam of the revolver holsters with guns strapped neatly inside. Nervously, I looked away and up to where there hung a picture of a stern-faced white-haired man whose eyes seem to follow every move I made.

Uneasily I moved away from the kiosk to find myself peering through the grimy window of a large room. It was filled with rows of slatted benches that were occupied by dark figures, smoking and drinking from the necks of bottles hidden inside brown paper bags. I could see still more shapeless figures, lying down unmoving, heads like skulls covered in tight wool. It was spooky and reminded me of the gloomy coal cellar at Warren Farm. I shuddered and stepped away from the window, for I hated darkness and the fear it brings. As I walked away from the room with slatted seats, I looked back at a sign above the door that read NIE BLANKES.

A short sharp piercing whistle; a grinding lurch; a clash of couplings; steel on steel screaming, seeking traction. Sounds and motion came together in a force of hidden energy that smoothed out to the musical click of wheels crossing expansion joints that were linked and cushioned on teak sleepers which rose and fell, creaking and groaning, linking the steel tracks that led us on a journey to who knows where.

I lay on my stomach on the middle bunk, head in hands, peering out into the speeding darkness, the gentle rocking motion and clicking wheels in sync with the memories of those I once knew caged in flintstone walls. It was then I began to sing to myself a sombre song they all knew before drifting into a deep, dreamless sleep.

I awoke to the shunt-shunt-shunt of the engine and its laboured breathing as it climbed, blowing out billows of soot and steam into the clear air above the Hex River Pass. I lowered the window in time to see my carriage poised on the edge of a ravine, and far, far below a valley floor shrouded in a blanket of mist pierced here and there by the tops of trees poking through the shroud like tips of broccoli. The red ball of dawn, balanced on a strip of black cloud, in turn wove its magic. The sun's sharp rays like golden chisels pierced the cloud base and sculptured on a rugged rock the imagined grizzled features of an ancient face, with frown lines of shadowed fissures and whiskers grown from foliage of green and gold.

A break in the mist drew my eyes down to a silver thread that wound through a jumble of black boulders, a winking trickle that played hide-and-seek with light and shade. The view through the window changed as suddenly as the track led down and away from precipitous slopes and deep wooded valleys and found, through a swirl of mist, an easier route around grassy slopes, before breaking at last into a more orderly, warmer world of gabled whitewashed houses encased in white picket fences. Cool emerald meadows, and vast fields of crops sprouting in lines, converged into one on the distant horizon.

There was so much to take in. It was so easy to slide from reality to imagination when every little scene that sped past would take the guise of whatever one wished it to be. For instance, a stretch of rolling hills brought back memories of the Downs, and the common cluster of houses surrounding a grand church with a single spire recalled visions of many such villages we had passed on the coach trip through Holland.

My reverie was broken by a strange musical sound filtering through from outside the closed door of the compartment, prompting me to scramble down from the bunk. After having slid open the compartment door, I came face to face with a figure in a white uniform with a xylophone strung across his chest on which he tapped out the same tune over and over again. I watched him disappear down the swaying passage. By this time my companions had awakened and moments later, dressed and orderly with Miss Mill at the head, we followed in single file behind the 'Pied Piper' and his tune, down the passage that ended at an entrance crowded with excited knots of people passing in and out of the dining car.

At the next inward flow we emerged into the brightly-lit dining car to be met by a waiter wearing a white jacket, black trousers, a broad smile and a white cloth worn over one shoulder. In one hand he carried a circular silver tray with which, with a flourish, he beckoned us to two abandoned tables littered with a variety of used crockery and utensils.

I watched in wonder as, with a remarkable association of movements and while balanced on the balls of his feet and swaying in unison with the rocking of the train, in seconds he had removed the assortment of equipment from the table to the silver tray that was now balanced on the tips of the fingers of his left hand. I stared apprehensively at the swaying mountain of plates and the crooked towers of cups, expecting to see them crash to the floor. Instead, I witnessed an extension of the miracle as with the tray still balanced delicately on the tips of his fingers, he whipped the white cloth from his shoulder and in a blur of movement wiped the tables clean. Then somehow, from somewhere, he produced a menu decorated with scenes of the Hex River that he handed to Miss Mill with an exaggerated gesture of civility.

I can honestly say that not once did I see him glance at the tray, not even when he spun on his heels and, with the tray balanced aloft, made his way to the kitchen at the far end of the dining car.

What a meal that was! For the first time I tasted foods I had never tasted before. What was more, I was able to choose what I fancied and leave what I disliked with no one standing over me, as Matron had at Warren Farm, forcing me to swallow to the point of regurgitation a mound of turnips watered down with cabbage water.

In my compartment the bunks had been unhinged and lowered to form two seats. A folding table on chrome legs hinged above the wash-hand basin had also been let down. It was covered all day with a variety of games played by my companions whose sole interest lay in winning never-ending bouts of Ludo, Snakes and Ladders, Draughts, and Tiddly Winks. Is it any wonder therefore, that as the odd man out who preferred to discover what lay in the moving countryside, I should have been the first among us to notice a startling change in the scenery?

Perhaps the change happened after I had dozed off, as I was wont to do, I can't remember exactly but nevertheless the contrast was amazing! I awoke from my nap to find that the countryside had transformed itself into a barren landscape of dry dusty grass, stunted camelthorn trees and riverbeds that were broken up into pools of green water. These had somehow encouraged patches of green grass to grow and had given life to straggling lines of tall, green-topped acacias that followed and marked out the river's course into the distance. The only sign of life along such rivers were small herds of thin, sad-looking cattle and goats that were either glued to the patches of green grass or could be seen wallowing heads-down in the murky water.

The weather, too, had changed to suit the landscape. Waves of dust and heat rose from the parched earth and were forced into the compartment by a warm slipstream breeze that glued skin to seat and covered the interior and occupants in a film of soot and dust. Through narrowed eyes, I peered out at an avenue of listless, scrawny gum trees that lined a dusty two-track road that led to a tired-looking homestead with a corrugated-iron roof. Everything was so startlingly different from the lush green of England.

The train reached Mafeking on the border with Bechuanaland just as the sun had begun to lose its influence. It was still pretty hot though and offered scant comfort to the passengers that spewed out onto the concrete platform.

We couldn't help bursting into laughter at a family passing our window, led by a mother carrying a handbag and basket and wearing a hat with a wide brim that hid her face. She was followed by a red-faced, sweating husband wearing a rumpled suit, buckling under the weight of two bulging suitcases and a little round birdcage tucked under one armpit. To add to the poor man's woes, he was being constantly harassed by his four noisy, out-of-control children who, rather than help, seemed capable of doing nothing except chase each other up and down the platform. They were some way off when it seemed the father rebelled. He left the two cases with the birdcage on top and deserted them for a pub on the platform, leaving his family milling around.

"The poor bugger's had enough of the dragon and the little shits," said William.

"Probably gone to get pissed," muttered Craig.

"See the way he lugged those suitcases?" said somebody

else, "Like a fucking donkey. Bet he has to beg for a shag."

There followed peals of laughter, during which I gave my tuppence-worth that was equally callous, but we were wrong, for soon the father returned with a porter. Nevertheless during the discussions that followed the family's departure, we ended up convincing ourselves our assumptions had been correct.

The station lights highlighted the shadows and the colours and shapes of cheering, waving well-wishers when, at last, with a sharp whistle and the wave of a green flag the train rolled out of Mafeking. At a crawl we crossed the Bechuanaland border, leaving behind an empty platform and the spirit of Baden Powell.

I remember waking once during the night with the urge to relieve myself and to hear the sound of protesting brakes as the train jerked to a halt, followed by a deathly silence in darkness so complete that my hand was a vague shadow before my eyes. I fumbled for the ceiling-light switch. The light above my head was so dim it did no more than illuminate the surface of my bunk. Moving carefully so as not to waken my companion sleeping below, I heard the sound of his measured breathing as I climbed down and moved to the sliding door, felt for and found the latch, lifted it and let myself out into the moonlit passage.

A frosty white light from the passage windows silhouetted my body and formed a shadow that mimicked my movements as I made my way down the passage to the toilet. On my return, I stopped to listen to a tap-tapping sound and the crunch of footsteps that seemed to come from outside below window level. Curiously I moved to the window, gripped the leather sash, lowered the window and leaned out into the cool, bright night. The contrast between the pallid light at his back and the moonlight was astonishing, as was the source—a silvery-white moon suspended in an arc of star-pricked blackness, illuminating a row of tree trunks as still as sentries clad in suits of silver armour, standing guard behind a huddle of corrugated iron huts on a platform bathed in moon dust.

Again I heard the mysterious sound, but this time the tap-tapping had a metallic ring to it, like the sound my hobnail boots made on the flint stone floors in Warren Farm, when if you kicked with your heels hard enough against the stone slabs it made the sparks fly.

I leaned out and looked back along the line of sleeping carriages. I searched for the source and found it when a figure and with it the sound of footsteps on ballast, appeared out of the shadow of the coaches bearing a swinging yellow light. As the light and sound drew nearer I saw it was a man wearing a peaked cap carrying a hurricane lamp. Every few steps he would stop and with the lamp held in front of his face, turn, lean forward and tap at something in the shadows.

Oblivious of my presence he continued this puzzling behaviour until he was directly below me. I thought at first he would pass on by, but suddenly he stopped and looked up in surprise, muttered something and raised the lamp to look at me. I could tell he was an old man by the highlighted wrinkles that deepened when he smiled. The waistcoat he wore had buttons down the front that gleamed like dull gold in the mix of yellow and moonlight, but duller where the light shone on the shaft of the hammer gripped in a fist flecked with hair. We looked at each other in silence. I wanted to say something, anything, but it didn't come out. He muttered something again then lowered the lamp, turned on his heels and moved on his tap-tapping way in the direction of the engine. I saw him, briefly, standing on the platform as the train pulled away and I watched that yellow light until it disappeared.

I often wonder what the significance was in that chance meeting at dead of night on a siding somewhere in what is now Botswana. It wasn't anything startling or mind-blowing that I feel may have had an effect on my life. To say there were no attached religious connotations might be untrue. I have never been a religious person—not that I don't believe in a Creator for I most certainly do—but mine is not the inconsistent God of the Bible. For example: as an act of repentance for the wickedness of his own creations, he decided to destroy both 'man and beast and every creeping thing and the fowls of the air'. What harm has a duiker or honeybird ever done that they should be destroyed? Furthermore, what god of love and justice with all his supposed powers, looks on ineffectually as his creations continue to destroy everything that he supposedly gave his son for? No, there are just too many inconsistencies in this man-made religion.

On the other hand, there are those that dispute the existence of a god in any form. These I pity for their ignorance. Who can believe for one moment that it was mankind or the birth of a breakaway planet that could produce something as beautiful and varied as nature in all her forms? Simplistic perhaps? And there are those that would argue the subject scientifically but again, that would be Man's perception. I find it much easier and far more logical to believe that Man makes his own Armageddon without the 'wrath of God' and his prophecies. Meanwhile, I am content in the belief that it is my god that conjured up that simple meeting with the 'ganger' that night in Bechuanaland. I remember it so vividly that it continues to provide me in times of trouble, with a peace of mind that only Mother Nature can equal. My god is a god without an agenda, who will one day rest with me when I am laid to rest.

From horizon to horizon I saw a wild sameness of anthills, some as tall as houses with narrow spires, each surrounded with nitrogenous mantles of dark-green shrubbery and stunted, weird-shaped trees spotted like measles on a carpet of withered grass that would sometimes melt into veils of pale-green, dotted with groves of rectilinear Mopani (Rhodesian Ironwood tree). In their shadows I would often catch glimpses of herds of impala nibbling on the fallen leaves.

In this vast wilderness, I remember above all the absence of humans. Wildlife there was aplenty, especially in the early mornings and at sundown, but the only sign of human habitation appeared at the small sidings and stations we passed through and along the banks of the few rivers with water.

The train stopped one time in the heat of the day to take on water at the entrance to a bridge spanning a large river choked with sandbanks and islands of reeds. Tall thorn trees filled with the nests of birds, grew right down to the water's edge with banks covered in a thick mat of green grass. The train moved across the bridge at a snail's pace, which gave me time to look down through a latticework of its girders at a village of mud huts, some of which seemed to hang precariously from where the bank rose steeply above a fleet of dugout canoes moored in its shadow. Further downriver I could see the shell of a large boat lying on its side like a half-eaten carcass. It was moored to a dead tree with branches invisible beneath a screeching, squawking, fluttering mass of snow-white egrets. Beneath them, oblivious to the cacophony, a small herd of cattle drinking in the shallows failed to disturb a pair of cormorants I spied roosting on a rock, wings spread out to dry and with beaks raised to the sun.

Soon after crossing that river, we stopped at a small station crawling with more black people than I had seen thus far. A cajoling, begging, beseeching tangled mass of arms reached up to the windows offering for sale, in woven baskets and enamel bowls, heaps of strange wild fruits—unknown fruits like marula (plum sized yellowish skinned fruit), wild plums, kaffir oranges (hard shelled juicy wild fruit), snot apples (bush fruit with edible mucilaginous layer), and the snow-white tangy seed of the baobab tree—that soon we would get to know and relish. Those that offered the fruit were in the main girls and boys, but they were soon pushed aside by eager women in bright cotton blouses, who tempted the passengers with beaded bracelets and bangles fashioned from vegetable ivory, and intricately embroidered cloths that were snatched up for a few pennies.

I can never forget hearing the screams of delight and the beaming smiles on the faces of those who made a sale or the absolute absence of malice in the expressions of the unsuccessful.

An elderly man with worn hands, raised above his head a polished woodcarving of a lion astride a buffalo, its teeth sunk in behind the boss and outspread claws that gripped the ribcage. The carving was indeed terrifying and made even more lifelike by the depicted pain of the dying buffalo, its muzzle drawn back from its teeth and its tongue hanging from the side of its mouth. I watched coins change hands at the next window and noticed the old man's reaction when, having parted with his piece for the handful of coins, he clapped his hands and tapped his chest in gratitude.

It had been an exciting and unforgettable experience that had left me feeling elated as the train moved on to the next stop, a small town of small houses with the funny name of Palapye. It was the last stop I was told, before Francistown that lay on the border with Rhodesia.

We slept through the stop in Francistown and while still asleep crossed the border into Rhodesia, passing through Immigration and Customs in the village of Plumtree.

We stopped at villages along the way with exotic and appropriate names, like Marula, so-named because of the large number of marula trees that grew in the area. Then there was Figtree, a name derived from a single large fig tree that still grew then in the centre of the town, which was used by Lobengula, one-time chief of the Matabele, as a meeting place for prospectors and hunters seeking admission into his territory.

As the sun rose the following day, waking us from our slumbers, I drew the blinds on a landscape that had changed dramatically. The endless vista of thorn and shrub had vanished and in its place as far as the eye could see, was a range of bald and rugged granite hills and rock formations named *amatobo* by Mzilikazi, a former ruler of the Matabele, meaning bald heads. The name was later corrupted and changed by the white man to Matopos.

Little did I know then that one day soon I would be climbing those domes, whalebacks and castles, and would sleep in the many caves that were still inhabited by leopards, dassies (African rodents) and bushman paintings. I didn't know it then, but one day I too would sit on Rhodes' grave amongst the sacred hills of the Karanga tribe, listen for the voice of the Mwari god and look out over what Rhodes referred to as a 'view of the world'.

Mr Robinson, the Deputy Head, was waiting for us when the train pulled into Bulawayo station. He was a giant of a man with the bearing of a Grenadier Guard and hands like spades, an impressive form who dwarfed his petite and pretty ash blond wife as they shook hands with and greeted each of us in turn. When the formalities were dispensed with, he organised the porters who were quick to do his bidding, and under his eagle eye the school bus was loaded with our luggage. 'Bus' was a very generous description as 'Lulu' (or 'monkey cage' to non-residents), was a 4-ton Bedford truck that didn't resemble a bus in the true sense of the word. It had four lines of wooden seats running the length of the bus facing inwards, a body encased in wire mesh with a cover of canvas that could be lowered in case of rain and a flat metal roof that, like the body, was painted in government green.

On instructions, the driver drove slowly along the streets of Bulawayo that had been decreed by Cecil Rhodes should be wide enough to allow a full span of oxen with wagon to turn.

We passed his bronze, modelled-from-life statue, then passed a plinth that supported a Maxim gun used in the Mashona rebellion of 1896; its muzzle pointing above a stream of traffic headed towards the columned colonial grandeur of the City Hall, surrounded by its beautiful gardens and manicured lawns, lofty palms and jacarandas. Was it pre-ordained or entirely coincidental that the same old building would one day resonate with my voice reciting poetry and singing an aria from the Pirates of Penzance?

After leaving the city suburbs, the full-width tarred road was reduced to two, parallel, asphalt macadam 'strips', suitably spaced to accommodate the passage of a car. These 'strip roads' as they were known, dated back to 1933 and were constructed mainly by unemployed Europeans as part of an unemployment relief scheme. This type of road had its advantages, so the theory goes. It was said to improve driver skills and discourage speed.

Unfortunately, I never had the chance to test the theory, as two decades passed before I owned my first car. By that time the majority of the roads in the country had been replaced by full width tarred roads, and the low-level Bailey bridges I had grown up with and which had been a feature of every river crossing in the country, had been replaced with high-level concrete bridges. They would have obviated the situation we had been in decades earlier, when Lulu became stationary about 5kms from our destination, behind a stream of vehicles taking turns to cross the Bailey bridge spanning the Umgusa River.

After leaving the Umgusa behind, the road wound its way through a narrow stretch of dense thorn bush smothered in a film of grey dust that billowed from the tall chimney of a cement factory. It looked completely out of place in the wild bush countryside that stretched as far as the eye could see. In that patch of grey, the only signs of life were the flocks of tiny mossies (Afrikaans: sparrows) that flitted from bush to bush like puffs of grey cotton wool. It was pollution at its worse that suddenly ceased about 2kms from the wire gates of Rhodesia Fairbridge Memorial College.

Chapter 15

Fairbridge 1948 – 1955

"When you close your eyes on a hot day, you may see things that have remained half-hidden at the back of your brain. That day I saw a street in the East End of London. It was a street crowded with children—dirty children, yet lovable, exhausted with the heat, no decent air, not enough food. The waste of it all! Children's lives wasting while the Empire cries out for more."

This is an excerpt from a speech given by Kingsley Fairbridge, the founder of the Fairbridge Farm Schools to a meeting of the Colonial Club at Oxford University in 1909.

Fairbridge Memorial College was up until 1946 a RAF training school. It was then known as Induna Flying School named after an unusual flat-topped hill called Ntabazinduna or 'hill of headman' that stood on the border of 2000 acres of bush bequeathed to the Fairbridge Trust. The word Induna is a derivative from the Ndebele word for 'headman'. No matter where one stood in the grounds of the home, Ntabazinduna was always visible, together with a small, pointed rocky hill that from a distance appeared to be part of Ntabazinduna but was in fact separated from the hill by a narrow swathe of open bush.

This rocky protuberance, known as Maxims Kopje, was the last place that the Maxim gun was fired by the British South Africa forces in the fight against Lobengula during the Matabele War in 1893.

My new home was a corrugated-iron nissen hut, one of twenty or more that were set up in two lines on brick plinths about three feet above the ground to protect the wooden floors from termites. This also inadvertently provided its occupants with the ideal hiding place for cigarettes, homemade marula wine, and apple cider.

Besides the dormitories there were other corrugated-iron buildings that included a chapel, two enormous dining-rooms separated by an expansive kitchen, a small staff tearoom, a lounge, a library and a prep room formerly an Officer's Mess that most believed was haunted and for good reason! I remember on more than one occasion visiting the prep room with others from my dormitory at dead of night and hearing the sound of male voices, coughs and the scrape of furniture on the wooden floors. It was bloody scary I can tell you, no less so in fact than a disused morgue that stood, strangely enough, only yards away from the chapel.

It was at least a year after I arrived before that morgue was pulled down, until that time it was a favourite place in which to scare the wits out of anybody locked inside. It was a simple concrete room, windowless except for a few air vents and a solid iron door that could only be opened from the outside. There were few of us that didn't unwillingly or unwittingly spend time in that morgue before it was demolished. Fortunately, the freezing equipment though still intact didn't work, thank God, so in theory there was nothing to be afraid of except the cold and the imagined images of bodies lying on the concrete slab.

Away from the dormitories stood the most impressive of all the corrugated-iron buildings. They were two immense aircraft hangars that made the two garaged buses inside, Lulu1 and Lulu2, look like dinky-toys in the vast empty space. Outside there was a fenced-off area that contained two obsolete aeroplanes. One was a Tiger Moth with a rudder and flaps that really worked and the other a Harvard with a cockpit and seats, a playground for souvenir seekers and budding pilots. Then one day a lorry pitched up while we were in school and when we came out to play the planes were gone just like that!

There were, if I recall, seven permanent brick buildings, the largest being the Headmaster's house. It had a gauzed-in veranda and a spacious garden that became the site for a self-contained cottage named the 'Rejects House' after those among the 'old boys' who had either been fired from or were between jobs. The Padre's house on the other hand, was a more humble abode and lacked a veranda, while the Bursar's residence though similar in appearance, made up for what it lacked in comparison with a beautiful vegetable and flower garden and a neat fowl run, wherein scratched and crowed the most magnificent, bad-tempered Hampshire cock and his harem of bountiful hens.

Besides the residences, there were three blocks of toilets with showers and baths, an enormous gymnasium and a concrete swimming pool that was oft-as-not under repair for cracks. It was shared equally when the summer rains fell with hordes of bullfrogs, water scorpions and all manner of drowned creatures.

The cricket pitch was in a prime spot close to everything and was used constantly by everybody for every type of sport. I remember in particular a titanic struggle between bat and violin in the early 1950s, when the boys played a two-day game of cricket against a team chosen from members of the Hallé Orchestra, captained by its conductor Sir John Barbarolli. They were in the country to give a series of concerts starting with one in the Bulawayo City Hall. I can't remember who won the match, but I shall never forget being one of the unfortunates who with free tickets, was forced on the following Saturday of all days, to sit through hours of composed torture in the Bulawayo City Hall.

That same cricket pitch incidentally, was used for another sport that was part of a series of initiation rites that dogged the life of a boy's rise from Junior to Senior. Unlike most of the initiations there was no pain, only acute embarrassment at being made to run around the pitch bollock-naked on a Sunday evening, just at a time that coincided with the passing by of the Senior girls on their way to church.

The first day or two in my new home passes as a blur in my remembrance. Why, I ask myself, and what have I forgotten that was worth remembering? Then I realise perhaps it was the excitement and mystery I shared that day with a hundred strangers that was just too much to comprehend.

There was one of us however who remembered that day— Geoff Crimes. He wrote: "We arrived about eight at night and were met and taken and put in 'Lulu'. I'll never forget that first journey through the dark streets of Bulawayo (very few shops were lit at night). All of a sudden your guts would be in your throat every two hundred yards or so as Lulu hit the drainage humps in the intersections. The first meal I cannot remember. I was taken to 'Ma' Laing's dormitory and put to bed. There were lots of kids all peeping out from under the blankets, all meant to be fast asleep. As soon as the lights went out the whisperings began: 'Where are you from new boy?', 'What's your name?' etc. I remember the following day was Sunday and we were allowed to miss church (hadn't got our 'whites' yet!). As soon as church was over the hoards descended on us to see 'what the new boys had brought with them'. Fortunately swimming was next on the agenda and that probably saved what little we had brought with us! It must sound a little bit traumatic (people nowadays seem to love that word!), but then I think that every kid who came out went through the same, and every kid who was there when a new bunch arrived did the same. I put it down to plain inquisitiveness and probably the realisation that a new arrival was someone with a link to 'home', as most of us referred to England, no matter how tenuous it may have been—Do I know him? Does he know me?"

Each day began at dawn, except for Saturdays, Sundays and school holidays. We were awakened by the sound of a gong that hung between two poles in an open space separating the two lines of dormitories. The gong, consisting of a short piece of railway line, was beaten at dawn, midday and in the evening by a Senior nominated by the Duty Prefect. For the first four years during which Fairbridge was run and funded by the Fairbridge Society, the sound of the gong preceded a flag-raising ceremony around the flagstaff. It was fine in summer, even pleasant when the sun rose early. But it was hell in winter when that freezing wind blew across the parade ground, turning skin purple. The poor little bugger whose turn it was to blow the Reveille on his bugle had to pause more than usual to draw in breaths of icy air that seemed to freeze the sound to an icy wail as we sang 'God save the King'.

Then one day in 1951, Britain handed over the home and its wards to the care of the Colonial government. That saw the end of the flag-raising ceremony (which we were glad for, because it meant an extra half-hour in bed) and the portrait of George VI that hung in the dining room was replaced with that of the Prime Minister, Sir Godfrey Huggins. Despite this severing of links with the past the migrants continued to arrive, but as the post-war living conditions improved back 'home' the flow of children became a trickle and ceased altogether in 1965.

We, the so-called 'chosen elite' of English institutions, earmarked as new 'white leaders' in a part of the empire creaking under the ominous weight of black nationalism, were left to our own devices after an order was received from the Fairbridge committee in London instructing the guardian Mr Robinson to destroy all documentation pertaining to The Rhodesian Fairbridge Memorial College.

My first and only junior schoolteacher was Mr Jackson, who must have gone through difficult times for the first few weeks after our arrival, deciding through a series of tests where each boy would best be placed in the educational stream. For example, due to conditions that had prevailed in Warren Farm, at the age of eight I was placed in Standard One but more by accident than design I rose two standards in the first year and by the end of the second year was on par with age to standard.

Mr Jackson or 'Sailor' as he was affectionately known, was an ex-Royal Navy Officer who had served in the war aboard a destroyer. He was short but incredibly strong, with a chest that resembled the bows of a battleship and legs like stunted oaks. For all his size, he was modest and quietly spoken.

When I first met him, had he worn a cassock I would have taken him as the double of Friar Tuck. The similarity between the two didn't end there, for he too had a round pink face that reddened by degrees according to how angry he was. Despite his homely and often placid appearance he was above all else a strict disciplinarian who frowned upon even the mildest of transgressions, including any disrespect shown to 'grown-ups' by not raising one's hat in passing or referring to the same by name rather than 'Sir' or 'Ma'am'. To swear was to commit a cardinal sin! I remember, for example, an occasion when he overheard me use the word 'bloody' while in conversation with a friend. That resulted in my receiving 'six of the best' for, as he put it, "using that word out of context."

As I look back, what I might have missed at the time but have subsequently come to understand, was Sailor's natural skills as a teacher for he was impartial and without favouritism. He was aware that in each of us lay a hidden quality that he nourished and brought to the fore. I was just one who, for example, battled to grasp the elements of Maths. He understood this and patiently endured my lack of reasoning but at the same time acknowledged that somewhere inside me lurked a leaning towards English Literature.

His observation paid off when in 1948 under his guidance I won a First Class award for Elocution in the first Rhodesian Eisteddfod that was held in the Bulawayo City Hall. He drove me to the event in his brand-new open-topped Morris Minor. I can still see him clapping in the front row when I stepped from the wings onto the stage and recited his favourite poem:

SHIPS

Stately Spanish galleon, sailing through the Isthmus
Dipping through the tropics by the palm green shores
With a cargo of ivory, apes and peacocks, sandalwood,
Cedar wood and sweet white wine.

Dirty British coaster with a salt caked smoke stack
Butting through the channel on a mad March day, with a
Cargo of Tyne coal, road rail, pig lead, firewood,
Iron ware and cheap tin trays.

He followed closely the ideals of Kingsley Fairbridge, that the young should be encouraged to become farmers, for Rhodesia at the time was still in its infancy and the road ahead lay in opening up the vast tracts of land that were as yet undeveloped. To this end Sailor formed a Young Farmers Club whereby each child, if he so wished, was allocated a piece of land on which to grow vegetables.

On my first attempt I grew a bed of lettuce that was delivered on the back seat of his car to the Bulawayo market. The crop was auctioned for Five Pounds, more money than I had ever dreamed of and made me rich enough to purchase a 4-part share in the ownership of a BSA pellet gun. Then did the world become my oyster! Dreams of gardening and its riches faded as the gates to adventure opened wide and led me to a veritable bush paradise in a world where nothing stayed the same, where the good was balanced with the bad, where we were 'kings of our domain' and where in a space of time I spent the best years of my life.

There was one proviso made however, for those who like me sought the company of the bush, and that was that nobody ventured into the bush alone. It was a hard-and-fast rule that came into effect when it was discovered that the more intrepid explorers among us, particularly over weekends and school holidays, were travelling further and further a field, sometimes as much as twenty miles or more beyond the boundaries of Fairbridge, to fish and hunt at places with mysterious names like Insiza, Bembezi and Nyamandhlovu.

The distances travelled increased even further with the advent of hitchhiking. Matopos, for instance, some thirty miles away became a favourite daily trip. The proviso on travelling alone remained in force for as long as I lived at Fairbridge. As to distances, well it was proven that such was the spirit among us that soon there was nowhere too far that a pair of legs and a little initiative wouldn't take us.

I read somewhere the words of a well-known psychiatrist who stated: "a child remembers best, the good times." How true that is and what could be better remembered than school holidays when discipline was relaxed and we were free to roam and explore the wonderful world that lay between the home and Ntabasinduna. It was a 3-hour walk north to the hill, along a narrow winding footpath that snaked through elephant grass high enough to hide a herd of cattle and with here and there a sprinkling of mubonda (Shona: wild protea) that offered some shade from the oppressive heat on a hot summer's day.

Nothing was hard-and-fast, we moved as the spirit moved on walks that could be extended to days, even a week or more in the school holidays. We slept beneath the stars or in the tangled undergrowth, with nothing to sustain us but tins of bully beef and loaves of bread supplied by the kitchen and whatever we shot with pellet gun or catapult. Water was sometimes difficult to find in certain areas, in which case we sucked donkey berries to ease the thirst. If we were lucky to come across the fruit of the 'kaffir orange' (hard shelled juicy wild fruit), we broke open the hard shell and sucked the juicy brown segments. There was always something to eat or drink from the veld (Afrikkaans: wise open rural spaces) sure, we went hungry and thirsty now and again, but that was part of learning and something to talk about over a roaring fire with nothing to disturb the night but the shriek of an eagle owl gliding silently through the darkness.

There was one place that we frequented more than anywhere else, east of Nthabasinduna. It was an area that adjoined the strip of bushveld we covered on the walk to the hill. There were no features such as a river or higher ground to separate the two, one simply stepped from one into the other unaware of the change in the countryside, until suddenly the long dry rustling grass and stunted trees disappeared and one found oneself splashing through water with soft green vlei (Afrikaans: marsh) grass brushing one's knees. If we wanted to, we rested in the shadow of a marula, a wild fig, or a flat-topped acacia with branches hanging heavy under the weight of tens of thousands of queleas (small grain eating birds), moving constantly as one in flocks that painted shadows on the earth.

Everything in this favourite place seemed so much grander than anywhere else, the anthills tall as giraffes and born from mantles of bush so dense that only snakes and squirrels could pass through and where the buck were so tame they ignored your presence until you got so close you could almost touch them.

We built ourselves a little tree house in a wild fig tree growing on the edge of a vlei where the flamelilies grew and huge green bullfrogs spawned in the shallows. The floor of the house was made from a door that we 'found' propped up against a tree outside the caretaker's storeroom back at the home. The roof was a few sheets of beaverboard rescued from repairs done to the inside walls of one of the dormitories. You could get inside the house if you took your hat off and bent double to get in the door, but there was room inside for a million mosquitoes and four bodies to lie prone and listen to the croak and splash of bullfrogs and the sound of nightjars calling to each other in the African dark.

Chapter Sixteen

Moses

At precisely six one morning, at the start of the school's December holidays and in the aftermath of a torrential downpour that had washed clean the streets and suburbs of Salisbury, the overnight express from Bulawayo, its klaxon blaring, rolled into Salisbury station.

A recorded impersonal voice from somewhere high above amongst the roof trusses, announced the arrival of the train and almost immediately the platform burst into life and I found myself swamped by crowds of hugging, kissing, sobbing and laughing humanity.

I grabbed my suitcase and fought my way through the jam-packed corridor outside the compartment and after buffeting my way like a ship braving a storm in the Bay of Biscay, I found a bench in a quiet spot at the edge of the crowds and sat down to wait for something to happen.

Hidden safely away in the inside pocket of my school blazer I carried a letter of introduction in a sealed envelope, but I trusted that the large badge emblazoned with a fancy 'F' sewn on the top pocket of my blazer would provide all the recognition needed for whoever was to meet me.

A clock hanging by two chains from the roof above my head read 07h00 and by then the platform was deserted except for a porter coming towards me. He wore black trousers, a waistcoat with silver buttons that shone like a row of medals and a pair of black thick-heeled shoes polished like an advert for Nugget shoe polish. He was pulling a barrow with a couple of suitcases and at his side were a clearly disgruntled man and woman who stopped now and again to argue. I watched them with keen interest until they merged with the light of day, then disappeared through the exit and into the shadows of moving traffic below a strip of blue sky. The hidden voice in the roof to announced the scheduled arrivals and departures of the day's traffic. I found myself glancing at the clock every five minutes now, the hands hardly seemed to move at all. Then bang on 07h30 and one-and-a-half hours late, Mr Murdock arrived. I saw him long before he saw me. I knew it was him—his actions were a dead giveaway as he dodged knots of passengers arriving to catch the 08h00 train. He moved at speed, head turning from left to right scanning the crowds, once or twice spinning on his heels to look back as if searching for something he may have missed. Then as he drew closer he began to veer off. I waved frantically until he saw me and waved back.

When he reached my side he was panting heavily. Beads of sweat littered his forehead. He looked flustered as he removed his hat and wiped his brow with the back of one hand, the other he stuck forward in greeting. His palm was sweaty and stuck to mine like raw dough. Then, letting go, he stepped back a pace, replaced his hat and placed his hands on my shoulders. He was a tall man, so tall he had to step back even further when stooping to bring our eyes level and avoid us banging heads, but even then the brim of his hat scraped my forehead.

I was shocked, for a moment, by two intensely blue eyes that stared out from beneath the brim. Fathomless they were, like the sun-polished sea off Las Palmas, the kind you can't lie to. They were framed by twists of hair the colour of ripened wheat, flecked with grey at the tips and set in a deeply tanned face, etched with fine lines that moved with every expression like wave lines on a sandy beach.

I had to make comparisons to determine his age. I always did that, for grown-ups to me fell into three categories: the young, the old, or very old. I compared him to my guardian, which made him 'old'.

The 'old' man straightened his back and turned to my suitcase. At the same time I remembered the sealed envelope and handed it to him. I stood idly by while he read the letter, then folded it carefully and tucked it into the pocket of his khaki shirt.

"Sorry I took so long George," he said apologetically, "but we had a cloudburst last night and the Mupingi came down in flood, so I had to wait for the waters to drop." Without waiting for a reply he impatiently hefted my suitcase. "Let's get going young man. We've a long way to go, I've left the car running and it's blocking the entrance."

Sure enough, in the street outside the entrance to the station, a dozen or more cars were backed up behind a fawn-coloured solid-looking car with broad chrome front bumpers splattered with gobs of mud. Between the headlights the grill gleamed like a set of perfect dentures. On either side of the car's body beneath the doors, running boards stuck out like a pair of clipped wings below side mirrors that protruded from the doors like chrome ears. Between the rear bumpers, breaking the sleek lines, was fixed an open boot covered by a sheet of canvas.

Irregular puffs of blue-grey exhaust smoke from the car had enveloped a small crowd of furious drivers and curious bystanders. I stood nervously beside the old man as he tried unsuccessfully to reason with the crowd, his voice drowned by the shouts of the exasperated drivers and the hooting of traffic.

At last the old man, clearly angry at the response of the crowd, was driven to prove a point. Instead of reasoning, he took on an indifferent attitude that seemed to grant him immunity from the curses and catcalls as he slowly untied the canvas on the boot. With infinite care he placed my suitcase in the boot, taking his time fastening the canvas then, with an air of insolent benignity, doffed his hat in the manner of a polite chauffeur as he opened the car door and ushered me in.

He chuckled to himself as he pulled off, waving to the crowd in the manner of a benign ruler and as we sped away I caught a view of his face in the rear view mirror. Our eyes met for a second before he winked and his face broke out in an insolent grin.

Caught up in the moment I found myself smiling as the car left the city centre. I was still smiling when a few miles further on we turned into a wide street lined with Jacaranda trees so tall that their overhanging branches formed a green tunnel. He drove slowly for my benefit, past imposing and fancy wrought-iron gates wearing brass name-plates scrolled with names like 'Clouds End' and 'Summer Place'.

We stopped now and again at the entrances of gravel drives bordered with lines of scarlet Flamboyant trees that led to stone mansions with grey slate roofs, nestled in groves of oak and silver birch, surrounded by lush emerald lawns and flower beds overflowing with summer colour. I remember we stopped briefly at the gilded entrance to a diplomat's residence guarded by a sentry in uniform and a high stone wall hanging heavy with bougainvillea and honeysuckle.

We drove on through less affluent suburbs of small stands and modest houses with corrugated-iron roofs painted red or green, fronts enclosed in gauzed verandas, and roads leading off that were narrow and littered with dustbins.

Soon we were driving through the outskirts of town and it wasn't long before, at a fork, the full tar road ended in strips.

We took the left fork marked with a signpost that read 'Mazoe 24 miles'. From there the road wound through gently undulating grasslands sparsely populated with trees that could easily be counted. Heavy rains had left the verges potholed and rutted by the passage of cars, donkey carts and cattle. The grass in the ditch alongside the road, fed by pools of rainwater, had grown tall with stems thick as pencils. From the branches of the odd tree that appeared above the dense grass, weaverbird nests hung like bunches of inverted flasks, while long-tailed widowbird cocks with heavy trailing tail plumes hovered in burdened flight amongst dozens of drab females. They were joined by flocks of doves and an array of red bishops, finches, and quelea feeding on the verges, rising in startled waves at the approach of the car on wings that fanned and whipped to life the fallen leaves that flipped and dipped like butterflies.

We had been travelling for perhaps an hour when, after a protracted conversation that had covered among other subjects a short history of my life leading up to my leaving England, the old man slowed down, pulled off the road and stopped in the shade of a tree. "Nature calls," he said, and I watched him disappear into the long grass. It wasn't long before he appeared doing up his flies. "How about you?" Embarrassed I shook my head.

"No thank you, Sir."

After he got back in the car, before closing the door he turned to face me. "Now that we've got to know each other George, please do away with the Sirs and the Misters. From now on, I'm Uncle Bob."

"Uncle Bob. Uncle Bob," I repeated beneath my breath as the car pulled off. "I have an uncle," I whispered to myself, "I've never had an uncle before." I glanced out the corner of my eye at Uncle Bob who was humming and tapping the steering wheel to a hidden tune that turned my insides warm.

At around noon we were no more than a hundred yards from the turn-off to Sipolilo when Uncle Bob spotted a figure sitting in the shade on the side of the road. He began slowing down trying to decide whether it needed help. From a distance the figure was sitting so still it appeared to be dead, then as we drew closer I could see it was a man with his head lowered and arms hanging loosely at his side.

He seemed unaware of the approaching vehicle. As we

drove closer, the rude noise of the car engine in the silence of the surrounding bush failed to catch his attention. Then as we drew alongside, his head slowly came up but he looked past the car as if searching for something tangible in the distance. At the same time he appeared to be stroking something in the grass at his feet.

Uncle Bob stopped the car and shifted the gear into neutral. He waited for a second or two before opening the driver's door then, after stepping down onto the hot dusty surface, walked towards the still figure. I followed, unsure, keeping to Uncle Bob's shadow until he stood in front of the seated figure. I watched as Uncle Bob removed a handkerchief from his pocket and wiped his brow.

"Good morning" he said, pocketing his sweaty handkerchief and reached out his hand in greeting.

Peeping from behind Uncle Bob's back I watched as the seated figure extended a shaking hand. The fingernails were chipped and broken, the finger joints swollen. The back of his hand was studded with scars and crisscrossed with prominent blue veins. From where I stood I looked down on a full head of unkempt snow-white hair that hid his ears and covered his shoulders in waves like the mane of a wild horse.

The man looked up, the movement causing the locks of hair to part like the dramatic uncovering of a foundation stone, revealing the face of the oldest man I had ever seen. I was struck by the intense brown eyes staring out like marbles from a face wrinkled and burned to baked leather. A snow-white beard covered his cheeks and jowls in coarse fur, except around the sunken lips where the fur had been stained the colour of polished teak by a pipe with a crusted bowl that peeped from his shirt-pocket like a guilty eye.

While the two spoke, the stranger continued stroking the fur of a tan-and-white dog that lay on its side at his feet, pink tongue protruding from its jaws, its lips pulled back in a snarl.

From its mouth dribbled a stream of pale-pink saliva alive with flies. I watched fascinated as a large green fly shining like cut-glass in the sunlight prodded at the surface of a sunken eye before it took off with a buzzing whine as Uncle Bob knelt down beside the still bundle. I watched as he ran his hands through the soft fur of the dog's neck and along the flanks, pausing and pressing now and again as if searching for a pulse.

"What happened?" he asked, looking up at the stranger. "Are you all right?"

"I'm fine" the old man said, looking up, a hand wiping at the deep slick creases below his eyes, "but I think Smudge is dying."

"I'm afraid she's gone," said Uncle Bob rising to his feet, patting the stranger's shoulder.

"You sure, Mister?"

The stranger leant over and swatted angrily at the swarm of flies that continued to buzz about the corpse, then stooped and gathered the limp bundle in his arms and pressed his lips to the dry nose. "Smudge, you stupid bitch," he whispered, he hugged the dog even tighter and buried his face in the dog's pelt. The stranger then seemed to quieten down.

"I'm afraid so," said Uncle Bob, reaching forward to stroke its head, "but if it's any consolation I don't think she had long to live, she shows all the signs of old age."

The old man then seemed to accept his dog's demise; he laid the body down at his feet then sat on a rock. He lit his pipe and related the history of his dog that he'd won in a poker game while he prospected for gold in a place called Essexvale, west of Bulawayo. The story took the form of a string of events, some of which were so exciting I remember them quite clearly:

"I drank myself to sleep one night, so drunk that I let the fire burn out and would have been victim to a pack of hyenas had Smudge, who was only a pup then, not kept them at bay all night. The next morning after having sobered up, I counted the spoor of four hyenas and recalled with shock a true story of a drunken hunter who in the same circumstances I found myself that night, was bitten in the face and dragged from a fire before the flesh of the cheeks and chin were torn away…

"I left Smudge to guard our camp one day while I went off to hunt for the pot and had hardly gone a mile when I heard her barks and yelps. I rushed back as fast as I could, firing shots and shouting, thinking it could be a leopard for I knew only too well their liking for dog meat, but when I reached camp it was only to find her astride a dead kaffir dog. She was at the same time fending off a bunch of kaffirs wielding spears and knobkerries, who on seeing me ran off at speed leaving the camp untouched. They were a hunting party and I reckoned they must have thought my camp was easy pickings. But they had reckoned without Smudge, who despite a spear wound had kept them at bay…

"Here it is, see here." He ran his finger along a jagged scar on the dog's shoulder where the fur had failed to grow back. "The wound was deep, so deep I had to stitch it up with a sail needle and twine, and do you know not once did she yelp, bless her, just whined a little, and when I was finished she licked my hand and limped off on the scent of the robbers who will still be running, I reckon."

He chuckled to himself, then faltered as he lifted the bundle of fur that became an extension to his beard as he buried his cheek in the pelt. I watched his shoulders shake a little before he raised his head once more and I saw fresh tears glistening in the cracks around his eyes.

"She sure as hell saved my life last night after a snake slid into my bedroll. Smudge sensed the bloody thing was there, wouldn't let me climb in and performed like a banshee when I ignored her, then I knew something was wrong the moment she gripped my wrist in her teeth and pulled. Oh Christ! I knew inside she was warning me, but like an idiot I lifted the roll. The snake reared ready to strike, she let my hand go and leaped past me, and I know I should have held her and pulled her away but things happened so fast I didn't think. I looked instead for something to kill it with, but before I could lay my hands on something, she had hold of it and was shaking it like a terrier does a rat. She had nearly bitten it through before it wriggled, turned and sank its fangs into the soft part high on the inside of her leg and hung on and it was then I lost my head, grabbed the snake, pulled it free, then stomped on it till there was nothing left but bloody skin. Smudge lay down for a bit, breathing like a blacksmith's bellows while I stroked and fussed her, then got up and limped around 'til she was too weak to stand, then crawled on her belly to her favourite place beside the fire…

"I tried everything. I slit the wound hoping to bleed out the poison but the fangs had struck deep in a difficult place. There was no place to tie a tourniquet, so I rubbed permanganate on the wound and bathed it in salt water. Before dawn she rallied and wandered round the campsite searching for water. I tried to give her some but her tongue was so swollen she couldn't lap, so I tried squirting water by mouth down her throat instead but she brought it up. I took her into the bedroll with me. She whimpered once or twice and coughed up heaps of phlegm. She was still alive when the sun came up, but she couldn't hear my voice."

We buried Smudge beneath a muhashe tree that was alive with wood pigeons and louries feeding on the scarlet fruit. "It's a tree sacred to the KoreKore," said Uncle Bob, "that nobody would chop down unless they chose to bring down the wrath of Mwari on their heads." After Moses had filled the grave, on his insistence we heaped stones atop the mound that he said would protect the body from scavengers.

It was as we were leaving this place to resume the journey, that the two men introduced themselves, and I in turn was introduced to Peter Wilson—or Moses, as he preferred to be called. He was given the name by a priest he'd got drunk with on his travels, who in an inebriated state, had compared Peter thanks to his looks, to the biblical Moses—and since then the name had stuck.

It turned out that Moses, before the tragedy, had been on his way to his home on the Hunyani River that coincidentally was not too far from Uncle Bob's farm. So Uncle Bob insisted he accompany us for the rest of the journey, for which I was grateful because Moses had found his niche in my affections.

As we prepared to load the old man's goods and chattels into the boot, Uncle Bob stopped what he was doing and pointed to the horizon where a thick bank of black cloud and thunder rolled slowly towards us as flashes of jagged lightning joined heaven and earth. It was still far off, but nevertheless the old man's few meagre belongings were quickly stashed in the boot—a patched canvas one-man tent, a few battered pots and pans, a canvas water bag, a half-sack of maize meal, the infamous bedroll and a wooden ammunition box. Last to join me on the back seat was a battered leather suitcase and the old man's rifle wrapped in a cloth.

Soon after taking the turn-off to Sipolilo the dust road wound its way through Mazoe, a sleepy village surrounded by green hills and orange groves. It was early afternoon and the sun played hide-and-seek between clouds of grey cumulus with black edging. They floated like bloated ships across the sky, casting constantly changing patterns of shadow on the countryside and the road ahead.

The road was corrugated in places, so much so that the uniform hum of the engine was often broken by the sound of stones clattering beneath the chassis. A constant flow of fine red dust sucked in by the slipstream smothered the interior in a coat of grit that stung the eyes and found a way to the roof of my mouth and ground between my teeth like sandpaper.

When I looked at my reflection in the rear view mirror, my face was transformed into a mask of damp ochre. Beyond the open window, the shade of leafy trees slipped coolly by and rays of dappled sunlight peeped and winked in playful insolence like the impish eyes of naughty children. All I wanted was to get out of the dust trap, spread my aching body, and feed on tomato sandwiches.

As if in answer to my prayer, Uncle Bob pulled on to the verge and stopped in the shade of a tall tree, its branches hanging heavy with leaves limp and polished in the midday heat. A short distance ahead on the opposite side of the road I saw a signpost marked 'Mtoroshanga' that pointed to a road heading east, in the direction of a range of hills shrouded in a bank of heavy cloud.

I watched the two men alight and head for a group of granite boulders grouped around the base of a tree a short distance away. In one hand Uncle Bob carried a brown paper bag that carried with it the aroma of fresh bread. In his other hand he carried a canvas water bag dripping with condensation. I suddenly felt thirsty and my stomach rumbled in anticipation. We sat facing each other. The rock under my bum felt cool, a welcome change from the clinging hot seat of the car. We ate in silence and washed down with cold water not the tomato sandwiches of my prayers, but raisin buns covered in a thick layer of sticky icing.

Moses gave a satisfied burp when he was finished and leaned back against a backrest of granite. I watched him remove his pipe from his shirt-pocket and deftly fill the bowl from a drawstring bag marked Springbok Choice Tobacco. He looked at me and grinned as he pulled the drawstring closed with his teeth and tucked the bag away in his pocket. I watched fascinated as he struck a match on the rock between his legs. In one smooth movement he placed the flaring match to the bowl and sucked on the stem. I watched the burning tobacco rise in the bowl and cringed as he tamped down the red-hot tobacco with his naked finger.

All around, the bush was silent save for the intermittent ear-piercing screech of a lone cicada, and the revenant call of a mourning dove that seemed to come from a bush with dark green leaves and delicate purple flowers.

Moses slid forward and stretched his legs. He looked around for a moment then his eyes rested on a point somewhere beyond me. I instinctively turned my head and followed his gaze as he took a long puff on his pipe. I watched the coils of smoke disintegrate in a passing breeze as invisible fingers ruffled his beard and parted a lock of hair exposing an ear lobe, pitted and peeling like flaky pastry.

He pointed with the stem of his pipe at the range of hills in the distance and said something to Uncle Bob. I didn't hear his words for my eyes and mind were focussed on the grey outline of the hills he had pointed to, their higher crests hidden in low black cloud, their shapes stirred intermittently by zigzagging stabs of lightning into constantly changing shapes.

It was in the omnipresence of the approaching storm that Moses seemed determined to look beyond his recent loss by reminiscing about his past. That seemed to please Uncle Bob, who encouraged him by assuming the stance of a keen listener, while I, always ready for a tale, settled back to listen.

It was tales of gold that had lured Moses' father from a quiet existence as a farmer in Somerset to the hard-fought life of a prospector and gold miner in the heady days of the Rand, where men made and lost fortunes in a single day.

Moses was twelve when the family set sail for Africa in 1878. His father, hard working and shrewd, spent the next five years consolidating his position in a consortium of mining ventures, before seizing the opportunity to diversify by purchasing a transport company and several upmarket properties. That made him wealthy and sought after by a succession of socialites.

"Mother and Father began leading separate lives in separate bedrooms," said Moses, "until one day she upped and left him, and on that same day I left the Reef and headed North at the age of 17 for a country beyond the Limpopo."

On the journey Moses teamed up with a 'down on his luck' young Englishman who too, had fallen into bad times after his brother had stolen his legacy.

"Family working with family seldom works out," muttered Moses, "the brother sold the legacy and kept the money to himself, leaving my poor partner high and dry. The smell of riches," he said, "does strange things to a man. It can change him overnight from an honest dreamer to a grasping unscrupulous bastard.

"I liked the man," said Moses, taking a final pull at his pipe before tucking it into the pocket of his shirt. "We worked and played hard. Our partnership might not have brought us the wealth we desired and it had its ups and downs but nevertheless it taught me the true meaning of trust, a virtue I learnt could be so easily squandered when wealth subjugates principles. It was a shame our relationship had to end the way it did, and in those hills." He pointed once more to the Umvukwes, now shrouded in dark cloud.

"We began prospecting in this area before chrome was discovered in the hills," said Moses, "before that there was little to be found other than a smattering of low grade asbestos and an unworkable vein of gold we found in the northern reaches. But despite its lack of riches, there was something about the Umvukwes that captured my soul. From afar they look pretty ordinary, nothing compared to the lofty beauty of the Inyanga or Chimanimani— whose views have left me speechless but remain inaccessible to me as if not of this world, unlike the Umvukwes where nothing remains the same despite their accessibility. Do you know?" his voice dropped and took on a dreamlike quality, "that each time I leave the Umvukwes I feel I know them better than myself, yet when I return there is always something new to see, a hidden valley perhaps or a cave that I have passed many times before but has somehow been kept from me.

"In winter I have seen the frost lie deep as snow on rocks that cracks like pistol shot as the sun warms the surface. Huge boulders big as houses split in two by the expansive force of nature, and behold, a year later when I pass the same spot, God has walked by and healed the cracks from which have sprung sweet-scented shrubs and trees that have provide shelter and food for dassies.

"It was in June 1896 at the time of the Mashona rebellion, that my partner and I were besieged for ten days in the same hills by a marauding gang of Shona warriors that had been part of a gang that had attacked Alice Mine. We would have perished from thirst had not a light drizzle fallen, it fell nowhere else that day but over the Umvukwes—it was a miracle!

"The following morning, though still feeling the effects of the siege, we climbed down from our refuge prepared to meet the enemy full on. But they were gone— moved out at first light leaving the ashes of their fires still warm and the bush around the camp still carrying their scent.

"We set off for the Hunyani River and on the way met up with Methuselah, heading a party of hunters returning to their kraal. Fortunately, he was a Korekore and an enemy of the Zezuru. He was willing to give us refuge so we lived with him and his family while we regained our strength, which is why we have remained companions ever since. In fact if the truth be known, it is he that has encouraged me over the years to return to my camp on the Hunyani whenever I take a break from prospecting."

"And what happened to your partner?" asked Uncle Bob.

"Oh him," said Moses, "well he just never got over the experience and when we got to hear of the European dead and wounded at Alice Mine, he packed his bags and returned to England."

We had been so engrossed in the old man's story that time had stood still. We had been aware of the storm since burying Smudge, the thunder had come and gone half-heartedly and once or twice drops of rain had fallen that had barely pockmarked the dust.

But it was as we were leaving that everything grew still. There was a deathly hush as birds and insects fell mute and leaves ceased to whisper. It came like a warning that in the future would become familiar to me, but right at that moment little did I realize that it heralded a storm.

A prolonged flash of lightning lit up the shapes of the two men as they left me standing and ran to the car, returning with the canvas that they pegged down in an open patch of ground. No sooner had we taken refuge beneath the canvas that the wind began to blow. It was no ordinary wind, but a living thing that tugged at the edges of the canvas with such power that my arms and hands ached in my feeble attempts to hold down the flapping canvas.

"We are in for one hell of a storm!" I heard Uncle Bob call out to Moses from the darkness beneath the cover, and no sooner had he spoken there was an unheralded flash followed by a crash of thunder that deafened me momentarily as the first drops of rain fell.

Curiously, I lifted the edge and peered out to see the heavy drops strike the parched earth in puffs of dust like bullets that peppered the earth with tiny craters. Above us the drops drummed like pebbles against the canvas, increasing in intensity until the sounds merged into a roar. Suddenly, the barrage ceased as swiftly as it began, eclipsed by a strange silence that is impossible to forget. It came before a rush of icy wind that was followed by another penetrating flash of lightning and a crash of deafening thunder. The sound on the canvas became a pounding, roaring, battering din beneath the weight of hailstones that pinned me to the earth.

Then, yet again, it suddenly subsided, a last final roar and the storm passed! There followed a smattering of rain before the wind died down altogether. When we lifted the cover, I remember the relief and joy as the glorious sun appeared from behind the clouds, it shone through swirls of gossamer mist that floated upwards and disappeared in the purified air.

I gazed in wonder at the heaps of hailstones lying around, reflecting the sun's rays. They added a mystic beauty to a scene of devastation in the aftermath of what had been, and would ever be, the most furious hailstorm I have ever witnessed. Trees had been stripped of leaves and lay like a green carpet upon the battered earth that had once had looked so perfect.

"Looks bad son, doesn't it?" I heard Uncle Bob say, and felt his hand on my shoulder, "But son," he said, "if you pass this spot in a week's time you will see things as they were, except the grass and trees will be greener and the birds will sing that much louder."

It didn't take long for the sun to dry out the canvas cover and by the time we left the place of stories the heaps of hailstones had almost disappeared. The boulders we had sat on appeared to have been polished by the storm's force and shone with renewed brightness. Even the road verges had all but swallowed the puddles, leaving the top soil cracked and peeling.

The road from there to Sipolilo wound its way through beautiful granite kopjes (Afrikaans: hills) with fantastic shapes, they were separated by clusters of huts, some of which to my amazement were perched on the summit of bald gigantic boulders. Intrigued, I asked about them.

"The sites were carefully chosen" Uncle Bob told me, "so the tribesman could hide from and defend themselves against the Matabele."

"And why do they not blow away?" I asked.

"Well George," he answered, "and it isn't a tall story if I tell you, a special kind of clay is used that sticks the huts like glue to the bare rock. There's a similar village not far from Paradise, maybe if we get the time I will take you there and get the tribesman to explain exactly how it's done."

The sun had passed its zenith when we reached the turn-off to Sipolilo, a village no more than a cluster of insignificant-looking tin-roofed houses, surrounded by copses of alien trees still bearing the remains of blue spring flowers and demarcated by white-washed picket fences and gates.

A signpost that read DISTRICT COMMISSIONER–DEPT INTERNAL AFFAIRS–DEPT MINES led us to two flag masts set in a triangle of gravel with separate flags fluttering in the breeze. One bore the insignia of the BSAP (the British South Africa Police), the other the Union Jack. A short gravel path led from there to the entrance of a brown brick building, from which dribbled a constant mixture of civilians and uniformed policemen.

Uncle Bob switched off the engine and strode off in the direction of the building. I watched idly as he stopped to talk to one of a group of mounted policemen, their horses tethered to a hitching post outside the building. The policeman raised his hand and pointed back over Uncle Bob's shoulder in the direction we had come. Uncle went on into the building and returned looking worried after having tried unsuccessfully to phone his wife.

Just then, an open Land Rover pulled up and stopped in a cloud of dust just feet away from Uncle Bob. Out stepped a figure wearing a beige pith helmet, long shorts, and jacket to match that of the horsemen. He slid from behind the wheel, removed his helmet and proceeded to dust down his uniform with vicious swipes of his helmet. Startled, I watched the horsemen spring to attention and salute the man, who ignored the salute and pulled from a pocket a green khaki handkerchief with which he dusted off a thick film of dust from the polished surface of his boots. Only when he appeared satisfied with his appearance did he stretch out a hand in greeting. It was obvious to me that he and Uncle Bob knew each other for they talked and laughed like friends meeting after a long absence.

The man with the fastidious habits I was to learn was Superintendent Peter Motherwell, member-in-charge of the BSAP Sipolilo and bearer of the bad news that rain had fallen overnight in the area. With a heavy belt of rain cloud still hovering above the Umvukwes and further north, there was a definite chance that the Mupingi would be impassable. The policeman offered to put us up for the night but Uncle Bob was anxious to get back.

We left Sipolilo without Moses. Talk of the floods had left him worried. His camp was close to the water's edge on the Hunyani. "If I strike out now," he said, "I'll make it before dark." After shaking hands, the old man drew me close to his chest. I felt the hard ridges of bone against my cheek and even deeper I could hear the beat of his heart. But it was the scent of him that I remember most: the brain-drugging smell of dried bushveld after the first rains; the heart-warming friendly scent of the campfire; and yes, it was there, clinging to the wool of his shirt, the sad, fresh odour of Smudge.

Saddened, I looked back at the old man standing beside his pile of meagre belongings. He cut a sad and lonely figure as he raised a hand in farewell and yet somehow I knew it would not be the last I would see of him.

We had travelled no more than an hour when as the car crested a rise I heard a murmur. It was no more than that at first, but as we descended it grew steadily louder, rising to a monotone roar as the full picture of the flooded river filled the windscreen.

Uncle Bob stopped the car at the side of the road, got out

and beckoned to me as he made his way towards a flat rock that jutted out above the raging river. I stood in awe beside him only yards away from torrents.

My God! What a scene... rumbling, tumbling, swirling waves that leaped forward and upward, each seeking to out-speed the other and in so doing smashing against rocks, exploding in bursts of ochre spray that were instantly transformed into spumes of effervescent scum. Detached from the maelstrom and buoyed by gusts of wind born of the speeding waters, they wafted above the waters like thistledown to settle at my feet in a carpet of yellow bubbles. Tall reeds were bent double, their silvery plumes dipped and drowned. I watched a whole tree float helplessly by, its roots sprouting like hairs on a scarecrow, its stricken branches stripped of bark, clinging to the bobbing trunk like arms on a corpse. I watched fascinated as it hit a rock with a thud, then turned broadside on like a stricken vessel against the iron markers that marked the edges of the drift.

Immediately a dam was formed against the trunk as debris from upstream smothered the obstruction in a tangled mass that rose swiftly. Then, as the contained waters breached the dam, it disintegrated in a silent explosion of debris that saw the flotsam disappear downstream, leaving the trapped tree behind, its trunk gleaming like wet marble.

While waiting for the river to subside we sat and chatted. As evening began drawing its curtains, suddenly the sun, hitherto hidden behind clouds, burst through in a blaze of glory that painted gold with nature's brush the river and the valley through which it flowed.

It was after dark before the river had dropped sufficiently for us to cross the drift. I seem to remember panicking, not so much from the actual crossing but more from when the car slid back into the river a few times while climbing up the steep slippery bank on the far side. After that the road must have been easier, and we were just in time, for as we arrived the rain began to fall. Through a curtain of raindrops trailing down the windscreen, I caught sight of the doorway and the figure of a woman with a shawl draped over her shoulders holding a lamp at eye level. That reminded me in an instant of another time, another place, when Jesus too held a lamp and knocked at my heart and a hundred others besides.

The journey to Paradise had been a memorable one that must have left me very tired, because I remember very little of what happened next. In fact, my last thoughts that night were of Aunt Ina as she helped me prepare for bed, and before my eyes closed I distinctly remember hearing the sound of frogs croaking to each other in the dark.

Chapter Seventeen

Paradise Farm

It was a knock on the door that dragged me from darkness and into the soft light of morning. Aunt Ina floated into the room wearing a smile and carrying a tray bearing a mug and a plate piled high with biscuits. After laying the tray on the bed beside me, she crossed the room and pulled back the curtains with a flourish, bathing the room in light that outlined her form beneath her cotton dress.

She sat down on the edge of the bed facing me. I was startled by the similarity between her and her husband. I don't know why but I had expected her to be stout, a picture-book farmer's wife with a round face, twinkling eyes, and shelf-like bosoms, but instead, I was looking into a pretty face framed in tight brown curls, lined, but still showing signs of youth.

She reminded me in many ways of Miss Mill, the way she engaged in conversation and listened intently to my experiences of the journey while unpacking my suitcase into a chest of drawers. When she was finished, she came and sat down beside me and gave me a big hug. In that instant I looked upon her not as a friend or aunt, but as a mother.

My first day on Paradise was spent exploring, never far from the cottage. The rain had cleared overnight and the sun was warm on my back as I wandered through the vegetable garden and orchard out back. Beds of vegetables were separated by hedges of pomegranates, neat rows of mealies (maize or corn on the cob) and molehills of sweet potatoes. From the nearby orchard came the fermenting scent of fallen peaches and oranges that had attracted myriads of yellow butterflies that flipped and jerked from blossom to fruit, or settled in carpets around the edges of puddles. I played my own game that day, chasing loeries, mousebirds, and bulbuls from the garden while Ina and I harvested what the birds left.

After the first few days life settled into a pattern. It began at first light with a pair of francolins calling to each other from a rocky outcrop at the back of the house, followed soon after by a chorus from the flock of guinea fowl that roosted every night in the fig tree that grew beside the path leading to Masikas kraal.

Bob told me the call of the birds was his alarm clock, and I knew this to be true for soon after the birds called I would hear the sound of his footsteps in the passage outside my door, which in turn was the signal that prompted me to throw on a shirt, shorts and takkies (trainers) and join him in the kitchen for a hot cup of coffee and rusks.

Wherever he went, I went with him. I was his shadow on the walks along the river, where he showed me the spoor of a leopard that had crouched to drink, the neat prints of a jackal beside a pile of wing feathers, and the fine prints of toktokkies (beetles) in the soft damp sand at the water's edge. He showed me a place on the river where he and a policeman, many years ago when Paradise was new, had shot two cattle thieves. He taught me how to follow the honeybird that led to wild bees' nests, and where a hammerkop had built a nest that was so strong it could carry the weight of a full-grown man. He took me on walks to Masikas kraal and showed me to the elders, sat and talked with them and drank kaffir beer from a calabash, while I played with my pot-bellied, shiny-black friends and made clay animals with horns of grass and baked them in the sun. One that was better than the rest I gave to Aunt Ina, who put it on the mantelpiece above the fireplace for all to see.

It was one of Bob's herders, Kurumidzai—*the fast one*—who taught me how to make urimbo, the sticky juice of a parasitic berry, that when chewed collects in the mouth like chewing gum and is wound around stems of grass, then stuck in an arc in the mud to snare birds coming down to drink.

Uncle Bob taught me how to fire his .410 shotgun that he used to shoot guinea fowl and pheasant. They were hung in the shed for days before Aunt Ina roasted them in a big pot, with a lid so heavy I had to use two hands and a lot of strength to lift it. That pot weighed less than Uncle Bob's *Martini-Henry* rifle that was so heavy I had to rest it in the fork of a tree. I fired it just once, which gave me no pleasure, only a bruised shoulder and burst eardrums. I can only remember him firing that rifle twice, once in mercy to dispatch a cow with a broken leg and once to shoot a jackal whose carcass he hung up on the fence of the sheep pen to warn off others. I never saw him shoot a buck for the pot, he always said he preferred to see them walking around.

Meals were taken at a table in an extension to the kitchen, which enabled the two to share a conversation and banter in person, while Ina busied herself moving with alacrity between pot-bellied stove, cupboard and a box on stilts in which she stored perishables t were kept cool by a trickle of water running over a bed of coke. I was always hungry then, especially at breakfast time when Ina served the bacon, eggs, sausages, and liver devilled in wild hwohwa (wild mushrooms), straight from the frying pan onto the plate whilst the bacon still hissed and everything bubbled. When we were finished we retired to the stoep (Afrikaans: stoop) for coffee. While they talked of mundane things, I stared up at the ceiling to watch the antics of Chifurira, the pink gecko, that Bob told me was an albino, like the sister of one of my friends in Masikas kraal. As they talked and the gecko ate, I could hear Sixpence, the houseboy, washing-up at the sink outside the kitchen door.

Lunch on the other hand was a choice. You either ate or you didn't, it depended on whether you were around. If I was, which wasn't often, I simply helped myself to either a couple of rusks doused in a mug of tea or made myself a sandwich from yesterday's joint of beef. Ina cooked dinner slowly, using, as she would often say, 'the aroma in the kitchen as her guide', and oh, my God, will I ever forget that mouth-watering aroma that followed me each evening as I passed the kitchen on my way to the Mupingi to switch off the pump!

The source of the Mupingi River lay at the northern end of the of the Umvukwes range, roughly sixty kilometres from where it joins the Hunyani. It was there, only a short distance from the confluence, that I came across a deep pool enclosed by a natural dam of moss-covered rocks, one of them long and flat that made it appear to float to the centre of the pond. A metal frame had been bolted to it to support a pump and motor that were protected from the elements by a roof of corrugated iron. It was so worn and rusted it appeared as perennial as the rock-fig tree growing from the bank above it. Its huge gnarled roots held in their crushing grip a huge boulder that had already cracked from the pressure, but even more striking was the tall curvaceous knobthorn that grew on the far bank. Its branches overshadowed everything including the farthest reaches of the pond, as well as a path that led to a natural river crossing of the Hunyani, over partially submerged rocks that vanished with the rains but for most of the year provided a path that wound through dense forest, open crop lands and cattle kraals, ending up in the dust of Masikas kraal.

It became my chosen duty to start that pump each morning at dawn. I would listen for the telltale sound of the water gushing into the tank that rested high above the cottage on a platform of teak sleepers. It was a vantage point from where Bob and I kept an eye out for bush fires and from where, on a clear day, it was possible to make out a darker shade of green that was the confluence of the Angwa and, to the east and beyond that, the light grey shapes of the Mavuradonha mountains.

Oh, how I miss, to this day, the evenings on the stoep, when we sat together as a family by the light of a hurricane lamp, listening to the splashing of a family of otters playing in the river, the 'krrik' of a disturbed moorhen scuttling amidst the reeds, and the gurgle of water flowing between rocks. It was the perfect background that gave deep meaning to the tales that each told me of years gone by. They were great storytellers and told me of how they met only weeks before Uncle Bob who, having fought in the Great War, was granted land in Monamatapa. They walked the sixty kilometres, from the source of the Mupingi in the Umvukwe range to its confluence with the Hunyani, in search of a suitable piece of land on which to build a farm.

Ina told of the day they decided on this spot and how in celebration they had swam naked in the river beside a pool of hippo. It was wild then, said Uncle Bob, and he spoke of the herds of game that roamed the hills and plains of Paradise, of Masikas kraal, a flourishing little village then, which remained neutral through the Mashona rebellion. Even though that was before their time, Uncle Bob had taken note of the tragedy and had acquired the habit of sleeping with his rifle lying beneath his bed.

They spoke sombrely of a severe drought in the 1920s, when Masikas kraal became a graveyard and the inhabitants who were able left the village, leaving behind the elderly and infirm to live on what remained of the crops and cattle. Scores of dogs, once used for hunting, were left to roam and formed packs of survivors that lived on the dwindling game, they in turn were hunted by the local farmers until none remained. The large game migrated to the Zambesi and the smaller game became so scarce, said Uncle Bob, that it was possible to go a whole day without seeing a single duiker or steenbok. "It wasn't only the blacks that suffered," he said, "for we, too, lost crops and cattle. We began to lose at such a rate that in the end we paid farmers who had a spare bit of grazing, to graze our livestock 'til the rains came, and because we had little money we paid them with a large percentage of our calf crop. But above all, water was the biggest problem. The Mupingi dried up completely and the Hunyani was reduced to a few stagnant pools."

"It got so bad," said Ina, "that the two of us, and a few of our labourers, deepened the pool. We dug night and day, taking turns, 'til we came to bedrock and we could dig no further, then we waited and prayed for the water to seep through. In the end it supplied us with enough water to survive. But even the indigenous bush that had pushed roots down to the limit began to shrivel as bushfires ate the bark and left Paradise looking like a battlefield

"So you can imagine how we felt when the rains eventually came. We have never forgotten that day, have we darling?" said Ina wistfully, stopping her knitting to glance at Bob. She then paused as she remembered: "We lay on the bare earth just there," and pointed with her needle into the darkness beyond the porch, "watching the dark angry clouds skirling above us while all around the lightning flashed and the thunder cracked and roared and we held hands. Do you remember, dear? And when at last the first icy drops fell, we undressed and lay down naked in the mud and sang and thanked God." All at once, I began to laugh as I imagined the two of them rolling around in the mud. Ina stopped knitting but my laugh must have been infectious because Uncle Bob leaned back in his chair and we laughed and laughed until the tears rolled down our cheeks, and Ina looked on, surprised it seemed at the effect her words had on us.

They told of the aftermath of the drought from which Paradise never recovered. The wildlife returned to the farm, albeit in smaller numbers, many of the large antelope having been decimated by hunters on the migration back from the Zambezi Valley. Sadly, the hippos and crocodiles never returned to the stretch of river that flowed through Paradise. Its waterways that were once kept clear by the foraging hippo, grew over and formed banks of sand and mud on which thick reed beds grew prolifically, thereby hindering the flow and reducing it to a trickle in the dry season.

Even the rafters and furniture in the cottage told a story. The former had been sawn from the Mukamba, the pod mahogany tree with hard black and scarlet seeds, some of which Ina kept in jars as a decoration in the kitchen and on the mantelpiece above the fireplace. It was a tree that was fairly common on Paradise, unlike the logs of Mukwa that had to be transported from Matabeleland to the carpenter who lived and worked in Masikas kraal. He was the same carpenter, I was told, that made the Murdock's furniture, the race and neck clamp in the dipping kraal and the donkey cart that Uncle Bob used to cart anything and everything around the farm.

I came across the carpenter one day while visiting my friends at Musikas kraal. He was standing up to his head in a trench, wielding a saw that appeared lengthier than the combined height of his two assistants. They were standing above him on a platform that supported a huge mahogany tree trunk they were sawing into planks.

Standing on the edge of the pit, I looked down on the carpenter. Each time the saw rose and fell, the poor man laboured under a shower of sawdust that stuck to his skin and scalp like icing on a fruitcake. As the cut grew longer, a fourth man hammered a wedge into the cut that kept it open and stopped the saw blade from jamming. The strength needed to lift and pull that gigantic saw was incredible. Somebody told me it took the men a full day to cut one plank perhaps longer, depending how many knots there were in the trunk. But it wasn't that I admired so much as the cleverness of the man to produce from those massive logs something as fine and pretty as Aunt Ina's dressing table.

Bob told me it took six months to build the stone cottage, and six days to build a pondokkie (hut) with a thatched roof, that they lived in while the house was being built. During that time, the two lived on tinned bully beef and sadza (porridge made from maize meal) with a treat now and then of bread that Ina baked in an oven dug into a termite mound. It was two years, he said, before they found the money to buy a wood stove. Until that time, Ina did all the cooking in a cast-iron pot with legs and in pots suspended on a tripod above the fire. She was still using the same pots to render down the tails of sheep to make cooking fat and prepare tripe which they were both very partial to, but which I ate under sufferance and with very long teeth. In fact, as I recall, everything Ina used in the house, from polishes to soaps and from glue to tannin, found its beginnings in those pots.

There were two days in each fortnight that began long before dawn. In fact, when Uncle Bob and I left the cottage on those days the bush was still fast asleep, except for crickets chirruping in the tall grass and the rustle of rodents searching for seed in the undergrowth beside the path that led to the compound. The compound was a circle of mud huts inhabited by the farm workers and each hut was surrounded by gardens of maize, sorghum, and sweet potatoes.

I followed Bob from hut to hut as he knocked on each door and called out "muka marume muka," (wake up my man, wake up). He didn't wait for any door to open. He didn't need to. The herdsmen knew from the knock that it was time to collect the herds of cattle from the fenced camps and drive them to the dip-tank that was centrally situated within a cattle kraal. It was built of stout poles to withstand the crushing weight of milling beasts with horns like battering rams.

It was a long walk to the dip, along a narrow path that wound around and between kopjes that looked menacing and silent in the dark. I kept close to Bob, especially when the pale ribbon of dust vanished into a tunnel of darkness and meandered through dense thickets, where lurked, in my imagination, all manner of fierce animals.

I was glad when the path entered an open plain crisscrossed with the tracks of cattle. We couldn't have been too far from the dip when Bob unslung his rifle and handed it to me. "Here you are. You carry it for a bit," he said, "and tell me when it gets too heavy." I carried it for what seemed like miles, shifting the weight from shoulder to shoulder, struggling to keep up with the tall frame ahead. It was pride and nothing else that in the end lifted me and saw me through, without help, to the gates of the dipping kraal.

The dip was a simple structure, a long narrow tank built of stone and cement. It was deep enough for the animals to plunge in without hitting the bottom and swim for a few yards, before climbing out into a shallow drip race where the beasts stood for a few minutes while the poisonous liquid dripped from the hides and flowed back into the tank. It was protected from the elements by a thatched roof that reduced evaporation, and ensured that the arsenical liquid remained at a constant strength.

We didn't have long to wait before the first rays of dawn crept out from behind the kopjes and trees and lit up the plain and a small herd of red hartebeest, grazing amongst a larger sprinkling of impala. We watched them while Bob pointed out their characteristics and within the blink of an eye they were gone, melted away like ghosts into the surrounding bush as the first sounds of the approaching herds of cattle broke the silence. It was thrilling to see the beasts arrive, driven by the herders, whistling and calling out a warning to each other as an errant beast looked to bolt from the herd. As the herd drew closer, the first rays of the sun reflected off the knots of horns, clicking and clacking, as the beasts bunched before the gate of the kraal and bellowed, and sniffed and snorted, scenting the ground. Hooves dug in to hold back the prodding heaving mass of meat and bone for a few seconds until the pressure was too great and they were bundled through. When the gate was shut, the beasts stood wide-eyed and trembling until they calmed down.

Now Bob had his own special way with his cattle, for once inside there was never a word spoken loudly or harshly. He and his herders knew each beast and kept the bad- tempered until last.

The first to go through would be a 'lure' batch of mature beasts which were very familiar with the dip, followed by the cows with calves, well spaced to avoid a cow leaping onto a calf when plunging. They were followed by the masses that went through in a continuous flow, stopping only for a few minutes in the drip race, before passing through a further race where the beasts with sores were treated with Stockholm tar, and grease was smeared on the ticks hidden beneath the base of the tail where the dip had failed to penetrate.

It became my proud job to count the cattle as they left the race. Everything was jotted down in a large black book that compared the number of cattle in each herd with the last count. If there were shortfalls, the herd was kept in a holding camp with grazing and water while the herders and I went off in search of the missing.

One Sunday Bob surprised me. It was at the breakfast table, when he brought up the subject of Moses. "What do you say we pay him a visit? Give him a surprise? Somebody at Masikas told me he lives about three miles downriver. It's going to be a pretty tough walk, but if we go now we should be back in time for tea and scones. Bring the binoculars George, they're hanging on the hat stand, and don't forget your hat."

Uncle Bob was right. The going was tough, and with the good seasonal rains the bush was even thicker than he had expected. We weren't much more than a mile down river before it became impossible to hug the bank and we had to make a wide detour through bush that was similar to that back at Fairbridge. What a walk that was! There were game trails everywhere. Bob pointed out the spoors of a lone hyena and wildcat, the strong pointed prints of duiker and reedbuck, and mounds of pellet droppings and urine patches from impala that stood by and watched us, until one snorted and the herd took off in all directions, weaving between the trees and clearing shrubs in explosive leaps.

As we worked our way back towards the river, we ran slap-bang into a herd of browsing kudu. I think they thought we hadn't seen them, but at the last minute one of the does flapped an ear and stood stock-still, staring at us through her beautiful bulging feminine eyes. As I stood there, I remembered Bob's words: 'If you see one, there'll be others. Look into the bush, not at it'. Sure enough, I concentrated and picked out the forms of others, including a bull with huge camouflaged horns. I don't know what scared them, but suddenly one of them gave a short sharp bark and in a flash they were gone.

Soon we were back at the river where it flowed through a shallow gorge, and instead of fighting our way through dense bush we clambered over rocks, which was hard going. It was so rugged that sometimes Bob handed me his rifle while he negotiated a difficult spot. We stopped for a breather and watched a troop of baboons across the river. On seeing us, they stopped the search for food and perched on rocks like spectators at a cricket match, all except for the leader. He was a huge brute, who sat above the troop in the fork of a tree and barked at us until, in play, Bob raised his rifle and took a bead on him, whereupon it barked the alarm, sprang down from its perch and made off taking his troop with him.

"Uncle Bob, do you think that baboon knew it was a gun pointing at it?" I asked.

"Oh, for sure, George," said Bob, "he's probably been shot

at a hundred times."

"But why do people shoot them, Uncle Bob, you can't eat them, they're like people?"

"That's true," said Bob, "but some people, especially farmers, see them as robbers and killers who steal mealies and kill and eat young lambs."

"But it doesn't seem fair, Uncle Bob. Me and my friends scrump fruit from the orchard back at the home, we've been caught plenty of times, but nobody shoots us."

"Yes, you're right George, and why do you raid the orchard? I did, too, when I was a boy, but the sad difference between us and them is, we stole the fruit because it was daring to do so and not because we were hungry, but the poor old baboons steal because they have to or they starve."

With that Bob rose to his feet and shouldered the rifle, "Come on George. Let's go find Moses."

It was by chance that we came across Moses and Methuselah fishing, otherwise we would not have found the tiny house as it was hidden away in a circle of trees between two rocky outcrops.

He was over-the-moon at seeing us again. It was the same old Moses, except he looked a lot happier than when we had last seen him. His friend Methuselah was a wiry old Manyika man with no shirt, which made him look a lot older than Moses, for his bare chest revealed a sprinkling of white hair and folds of loose skin on his skinny frame. He spoke pretty good English as a result of having lived for years with Moses, who couldn't speak a word of the native dialect. All the time the two spoke they never stopped catching fish. It was sort of a reflex action, in and out, in and out, and each time they lifted the fishing poles out of the water there was either a sinde (sardine) or marimba (barbell), which they dropped into a billycan that was already brimming with fish.

"Well that's it," said Moses, rising to his feet, "that's supper.

Methuselah, toss the bait and let's go." I watched the lump of sadza plop into the water. Immediately the river came alive with fish snatching at the lump of dough and in seconds it was gone.

Their house was built from stone, without mortar. The two had gone to a lot of trouble, chipping and facing each stone so that there were no gaps between each course, which had made it possible to plaster the inside with a mixture of mud and manure. The lintels above the two windows and above the door had been shaped with an adze (edge tool used for carving) and the door likewise. The windows were fixed and covered in mosquito gauze, while the roof and chimney had been fashioned from flat galvanised sheeting painted a dark green to match the surroundings. Even the rocks holding the roof down had been carefully selected, to be wide and flat so that they could not easily be seen by a passer by.

It didn't look like much from the outside, but when Moses invited us in I was surprised at the amount of space inside. It was a single room divided into three by drops of hessian hanging from the rafters. In two of the rooms there was a bed and a wooden ammunition box used as a bedside table. The third room served as a kitchen-cum-living room, with two easy chairs and a tiny wood stove with a pipe coming out the back that was connected to the chimney. It was cool inside, though with the dagga wall it must have been warm in winter. Out back was a well-worn path that led to a long drop (hole in the ground toilet) enclosed in a flat iron shell with a roof. There was no door, just a strip of hessian and inside a heavy wooden box-seat with a hole cut in the centre. Within easy reach of anybody sitting on the box was a pile of old newspapers and a bag of quick lime.

We sat and chatted over a cup of tea Methuselah had brewed on the wood stove and ate biscuits made from maize-meal baked to a golden brown. I learnt in the course of conversation, that although the river ran through many farms the frontage did not belong to the farmers but was common ground for a certain distance from the high-water line. So in essence, Moses and his companion were not trespassers, but anyway, as Moses pointed out, they should be welcomed as the eyes and ears against rustling and poaching from across the river.

The two led the 'life of Riley'. They lived on whatever the land had to offer. Methuselah's relations, and there seemed to be many, gave them enough money to enable Moses to buy the ammunition he needed for his old Martini Henry rifle, the odd item of clothing and a bottle of brandy Moses would keep in the box beside his bed along with bottles of Methuselah's home-made brew of marula and wild plum wine.

Before we left for home, they took us for a walk down river and pointed out a place where animals came to drink. It was there that the river flowed through a narrow plain of grassland, cropped short by cattle and game. The banks on either side were nude of vegetation, besides the swathes of reeds that sprouted either side of the places where the animals waded in to drink and cool off. A little further down from there, at a spot where a bank of mud and sand reached out into the shallows, Methuselah pointed out the spoors of makarwe (Shona: crocodiles) and pointed to one lying on the far bank. Try as I might, I couldn't see it until Bob painstakingly directed my sight with the binoculars, to where it laid mouth wide open and motionless like a log of wood.

The sun had begun its descent when we said our goodbyes to the two men. I would see neither man again.

Ina wrote me a letter, I can't remember exactly when, telling me of the death of Moses from pneumonia and a short while later I learned of the death of Methuselah. Both were given a ceremonial funeral at Methuselah's home village near Rusapi, where according to Bob, they were buried side by side in Methuselah's family graveyard.

Tea and scones with homemade strawberry jam and oodles

of fresh cream were waiting for us that day when we got home. In the course of conversation over tea, it was decided that in the morning we would be off on a trip to Sipolilo to do Christmas shopping.

I couldn't wait and there wasn't much sleep that night, I can tell you. I was up and about before sunrise and took a walk to start the pump. On the way back already the cheeky mousebirds were busy in the pawpaw trees, hopping from fruit to fruit, pecking their annoying holes, while Tip Tolls flashed their yellow bums disdainfully at me as they flapped past, heading for the tomato vines. Go-away birds flew past in clumsy flopping flight, landing in the trees outside the orchard. They quarrelled with each other before making peace, then looped down to the fruit trees and lopped from branch to branch in the search for ripe fruit. I remember thinking to myself how great life was and how good it was to be alive.

Sipolilo was buzzing when we arrived and the only trading store in the town was crawling with black people who had arrived in a bus that looked ready to fall to pieces. It was covered in a layer of dust so thick that the logos on the sides were illegible. The roof, invisible under a roof rack, was piled high with cases, boxes, furniture, wickerwork baskets packed with chickens, bicycles and a goat with its legs tied to one of the rack supports. Its passengers, arms filled with still more goods, streamed from the store and packed the bus so full you could hardly see the heads in the windows.

Bob looked at Ina, and shook his head: "Same old story isn't it dear?" I heard him say, "they'll get halfway to where they're going and the bloody thing will break down. Then they'll unload all that m'pashla (Shona: belongings), stack it on the side of the road and wait hours, maybe even days, for another bus." He turned to me with a grin: "And do you think they'll learn not to overload the bus?" He shook his head. "To them George, it's all part of life; accept the inevitable, be patient and you'll get to where you're going." Those words of wisdom meant nothing to me then for I was ignorant of the ways of black people, but as I grew older his words would ring true.

Meanwhile, the crowd in the shop had not lessened so we drove to the hotel for breakfast, then sat around thoroughly bored, drinking coffee. .

The bus was gone when we got back to the shop and so were most of the customers, so we split up to do our shopping. I hadn't the slightest idea of what to buy. I had the princely sum of five shillings to spend (equivalent to about 10 weeks' pocket money) which was a fortune in those days. I remember it well, walking round and round the shop in a quandary, and in the end settling on a penknife for Bob that had a single blade and a round pointed tool that the shopkeeper told me was used for prising stones from the hooves of horses. For Ina, after much deliberation, I chose a china figurine of a lady with a parasol that ended up on the mantelpiece beside my clay mombe (Shona: cow).

As was customary on the night before Christmas, the sabhuku (village headman) of Masikas kraal invited us to a night of celebration that began soon after dark. Fires were lit, and a crowd of bare-breasted young girls wearing short hide skirts, and a few of the older women, formed a half-circle opposite the men of the village and danced to the throbbing sound made by young men hammering tom-toms with such energy that my eardrums threatened to explode. That was a signal for everybody to sing and dance.

I glanced across at Ina and Bob, who to my surprise were clapping their hands in time with the rhythm, while at same time bending their bodies forward and backwards swaying to the beat.

Suddenly one of the girls, after much prompting and giggling from her fellow dancers, broke free from the others and came dancing forward to choose Bob as her partner. Poor old Bob, I could see how bashful he was, and Ina made things worse by calling out to him above the singing, urging him on as he tried with frenzied motions to keep in time with the tune. Then Ina broke ranks and swayed over to join him. To cheers and laughter from the crowd, they gyrated and stamped around in the light of the fires, surrounded by the girls with dusty bobbing breasts and smooth sweaty bellies. With perspiration running in rivers down their faces they both decided enough was enough and left the dancers to join the sabhuku, who as headman, found it his duty to serve them and me a calabash of kaffir beer and a plate of food.

It was my first, and last, taste of 'kaffir beer' and kraal food. The beer, as I recall, was vile, but I held my breath and with everybody clapping and cheering drank it, but the plate of fatty meat and mowa (a type of spinach) was so horrible it left me 'between a rock and a hard place': to refuse it would be disrespectful and yet I knew that if I did eat it I would be violently ill, which would also display bad manners. So I did the next best thing and when I was sure nobody was looking, I nudged Ina. Understanding my plight, she took the plate from me and handed it to a wide-eyed hungry-looking child standing behind us who gulped the food down and in so doing, saved me from 'a fate worse than death'.

I can't remember the walk home that night so I guess Bob must have piggybacked me all the way. To tell the truth, I can't even remember getting into bed on Christmas Eve, but I do recall clearly waking up on Christmas Day to the sound of drums coming from the kraal and the weight of a sock lying across my feet, crammed with gifts. There were sweets and Dinky-toys, fruits and nuts, and homemade biscuits, and a tin of condensed milk.

It was the happiest Christmas of my life, made even more unforgettable by the gift of a sheath knife that came with a leather belt. The curved knife was at least nine inches long and had a handle that was hollow with a screw top for carrying fishing hooks and twine. It was so well balanced that after a bit of practice I was able to take the knife by the blade like a knife thrower in a circus, and from ten paces with a dextrous flick of the wrist would bury the blade in the trunk of a tree. Kurumidzai tried unsuccessfully to teach me to carve the figures of animals from the soft sapling wood of the mutiti tree with its pretty black and red beans, but because I wasn't much good at carving, I collected the beans instead in a jar and gave it to Ina who placed it on the windowsill in my bedroom.

The last week of the holidays just flew past. There was so much to do and remember. However, there was an incident in that final week that was to put me off hunting for life.

It happened one afternoon after Bob handed me the .410 and a pocket full of cartridges. He suggested I take a stroll alone to a valley not far from the cottage where game birds were plentiful. I knew the area quite well as I had been there with him quite often. It was the site of an old kraal that judging from the huge tracts of re-growth that once were fields, would have been a lot larger than Masikas kraal in its heyday. It was from this same site that Bob had collected artefacts that he kept in a box in his storeroom. They included spear and arrowheads, pottery and a collection of primitive blacksmith tools. There was little that remained of the kraal itself, save a gravesite of mounds of stones and a circle of large rocks that Bob presumed was once a meeting place for elders similar to that to be found in Masikas kraal.

The site I have described has no relevance to what was about to happen, other than it being the area in which I came across a large flock of guinea fowl that would become the catalyst for a tragedy.

I heard the rustle of the birds first and froze when I caught sight of their blue and scarlet heads weaving in and out of the patches of long grass. As I crouched and pulled back the safety catch, suddenly there was a kek-kek-kekkkkk alarm call and one of the birds flew up in my face. Instinctively I swung the .410 from left to right as dozens more flew up in a flurry of wings. I fired both barrels in quick succession and watched one tumble from the sky in a cloud of feathers. Elated, I rushed through the waist-high grass to where I had seen the bird fall, I could hear it flapping in the grass and I stopped for precious seconds to reload, then all of sudden something leaped out in front of me, so close it caught me off balance!

Stumbling backwards, I tripped on something and as I fell, I remember putting out a hand to cushion the fall and spontaneously pulled the trigger. The crash of the shot numbed me and when I got to my feet, everything was quiet except for the pounding in my chest. I stood for a while collecting my thoughts.

Then I heard movement in the grass. Nervously, I crept forward, parting the grass with the muzzle, searching. Just ahead I could see where the grass was flattened and a little beyond that a mound that looked like an anthill, until it moved and I came face to face with a reedbuck doe, down on its front legs, with one of the hind legs flecked with blood, splayed out broken and useless behind it. Blowing and snorting, it struggled again and again to get to get to its feet and all the time I stood by in awe and dread, not knowing what to do, wishing and praying that the poor beast would find its feet and bound away, but it didn't. I was at my wit's end when it lay back, raised its head and stared at me accusingly.

I heard myself call out, "What have I done! What have I done! It wasn't me!" a mix of guilt, pity and anger wanted the beast dead. In fact, I begged it to lay down its head so I wouldn't have to look into its eyes any longer… then calmness, when all at once I knew what I had to do—I knew what Bob would do. I remembered the cow with the broken leg, raised the gun and pointed it at the buck's head. It was looking straight at me when I closed my eyes and fired. The first shot missed. When I opened my eyes it was still looking at me. This time I kept both eyes open and fired again. The head fell back blood bubbling and snorting from its nostrils, but it wasn't dead, the belly was moving and there was a thundering in my ears. I pleaded and pleaded, "Please die! Please die!" but it wouldn't! The belly continued to swell and heave like there was something inside trying to get out. I was in such a state that I can't even remember reloading and firing two barrels into the belly of the beast, but I did. When I came to my senses, the carcass was still except for the rippling of nerves along its flanks, the sight of which caused me to throw down the rifle in disgust and flee like the devil from that place to the cottage.

Ina was in the kitchen when I got there. Ashamed and wretched, I blurted out what had happened. She didn't say anything, which I was glad for. Instead, she told me to sit on the porch and rest. When I was rested, she sent me and Sixpence to retrieve the rifle.

It was late in the afternoon when Bob came home. I was out front in the orchard when I heard him call me from the porch. It was a long walk to the porch, made even longer with the thoughts that rushed through my mind. I remember conjuring up all sorts of excuses, excuses that filtered down to nothing when I stood before him looking down at his boots.

"So tell me what happened."

I told him. Everything, from beginning to end, and when I was finished, I waited for the tirade I was sure would come. But it didn't. Instead, he said, "What's done is done. I think you've learnt your lesson." He was right, I had.

I remember how miserable the last few days of the holiday were, for not only was the death of the reedbuck still fresh in my mind, but the thought that I was about to leave Paradise weighed heavy on me. I was haunted too, by the thoughts of what lay ahead. My Junior days were over, and from the stories that had filtered through from the Seniors, I knew that my first-form year was going to be a trying one. More saddening than that was the thought that I would be leaving Paradise and the couple who had made me feel part of their lives. I looked upon them as my Mum and Dad. I loved them as much as a good son should and I knew that they in turn loved me.

I returned to Paradise for all the school holidays in my thirteenth year, and it was in April 1953 that I spent my last holiday in Paradise. I was fourteen then, and Bob must have thought I was old enough to be told of his own childhood and the stormy road that had led him and Ina to Paradise.

Chapter Eighteen

My Senior Years

So I returned to face my first year of senior school. As I had expected, it was not easy at all. There were rules to abide by and there were those seniors called 'prefects' whose duties were to lead and control the mass. It was they who set out the list of home rules and added to the list when and as they saw fit. It was they who meted out the punishments for breaking the rules—except in exceptional circumstances when the transgression was so severe as to warrant a sentence by the headmaster or his deputy. It was they too, who decided what form a punishment should take, whether it was a caning, manual labour or detention. That wasn't to say they weren't capable of conjuring up even more original forms of punishment. For instance, I was caught smoking one day, and rather than receiving a caning, which would have been an easy option, I was given instead a packet of Tom-Tom cigarettes to chain-smoke, which left me extremely sick and high as a fly with a migraine walking upside down on a ceiling.

They ruled with an iron fist yet frowned on thieves and bullies, and strangely enough, like everybody else ignored the tradition of initiations.

It was to one of these prefects that I was assigned fagging duties in my first year. He was a fellow called Frank Jennings, built like a tank (in fact that was his nickname) and a sportsman of note. He wore rugby shorts like parachutes that took as much cleaning as his dozens of jock-straps, that were often as not stained with skid-marks as deep and broad as tyre marks on a muddy road.

Whatever he wore on the sports fields, two fags took turns

in washing and whichever of the two fags was not assigned washing had the job of polishing and shining his huge footwear for every occasion, or brushing his longs and blazer ready for the morning. Despite these wearisome mundane chores, fagging had its advantages, for as his servant one fell under his protection. I remember one occasion when one of the fags was smacked about by a feared fifth-former with a penchant for initiating first-formers by hanging them up by their arms before brushing their balls with boot-polish, which the reader may be assured is not only painful but is very difficult to remove. Nevertheless, the bully got his just desserts when, on that same day, the 'owner' of the persecuted fag organised us into a vigilante group and that evening after supper twelve of us ambushed the bully from the shadows. As somebody said afterwards, it was like ants attacking a dung beetle, and in a minute or two it was all over. We left him bruised and battered while the prefects turned a blind eye.

Keeping in the same vein, what I am about to write about isn't easy.

I don't remember how I felt after the rape. It was long ago and I was in my tenth year. Time has mercifully clouded the critical days of my adjustment. I remember, however, contemplating when I was about thirteen and about to become a senior, to confiding in Miss Mill but I was afraid of the repercussions.

For sixty years or more I have kept it close to my chest, but whenever I sit down to write it haunts me like a dreadful secret that requires release.

I haven't told a soul until now, so perhaps now is the time to relieve myself of this burden. At the same time, I would remind the reader that behind every evil deed there lies a root cause.

Padrě appeared as an upright religious man under whose guidance and teaching many others and I were confirmed into the Anglican Church. He was also the founding head of the

Fairbridge Cub Scout Troop. He was respected and revered by the headmaster and staff but in the eyes of his flock of young boys, he was what we called a 'moffie' (a derogatory term for a gay man) who also had a craving for a young penis.

Godfrey was the home's part-time tractor driver, altar boy, the organist in the school chapel and Padrě's seduced 16-year-old lover, but the youngest amongst us were unaware that Padrě wanted more and had his choice among the Cubs he accompanied on camping trips.

But children are wont to speak in their innocence, and Padrě's exploits became common knowledge. One day a deputation was chosen amongst the molested who approached the headmaster and told their stories. This so enraged the headmaster that they were beaten and warned against spreading such malicious lies.

I was one of a group of junior boys who were tasked with the job of harvesting a field of cotton one day (cotton was grown to help fund the home). I was thrilled to the core when Godfrey invited me to sit between his legs on the tractor seat and steer the wheels between the furrows while he groped up the leg of my shorts. He fondled my penis and when the work was finished for the day he let me drive back to the hangars.

It was late afternoon and everything was quiet when he parked the tractor. He took me by the hand and led me to a storeroom. Once inside, he pulled me down beside him then laid back and opened his flies.

I stared at his penis. It was the first one I had seen so close. I wasn't afraid when Godfrey took my hand. I was so under his spell, hypnotised and persuaded by his kind words and kisses. It seemed a natural progression, based on past memories, that he should remove my pants and take me in his mouth and draw from me a pleasurable response. But when he cupped my head to his groin it must have been then that I panicked, and struggled in horror at the size and the rank stench of stale urine.

I couldn't, wouldn't, take it in my mouth. It was at this point that fear, combined with hysteria, forced from me a scream and I begged for mercy, but the more I screamed, the angrier he became, and as I struggled, he clamped his hand over my mouth. "Ssh…Ssh…" he whispered, "If you don't shut up, I'll have to hurt you. You wouldn't like that, would you?" He toned his voice to a whisper, "Lie still, it's not going to hurt." I could hear my voice above his breathing, a far-off sound, muffled to the cold concrete as he turned my face to the floor and straddled me. I can still taste my tears against the skin covering my mouth and the vibrations of my muffled screams against the palm of his hand… "You'd better not tell a soul," he said, pulling up his trousers, "you're a new boy, nobody will believe you, and if you're good I'll give you another ride on the tractor. You'd like that wouldn't you?" and with that, he was gone.

The priest was still there when I left school, but years later I learned he had been transferred to a school in Ndola, the capital of what was then Northern Rhodesia. It was there, as if in answer to a prayer that he was jailed for sexually assaulting minors.

There is often, however, a downside to justice, and no more so than in the case of this devil priest. He was married to a lovely kind woman with a daughter, a sweet little thing who I recall pushing around their garden in her dad's wheelbarrow. It makes me sad to think of what might have happened to that little girl and her mother. Godfrey was eventually dismissed, for drilling holes in the ceilings of the bathrooms of a number of the housemothers. But that was long ago and change was everywhere. I began wearing underpants and grey shorts, a Milton blazer with the badge of an elephant with the school motto in Latin (that I have forgotten), and a blue shirt with a striped tie and a hat I was allowed to shape like a trilby.

Days began that much earlier now, the two Lulus would wait outside the dining room, motors purring impatiently, ready to begin the 10-mile drive that crossed the Umgusa. We would pass the rich suburb of Kumalo or 'Jewmalo' where the rich people lived; past the WELCOME TO BULAWAYO sign and into Selbourne Avenue, which was lined with silver-oaks and bougainvilleas, across the Matshomslope river— wherein Sir Roy Welensky once swam bare-assed and upon whose banks was situated Evelyn High, the sister-school to Milton High.

Lulu dropped us off on the first day of high school in the car park outside the tall wire gates. The seniors left us stranded and walked through with a stream of pupils who knew where to go. Someone must have noticed we were 'new boys' and led us through the gates, around a circular bed of roses, where we glimpsed the wide tarred quadrangle filled with blue blazers, the hum of voices, and across the quad the stately red-brick Beit School Hall, with its bell tower, red pillars and arched windows.

We stopped at last outside Charter House, one of two boarding hostels with attached classrooms. The other classrooms, and there were many, were built in a circle surrounding the Quadrangle, and beyond the classrooms were acres of sports fields. Strangely enough, the school lacked a swimming pool, so all swimming activities were carried out at the Olympic-sized pool at the sister-school little more than a mile away. Out of a total of 600 boys, the school hostels boarded perhaps a hundred, the balance being made up of day-scholars.

Everything went smoothly for the first few weeks. I had a different teacher for every subject and a few have remained in my memory. Mr Quirk the music teacher, with shoulder-length hair that was frowned upon in those days, taught me how to sing and drafted me into the chorus for every Gilbert and Sullivan operetta that was co-produced with the sister-school. I felt quite important then, a 'cut above the rest' in fact, for the home had to lay on special transport for me to attend rehearsals.

My history teacher was an attractive lady, whose name escapes me, but who I remember had a soft spot for the Fairbridge scholars, due perhaps to her ties to the war and a husband who still bore the mental scars of a war spent in a Japanese prisoner-of-war camp.

My Latin teacher was nicknamed 'Vampire', because he had a very short neck and his head seemed to rest on his shoulders. It wasn't only his looks that made him unforgettable, but also his habit of standing behind his pupils and rapping them on the head with a ruler each time they made a mistake when quoting the present, past and future tenses of verbs. We read from textbooks as old as Milton itself, their flyleaves smothered with caricature drawings of past teachers and clever little verses:

*Latin is an old language as dead as dead can be,
First it killed the Romans, now it's killing me.*

Like many scholars, I developed a dislike for Maths. Not the straightforward commonsense genre that with a little reasoning and the rare flash of brilliance I was able to get my head around, but Algebra, Geometry and Trigonometry. I believed they were contrived stumbling blocks invented by someone with nothing better to do than to make life a misery. It was this train of thought that, besides being an excuse for my ineptitude, inevitably brought me into conflict with Gifford, my Maths teacher. He was a former World War I ship's captain, with two shattered ankles that had left him with a bad limp in both legs that caused his feet to flap with each step. It became much more noticeable in winter when freezing gale-force winds swept across the quad and I looked on with feelings of pity, and a hint of malevolence, as he crossed the tarmac, head down, white hair flowing like an ensign, coat flapping like the sails of a yacht tacking against the wind.

It wasn't long before I became his nemesis through the

habit I had of constantly raising my hand and questioning each step through an equation. I realise now how off-putting it must have been for the others in the class that, because of my inability to grasp things, I would be asking the same questions the following day and the day after. So it didn't come as any surprise when I was downgraded and handed over to Pete Mans, an alternate Maths teacher who was considered more suited to my temperament. He was a complete antithesis to Gifford, being young, patient and with a pragmatic approach to each of his pupils. It was in fact thanks to him that I was able to scrape through with a pass in all my end-of-year Maths exams. All that is, except Algebra and Trigonometry that I fortunately learned the value of when school was just a memory.

He was also the coach of the Under Fifteen cricket team and gauged my potential as a bowler. Isn't it strange how every schoolboy cricketer wanted to be a fast bowler? I think it was the power one had over a nervous batsman. There weren't helmets back then, nor were there thigh guards and such like. Even 'boxes' were only worn when one became a Fourth-former—something to do with size I guess?

"You'll never be a pace bowler," he told me, which caught me a little off-guard. "You haven't got the build either, but if you concentrate on line and length, with your accuracy you'll do alright as a medium pacer."

I fell under his wing while he taught me all he knew, but he kept me in suspense for weeks before he decided the time was right to give me a place in the Under 15A team to play Chaplin High in Gwelo. What a game that was, and we won easily!

Partially (say I in all modesty), through my prowess, I set a new school record by taking nine wickets for less than a hundred runs! A miracle that warranted mention by the headmaster Pop Downing in Assembly. To add to my short-lived burst of fame, somebody wrote my name in white paint beneath a verse painted decades ago on a portion of wall in the quad that had been set aside for budding poets and graffiti artists to hone their skills:

In Jerusalem there's a wailing wall,
At Eton there's the wall game,
Milton boasts a wall for art,
So here you are free to draw on this wall.

So it could be said I left my mark for posterity, if not on the wall then surely in the archives somewhere, waiting to be unearthed by someone who may point a finger and say ' I remember that day'.

But, my patient reader, despite my lacklustre performance as an academic, what my teachers taught me didn't go entirely to waste. Somehow I must have ingested a certain amount of their wisdom. How else would I have passed a bookkeeping and correspondence course in Pulp Technology when I was in my thirties that enabled me to become manager of a Pulp Plant and later still the owner of a satellite business in South Africa that served a leading company? Not bad, I guess, for a teacher's 'worst nightmare'. It makes me think sometimes that, if there is a life hereafter, my former teachers will be looking up or down, whatever the case may be, either in abject amazement or doubled up with laughter.

'Initiations," say those who were never put in the position of experiencing them, or if they did were ignorant of the consequences, "are a means to becoming a man."

"Gives you balls!" I was told, and "strengthens your character."

"Tit for tat," a senior told me patronizingly, as I was about to run the gauntlet. "Never mind" he said, when it was over, "It was your turn now, but next year will be your revenge, for it will be you that wields the 'lambs tail'."

We 'ran the gauntlet' naked after dark, the length of the gym and back. At first we ran like hares to try and escape the blows from two lines of seniors armed with 'lambs tails' (wet towels wrapped up tight and dipped in salt for extra sting). It was the wrong option we learned too late. We should have walked rather than run and taken the blows in our stride. What blows were dodged through speed were repeated a hundredfold, when blows were aimed at the ankles and brought us down in a heap of perspiration and even piss. There were those among us that pissed through fear, confusion and panic, as we all tried to gain our feet at once. It was bloody awful, that slippery, slapping noise of flesh on flesh, and the memory of extricating myself from the pile and crawling for the finishing line on hands and knees, oblivious to everything but the shouts and screams of those behind me. I dreaded most of all the end-of-term trip from school, when what should have been a happy day invariably ended with another form of torture known as 'belly-tapping'. It entailed being held down while one's belly was rapped continually in the same spot with an assortment of objects from toothbrush, comb or ruler, until the bruised skin turned red then purple. It wasn't the pain that pissed me off but the embarrassment that came from having it done in the presence of girls, including the curvaceous and attractive June Rimmer by whom I was secretly smitten.

Belly-tapping, I learned from one of the perpetrators, was loosely based on the principle of the Japanese water torture that was used to extract information from captured prisoners-of-war.

If I am to be honest, then let me end this talk on initiations by pointing out that for reasons I have still to fathom, I got off pretty lightly. If I think back on those who suffered most, they would have been distanced from the norm by being either excessively slim, (some might say skinny), or excessively heavy, (some might say porky), or possess some other abnormality such as in my case, a longer than normal nose, and a darker than average skin that tanned beautifully but assumed the skin tone of a scaled fish in winter. So why is it that I managed to escape the excesses? I put it down to being a loner with a handful of friends with the same interests, two of whom were Fifth-formers that in a contrived way I used as protection. In this way I avoided having my testicles painted with boot-polish, or forced to compare the size of ones penis using a boot that was hung by a piece of string looped behind the crown.

I look back now and think to myself—what was the debasement all for? Did it make me any more of a man? I don't think so, for I am no more or less of a coward than I was then. Did it change my character in any way? To begin with, I haven't been analysed and am not likely to be, nor have I any inclination towards that kind of sanitation. But one thing I will say and what I am about to tell the reader is positive proof that whilst I might look upon my years at Fairbridge as having been among the best years of my life, there were others that would not share my sentiments.

Take for instance, a conversation I had with a man I grew up with for all those years in the same dormitory and who I met again when I was about twenty and about to enlist for my National Service.

I couldn't believe this was the clever, skinny, be-spectacled boy who everybody, including me I am ashamed to say, had bullied and teased because he was 'different'.

"I left Fairbridge just after you, Joel" he said. (It was my nickname, and I wished he had forgotten that slang-name for a turd that was used by those who wished to annoy me or were looking for a fight.) God! How I hated that name back then, but now coming from his mouth it was payback time, and I did no more than clench my fists and grin.

"Robbie (Robinson, the Head) wanted me to stay on and get my Cambridge, but it would have meant another two or three years at Fairbridge and I didn't want that, I'd had enough. You were lucky, Joel, you got away for most of the holidays. I used to watch you lucky bastards pack your cases and wonder why I was overlooked every fucking time. I don't know, perhaps I was too shy, didn't shout loud enough or play any sport. Nearly ten years I spent in that home without once being invited out for a holiday. Anyway, it doesn't matter. I don't take any shit anymore. My gang are my friends. We share everything, digs, booze and birds."

I had to smile at his fake bravado and the oversized leather jacket he wore on his skinny frame that gave him a fake pair of shoulders. I remembered him from old, quiet and friendless, incapable of malice, a 'dorm hanger' who had never set foot in the bush, eaten birds or smoked cow shit.

We spoke at length about the past and almost inevitably the subject of initiations cropped up. "I just wish," he muttered, "that I could now meet up with the belly tappers, the bum rushers and those seniors who tied their boots to my cock and measured to see what an erection would do for me, and for good measure polished my balls with boot-polish." He stopped for moment, slurped his beer and studied the ceiling deep in thought. "Who do you reckon, Joel, had the longest cock in our dorm?"

"Certainly not me," I said, although I had a fair idea who he was hinting at, but I didn't tell him. I didn't want him to know that I, like him, had felt many times the dormitory prefect's enormous penis between my thighs after lights out.

"Ah well," he sighed, as we left the bar, "according to my birth certificate, I may well have relations back home. Who knows, perhaps one of these days I'll get there."

I do not know if he did. I certainly hope so.

On a hot blistering day in October 1953, in my fifteenth year. (October was better known as 'suicide month' to a

Rhodesian, when according to folklore, the heat that ushered in the summer rains was said to drive people to suicide and other strange things). On the same day, Billy and I bumped into a friend in the shallow end of the pool. We hadn't spoken to each other since the time we had spent a week together on a gladiola farm with a small vineyard and dairy, at a place northeast of Bulawayo called Nyamandhlovu—a name that literally translated from Ndebele means 'the flesh of the elephants'.

It was a week neither of us had forgotten and each recollection of the farm brought on peels of laughter, especially after I brought up the incident of the Friesland bull with only one testicle. We teased it one day from what we thought was a safe distance until it charged us! We ran screaming down the road from the dairy and took refuge, just in time, in a side barn, where coincidentally we came across a cask of home-brewed wine, which we drank like water and ended up as drunk as coots.

By the time we had exhausted the memories and firmly renewed our friendship, the pool was crowded, as was the wooden bench on the grass beside the pool reserved for staff members, including the headmaster's pretty wife and the crème de la crème of the female staff, all dressed in sexy summer dresses.

They were in unusually high spirits that day, a state of being that we put down to either the temperature of the sun or, as it transpired, might have resulted from a staff party held the night before in the staff room that lasted until the early hours.

Whatever it was, the fun began when two hefty seniors were seen wrestling on the diving board, each trying to toss the other into the pool. Before plunging from the board one of them lost his trunks, revealing his naked loins and buttocks. The sight drew forth loud catcalls and whistles from the bathers, and from the ladies a moment of shocked silence, followed by screams of delighted applause and an inadvertent loss of decorum when they revealed, through their excited motions, yards of exciting thigh and delectable flashes of underwear.

It was this unexpected turn of events that drew me, my new found friend and a dozen others to the side of the pool directly in front of the wooden bench, where I hunched on the lip of the pool, chin on hands and stared through my eyelashes at the scene unfolding barely ten feet away.

Miss A, my housemother, was the first to catch my eye; reminding me of a wild gypsy with flashing eyes and long black hair that she always wore tied back in a scarf.

We all loved her, either covertly, when she was the subject of after-dark discussions when her body was admired in detail, or overtly, when a simple goodnight kiss at bedtime became a competition amongst us as to who could best imagine and describe the feel of her breasts against his chest. We knew she loved the attention, but on reflection I get the feeling it was her way of stirring up jealousy amongst us—a kind of divide-and-rule tactic. But right then, conspiracy theories aside, here she was displaying a whole lot of thigh and a scintillating pair of lace-trimmed knickers, which I often saw amongst her others in all their tantalizing shapes and colours on the tiny wash-line outside her flat.

On her left sat Miss R, a junior schoolteacher, with a glorious set of breasts and lips that were the source of many a wet dream. She seemed unaware that at that moment her dress had risen high, exhibiting not only her lush thighs but the bulge of pubic mound through her skin-tight underwear.

The Head's wife too, and the part-time librarian sitting beside her seemed unable to control their alternating flashes of pink and white gusset that appeared teasingly each time they opened and closed their legs. Me, well, I must have felt like any other fired-up adolescent clinging to the side of the pool, so suffused with lust that I had to keep adjusting the leg of my trunks to ease the strain of an erection that defied the cooling effect of the water. I turned to my friend, our eyes met, and reading my thoughts, he smiled and sidled up to me until our shoulders brushed. He leaned forward and whispered in my ear.

"Nice isn't it? You randy bugger. Bet you've got the horn like me. Here, feel it." He took my hand and brushed it across the bulge in the front of his trunks. At the same time, he slid his hand down, took hold of my penis and proceeded to squeeze it and rub the material of my trunks against the sensitive tip. Right at that moment any sense of guilt or feelings of apprehension I might have had, swiftly vanished before the onslaught of a rush of voluptuous sensual pleasure. As if in a trance, I reached for him in turn and together we fondled each other, blind to the sights of what had brought us to this point. I remember swimming away with a mixture of guilt and pleasure. Guilt that was short-lived and pleasure that was prolonged, until I met Caroline.

It was one of those blustery winter days of scudding clouds that played havoc with a sun that appeared sometimes in patches of blue, and warmed up ever so slightly the corrugated-iron walls of a shack I had built from sheets of iron and gum poles left behind by the RAF.

I'd made a mistake with the dimensions of the shack and as a consequence of my lack of skills, the end result was it looked uncannily like a privy, being taller than I had intended and with so little floor space that there was just enough room for four small people to sit down with knees drawn up. As a further insult to my capabilities as a builder, someone soon after its completion had scrawled on the door in bold white letters the offensive words: 'Bowley's Bog House'.

Still, it had served its purpose as somewhere to smoke without being seen, and was quite unintentionally a vantage point from which I could view the comings and goings of Caroline to the Girls' Pets Corner (a fenced-in area set aside for pets).. I had secretly admired her but had never had the courage to approach her, until this day of strong winds that played havoc with her dress while she was bent over, seeking to catch a rabbit in one of the runs.

It seemed a heaven-sent opportunity to get to know her. In no time at all I joined her, chasing the damn rabbit round and round the run, cornering it at last against the fence. After handing the animal to her, I watched her hug it to her breast. As she stroked its long ears, I remember thinking how pretty she looked and how envious I was of the rabbit clasped in her arms.

We stood and talked while she calmed the animal down. At first I was so shy I couldn't seem to find the right words, then as the conversation progressed I found my composure and wit and drew from her peals of laughter when I described how she looked chasing the rabbit around the run. She, not to be outdone, countered with a far from complimentary description of my strange looking shack.

"Let's put the rabbit away," she said, turning her back on me as a gust of wind that flattened her dress against her form and outlined to my delight the shape of her legs and smooth bottom. "Then perhaps you can show me what your strange-looking house looks like inside." With that I turned and followed her to a hutch. As she stooped to open it, the wind blew and lifted her dress waist-high, revealing a heart-melting strip of translucent flesh above a waistband of sky-blue panties. Shocked and excited, I pretended too late to look away. Our eyes met and she smiled seductively. "You've been staring at my knickers, haven't you?" I was struck speechless by her frankness and felt my cheeks smoulder and my penis wither. "Err, no," I stuttered, "it was the wind... I couldn't help it... I'm sorry."

"Sorry for what? Have you never seen a girl's knickers before?"

"Of course," I said, looking away from her laughing eyes, staring instead at my shoe scuffing the ground.

"So why are you so shy? Do you want another look? Here..." She raised her dress as far as her knees then, as I turned my head in embarrassment to look away, she dropped the hem and laughed. "Come on George, I'm only teasing, let's go and have a look at your hut."

For close on a year Caroline and I had been what could be loosely termed as boy and girl friend. I say loosely, because unlike my friends who went through girls like chewing gum, in relationships that were short and sweet and were, according to them, cornucopias of sex, ours, after an interesting beginning, had dragged along platonically with the added spice of an occasional kiss and cuddle in the shadows. I was in love and proved it to myself. My uncontrolled fits of immature jealousy that since I had turned fifteen hung over me like a cloud, gnawed at me each time I saw her talk to another boy. It didn't help that because of her attractiveness and flirtatious style I was rapidly acquiring an inferiority complex. I was about to throw in the towel when she invited me to spend a weekend with her and her friend Angela on a plot near Bembesi Dam, about forty kilometres from the home.

I knew the dam well. It was a muddy shallow stretch of water filled to capacity with barbel. We caught them by tying a baited hook to a piece of string tied to a sapling that was stuck in the mud about twenty paces from the shoreline. It was a lazy method of fishing that entailed sitting on the shore while smoking and talking crap until the sapling bent and one simply waded in, retrieved the fish and sold it to the locals.

I've always been interested in oddities and Angela's parents were no exception. They were what I term 'free souls' for never till then had I seen or been in the company of a couple who, despite being in their late forties were so much in love with each other.

I lost count of the times they kissed in a day. It was a kiss good-morning at breakfast; a kiss and a bear-hug when he left for work on the Saturday morning; the same again when he returned at lunchtime, and an extra-long kiss at night as they went to bed that seemed to last the walk to their bedroom. I saw him grope her bottom in passing a few times as if I wasn't there and found him fondling not one but both of her breasts in the kitchen one Sunday morning before they left for church.

I decided on the Saturday afternoon to go for a walk by myself around the dam. When I returned the car was gone and the house was empty, or so I thought until I walked through the house towards my bedroom and passed the girl's room. The door was ajar and as I passed I heard the sound of bedsprings and a voice called out: "Hey, George, where are you going?" I stopped, retraced my steps and poked my head around the door. I was shocked to see Caroline sitting on the side of the bed, unmoved by my presence, dressed in her bra and knickers.

"Oh shit," I squeaked, " I'm sorry, I was just on the way to my room."

At a loss and making a feeble attempt to appear unshaken, I took a step inside, one hand firmly gripping the door handle, the other glued to the door. I glanced around nervously, pretending to look for her friend. "Where's Angela?" I croaked, avoiding her eyes.

"She's gone shopping with her Mum and Dad, George, which means we have the house to ourselves." I tensed at her words ready to flee and would have done so had she not risen from the bed in her state of undress. She reminded me briefly of a picture in a book of 'Old Masters' in the school library, in particular a well-thumbed print of Bottecelli's painting of Venus rising from a seashell. I was quick to notice however that while Venus had modestly hidden her naked mons veneris with one hand, Caroline on the other hand might have been misled into thinking that because she wore pants a hand wasn't necessary to hide hers. In actual fact, because her flesh-coloured panties were so tight and transparent, I could see the pubic patch and a mouth-watering fleck of hair that had escaped the confines of the gusset and was coiled up in the crease of a thigh.

"Stop staring, George! What's the matter? You've seen my knickers before, now come and sit down before you faint" she said, pointing to the bed, "and have a cig. Do you want one?"

"No thanks," I managed to get out, "I stopped long ago."

"Oh why, I thought all the boys smoked?"

"No, not all of us," and I told her of the time I was forced by a prefect to smoke a packet which made me ill.

"Oh dear" she said, "Well you don't mind if I have a puff do you?" Without waiting for a reply she crossed to a chest of drawers and bent over to remove a packet of ten *Star Cigarettes* and a box of matches, leaving me entranced and excited by the division of her buttocks that I could see clearly through the taut nylon. Then without a care in the world she sat on the dressing table stool, facing me, legs apart, unaware that her gusset was stretched to the limit.

She took forever to smoke that cigarette and I can't remember a single word spoken between each puff. But I can still remember the relief I felt when I didn't have to pretend not to stare anymore after she rose, threw the stompie out of the window and sat beside me on the bed. Without warning she pulled me forward, clamped her lips to mine and thrust her tongue between my lips, lapped at my cheeks and palate with catlike darts of her tongue. In and out, in and out as she forced me down across the bed and we were jammed and squashed against each other in a newfound sexuality.

This time it was I who captured her mouth and forced her lips and teeth apart none too gently. I tasted her last cigarette, saliva, and a mix of tastes that became an aphrodisiac with a force that willed my hand with a life of its own to seek and find her own mons veneris, so smooth and slippery, it brought back to my tangled mind memories of a bed and mirror in another place. Slipping to the floor, I knelt between her splayed legs, aware of her warm silken skin against my cheeks. In haste, with fumbling hands I reached back and tugged at my shorts and after a frustrating struggle managed to kick them off, leaving me exhausted. My eyes were drawn to the crotch of her panties, tight as an onionskin glued to the swell of her vulva. In a sudden surge of lust, I pulled aside the gossamer gusset and found her sweet inside, her shell-pink, white with dew, marshmallow soft between her succulent lips, coated in a constant flow of rich briny nectar. I found the familiar knot of her swollen bud, kissed it, nibbled it, lashed it with my tongue, sucked it until she cried out in ecstasy and lay trembling, while I lapped away the remains of her cream. I felt for my penis, rubbed it a few times and came in a knee-jerking, buckling flood.

My first attempt at true lovemaking proved to be like a stroll along a well-worn path, a rekindling of past memories. I knew what the reaction would be from Caroline when I kissed each part of her. The taste and scent of her wetness, the sensitive clitoris, the cries of ecstasy when she came, were no different in essence from the woman from the past.

This in itself negated any blind instinctive first-time fumbling and haste to enter and spend.

There was of course a fundamental difference—ours was a natural progression that stemmed from young love, whereas, and I realised in times to come, hitherto I had been used as a child to assuage a hidden lust.

Chapter Nineteen

Bob's Story

In December 1954, just a few weeks away from my sixteenth birthday, I returned to Paradise.

Neither the old folk nor the farm had changed much. Sixpence had been promoted from kitchen-boy to houseboy, and the youths in Masikas kraal were still my friends, even those my age who, like their fathers, had become herders on the farm.

We spent Old Year's Eve, the night of my birthday, with the Motherwells in Sipolilo. He was, as you will recall, the Member in charge of the Sipolilo branch of the British South Africa Police.

After a meal we sat together on the stoep, and as I drank my first glass of cider, I listened to talk of the 'old times.' Moses and Methuselah were brought up in the course of conversation and Bob and I learned that since the demise of the two, rustling and the theft of fencing along the riverfront had become a real problem, just as Moses and Methuselah had intimated would happen in the absence of their presence on the Hunyani.

"It's a difficult one," said Motherwell. "I could increase the patrols along the river, but that would mean leaving me a bit lean on the home front. I'm going to have to ask farmers like yourself to be a bit more vigilant and maybe spend a bit more time patrolling your own borders."

"I don't think that would be too much of a problem," said Bob, shrugging his shoulders. "I'll set up an ambush or two on the river like we did in the old days, take out a few and the word gets around, end of problem."

"It isn't that easy any more," replied Motherwell, shaking

his head. "Ever since Prime Minister Todd took over, we've been told to rein in a bit, avoid confrontation with the locals. Word is," he said in almost a whisper, leaning forward as if afraid someone might hear, "it seems, Bob, that the natives on the mines and in the towns are getting restless. I hear from higher up that Todd is talking to the troublemakers, so you see what you are suggesting may well land you in the dock, so be careful."

Bob nodded his head. "I've heard all this before but it'll come to nothing you'll see, but one thing's for sure despite these clandestine talks, whoever steals my stock, be they black or white, should beware believe me," and I knew by the tone of his voice he meant what he said.

It was another good rainy season and the Hunyani was running strong which coincided with Bob's sudden craze for fishing. Bob, despite having told me on more than one occasion that fishing was a lazy man's sport, had brought a whole new set of rods and tackle, and was spending all his spare time fishing. That pleased Ina because, knowing his favourite fishing spot, she knew where to find him if the need arose. She was pleased, she confided, because it gave them more time together. It was good for me too, because I was partial to fishing and it gave Bob the time, because he must have considered me old enough, to relate to me the story of his early life and the terrible incident that led him to Paradise.

But before I get to that, let me tell you of a photo album I found wedged between two reference books and a mysterious black book I came across between a set of old classics and poems by Dickens, Kipling, Shelley and Longfellow. They were all bound in embossed cloth bindings and had timeworn yellow pages with flyleaves alive with esoteric verses and messages signed with faded names. However, there was a little black book that seemed out of place amongst these grand books for it had no title on the spine. It was only when I opened it that I found on an otherwise blank flyleaf the title—A Soldier's Tale—and beneath the title the simple word 'Anonymous'.

Oh, my God! After leafing through the first few pages, it was like opening a window onto a whole new surreal world! Every few pages were studded with pen-and-ink drawings of men in battle, so detailed and lifelike that I could see for instance the expressions of triumph or pain on the faces in the drawings.

I remember sitting down on the floor before the bookcase that afternoon, so engrossed that I was still there when Bob came home, and Ina who had been in the kitchen all afternoon and had thought I was with Bob, came searching through the house calling my name.

That night I took the book to bed with me and read until the hurricane lamp ran out of paraffin.

Between fishing and reading, I read the book from cover to cover over the next day or two. It was only on replacing the book on the shelf that curiosity got the better of me and I took down the photograph album. It was filled with old-fashioned sepia photos of people and for me, monotonous pictures of buildings and countryside scenes. That was, until the last page when, like a bolt out of the blue, I was confronted with rows upon rows of stern-faced soldiers in uniform, either sitting with ankles crossed or standing between the shoulders of those in front. There were pictures too, of troop carriers laden with smiling, laughing, waving troops, carrying rifles and backpacks.

Amongst all the photos, there were two that interested me the most. One was of a tall, handsome young man in uniform, who I was sure was Bob, with his one arm around the shoulders of a stern-faced man almost his height, and his other arm around the waist of a woman with a round face and broad smile. I knew without thinking that the man and woman were his mother and father.

The second portrayed the man who I presumed was Bob, with one hand around the barrel of a rifle at his side and the other across the shoulders of a soldier, his height and build, with a thick mop of fair hair. I wasn't sure at first whether to take the album to Ina and ask her about the photographs. Would she think I was snooping, I wondered? But it didn't take long for me to thrust aside any misgivings I might have had, and after making sure she was alone I strolled into the kitchen and laid the album on the table. "Look what I found, Aunt Ina," I said, feigning surprise.

"Gosh" she said, her eyes lit up, "it's years since I last looked at these. Come on, pull up a chair and I'll show you what Bob and I looked like when we were young."

Ina forgot all of what she had been doing and for the next hour or two she diligently went through every photograph, pointing out her and Bob's relatives and dozens she remembered but couldn't give names to, referring to them as 'he and she, who did this and that, lived here and there, were good or bad'.

I must admit I had begun to lose interest until she reached the long awaited final page. Suddenly I came to life and the questions flowed. "Isn't that Uncle Bob and his Mum and Dad," I said, pointing to the photograph.

"Quite right," she said, "It was taken the day he and Ginger left to go to the Somme."

"Aunt Ina," I almost shouted, "what was that name again?"

"The Somme," she repeated, "It was a battlefield in France."

"Yes! Yes! I know, Aunt Ina," I cried, "I've just read about it. Gosh! I know Uncle Bob fought in the Great War, you've mentioned it before, but I didn't know he fought at the Somme."

"Yes, he did, and that's Ginger." She pointed a finger at the photo of the two men. "They grew up together in Yorkshire."

"Where does Ginger live now?" I asked.

Ina closed the album and rose to her feet. "He died," she said softly, and before I could ask another question she handed me the album. "And that's enough questions," she said lightly, "now just go and put the album back where you found it, and be a good lad and go and find Uncle Bob and tell him its time for tea."

I found him in the usual spot. He was threading a worm when he heard me approaching and turned his head.

I was looking at him in a new light. He was no longer the patient father-like figure I had grown to respect and admire. Instead, he was now and would forever be my hero.

"So you've decided to join me?" he said, "I'm glad about that, I was beginning to think you'd deserted me." It was polite banter but I felt its sting. "Come and sit down," he said, patting the ground. "The fish aren't biting; all I'm doing is drowning worms. Still there's been plenty going on. You see that patch of reeds over there with the rock growing out of it?" He pointed the tip of his rod in the general direction. "Keep your eye on it." Then he dropped his voice to a whisper. "Keep dead still."

We did just that for ages, whilst all I could hear was the sounds of the river and the cluck, cluck, of a moorhen hidden in that patch of reeds. Suddenly the sound pitch of the moorhen changed and from out of the reeds popped half-a-dozen little black chicks. They swam happily in circles around their mother until something spooked them, and in the blink of an eye they disappeared. Uncle Bob chuckled to himself, and turned to me. "That's only the second time in my life that I've seen a moorhen chick, George. I must have passed by them a thousand times but the slightest movement scares them.

"Ah! Yes," he said, with a deep sigh of satisfaction, "it's at times like this, my God has me believing there is more to life. Would you believe it, George, it was only yesterday a heron rose from over there," he pointed down stream with his rod, "with a fish in its beak that was so heavy, that if it hadn't dropped it, the poor bird would have nosedived into the water. It's sights like that have been too few all these years. My wife spends a lot of time here now instead of on the stoep, sitting and chatting sometimes till after dark. Which reminds me, she might be along just now with some tea and cakes. I could do with it, how about you?"

"Oh God!" I replied, "I'm sorry," I said, jumping to my feet, "I forgot she told me to call you for tea. Oh hell, that was ages ago. I'm going to be in the soup. Here, let me carry your rods."

"No, don't worry," he said, rising to his feet. He took the rods and placed them clear of the water's edge. "We'll come back after tea, Come on, I'll race you home."

Tea had long gone and after an hour or more we hadn't caught a single fish. They were there, I could see the swirl of water beneath the surface, and now and again one would leap out of the water in a flash of silver and snap at a dragonfly or swim after an insect struggling on the surface.

It was Bob who broke the silence. "George, you're very quiet, you normally talk the hind legs off a donkey. Is something the matter?" I was caught off-guard at first. I knew what I wanted to say, but it was just a case of finding the words, hence it took a moment of awkward silence before I took the plunge.

"Uncle Bob," I said, "I've just finished reading a book about the Great War."

"Oh, I know that," said Bob, "who do you think it was who put the book on your bedside table the other night after you fell asleep with it lying on your chest. There's only one thing that puzzles me though. Why on earth did you choose that book when there's a hundred books to choose from?"

"It wasn't a case of choosing, Uncle Bob," I said defensively, "it looked different from the other books on the shelf. All the others except that one, had titles on the spine, so I had to pull it out to look for a title and I'm glad I did because it's the most sad and exciting book I've ever read. I finished it yesterday and when I put it back on the shelf, I came across a photograph album with a picture of you and your mum and a fellow called Ginger. Who was he, Uncle Bob?"

"He was a good friend of mine, George, that I grew up

with." There was no stopping now; I had to know first-hand.

"Uncle Bob, did you and your friend go to the Somme?"

"You have been talking to Aunt Ina haven't you?" said Bob, shaking his head with a grin.

"Yes I did, but why do you ask?" I hesitated for a moment. "Uncle Bob, the book I just read was all about the Somme. I couldn't believe it when Aunt Ina told me you and Ginger had fought there. The man who wrote the book also fought there. Did you know him?"

"No, I didn't," he answered, "there were thousands of us, any one of us could have written the book."

Over the next few days I badgered Bob at every opportunity to tell me his story, until one afternoon he relented. We were sitting beside the river fishing and out of the blue he turned to me and said: "Okay George, I'll tell you my story. I was only a year or so older than you when I joined up so I guess you're old enough to hear it."

Bob told me his story over a number of days. There were often interruptions in the telling that necessitated me having to remind him each time where he left off. The interruptions, I would add, were more of a help than a hindrance, because they gave me time to jot down in a feint-lined exercise book I kept as a diary in my suitcase, the highlights and gist of the story while it was still fresh in my mind.

I must confess here and now that I have ignored, or conveniently forgotten much of what he told me concerning the different characters that were either neighbours or family friends. I have forgotten or perhaps he never mentioned the name of the village where he was born. I have searched for it on maps of Yorkshire in the hope that a name may jog my memory and proclaim its rebirth, but to no avail. So I have decided to rename it 'Lapwing', a suitable name I think, for reasons that will become apparent.

The battle scenes are as authentic as those described by him, although a lot more gory as I am now much older and better able to see the scenes through Bob's eyes and the anonymous writer, rather than the less offensive toned-down version Bob gave to me.

Lest I forget, Captain Wilkinson of the 17th did not exist by that name but he was there. Neither did he wear a patch over the eye. All right, so I am an impressionable 70. Bob didn't give him a name, so I have decided to use my poetic licence.

Bob once had a friend called Ginger, aptly named on account of his thick head of auburn hair. They were born within hours of each other in March 1898 and were attended to by the same midwife. For the past fifty years she had witnessed most of the arrivals and departures of the citizens of Lower Lapwing, a tiny village named after the large flocks of Lapwings that nested nearby and followed the ploughmen in dense grey flocks, searching for titbits from the freshly turned Yorkshire soil.

The life of a farmer's son, even at age six, began before sunrise. Bob was awake and up before his father had finished washing his face at the sink in the kitchen. From his bedroom, as he tied his laces, Bob would hear like an alarm clock the growls, spits and protestations that carried through the house when the ice-cold water came into contact with his father's skin. Bob meanwhile, with his mother tucked up in bed, had no one to enforce his toiletries so mostly he dispensed with the early morning wash.

Even in the harshest of winters Bob was up before sunrise, helping his father clear the snowdrifts from the path leading to the front door. Before he left for school it was his job to light the woodstove, fill the kettle from the outside tap and place it on the hob ready for his Mum's and Dad's early morning cup of tea.

School began at nine o'clock but the Bob and Ginger would always meet up early before they set off on the long walk to school, partly because it gave them more time to play on the way and partly because their mothers wanted them out of the way so housework could begin. "By the time I left the house," he said, "Father was already out on the pastures with his two dogs, tending to the sheep."

Up the long winding road they meandered, carrying rush dinner baskets over their shoulders and shabby little coats on their arms to protect them should it rain.

On the way they would meet up with the children of farm workers that lived in the hamlets further up the Downs. Though stained with the marks of poverty, those children were strong and lusty and to the boys' amusement, in place of gloves they carried hot potatoes in their pockets to keep their hands warm and serve as a snack between lessons.

Bob and Ginger, though born of landowners who were a class above the rest, grew up untainted as yet with class distinction. When let loose from control, they quarrelled and fought with the hamlet children, in peaceful moments squatted with them in the dust of the road to play marbles and five-stones, or climbed into the hedges in a search of birds' nests and blackberries. In winter they slid on ice puddles and made snowballs, soft ones for friends and hard ones with a stone inside for the 'enemy'.

In the early hours of the day there was little traffic on the road other than farm labourers from the hamlets on their way to work, or farmers on their way to visit neighbours who thought nothing of creating an obstruction by stopping their carts in the middle of the road to exchange greetings and news from their driving seats. Theirs was a practice that stoked the ire of the two boys who, to escape the obstructions, were forced to move along the verges. More often than not the verges were wet and muddy, so shoes that had been so painstakingly polished the night before in preparation for the daily inspection by the headmistress of Lower Lapwing Primary, had to be cleaned again but with far more difficulty.

Going home in the afternoon, on the other hand, there was always more to be seen. It was time to wave at the endless stream of carts loaded to the gunwales with goods and produce purchased or bartered for in the markets to the north. They would stare at the drivers of the carts dressed in their Sunday best, wearing smocks edged with lace and smart leather jerkins that complimented ruddy weather-beaten faces half-hidden beneath the broad floppy brims of straw hats. Further down the road the boys often met up with the squire's gaily painted trap, and a grand sight it was, a heady stimulus that encouraged the boys to bow and the girls to curtsy to the pink-cheeked squire and his entourage of ladies waving white handkerchiefs. In the manner of a monarch, the squire would acknowledge their existence by tapping the brim of his hat with his whip.

There was always something for the boys and their friends to eat on their journeys to and from school. In spring they ate the young green shoots from the hawthorn hedges, which they called bread-and-cheese, and sorrel leaves called sour-grass. In autumn there was always an abundance of blackberries and crab-apples to tickle their taste buds. It was not so much from hunger that they partook of nature's bounty, but more so from force of habit and their inborn love of wild food.

Life for Bob and Ginger was not all work. There were no 'bought' pleasures for the growing lads. Pleasures were the change of the seasons, the trapping of rabbits in the meadows that crept down to the river where bulrushes that grew so thick along the bank they hid the boys from the local Estates gamekeeper while they busied themselves poaching trout.

"We were opposites in habit," he told me, "but alike in so many other ways. Ginger excelled on the sports field and, unlike me, wore girls around his neck like a string of beads. One I remember was a comely barmaid who cured him for a while of his wayward spirit after her husband caught them kissing."

It was in these most natural of times that Ginger and Bob were conscripted and prepared to leave for the hell that was the Somme.

Bob could never remember seeing his mother cry. It was strange and unsettling therefore, that he should feel her tears soaking the collar of his greatcoat and the warmth of her heaving breast trembling against his chest. "I distinctly felt her recoil," he said, "when her hands touched by accident the cold smooth rifle barrel that hugged my back like the arm of a cold friend."

Locked in her tight embrace, his mother, always a tower of spiritual strength and understanding, suddenly appeared to him frail, helpless, lost even. He instinctively tightened his hold, and with his chin resting on her hair, looked beyond and into the eyes of his father. In his mind's eye he caught the image of him, burdened with religious dogma, on his knees beside his bed, praying out loud to his God for a bountiful harvest, a lamb for a barren ewe, and even now a silent prayer for his son. In the aching sadness of farewell, Bob remembered the hidden strength of his father's arms and smelt his earthy scent as love burst through like a brilliant sun that kindled the instantaneous rush of emotion. No words were necessary. It was all spelt out in the trembling shoulders and the hidden tears, when love bathed the three in an aura so strong that he continues to feel its presence.

The Somme

"The road to the front," he said, "wound through a countryside of stunted tree trunks split and torn by countless shells, past once proud farmhouses and villages reduced to heaps of rubble and shattered walls from which roof trusses protruded like the ribs of devoured prey.

We were forced to detour round the bloated bodies of two horses, still lying in their traces beside the remains of a cart with one wheel arched skyward, draped with a red cloth that reminded me of blood on the white belly fur of a dead rabbit. Beside the overturned cart lay the body of a woman violated by the force of the explosion, her fingers covering her bloody face. Beyond her, seen above the belly of a dead horse, a young girl stood mesmerized and shaking, her eyes filled with terror. I wanted to run then, back from whence I'd come, and would have done so had the close knot of bodies not propelled me forward through the landscape of murdered fields towards the sound of gunfire.

We spent the first night on French soil on the verge of a road that was nothing more than a series of enormous shell-holes littered with pieces of uniform, broken weapons and the twisted wrecks of vehicles. Either side of the road resembled a lunar surface, watered by a miserable drizzle that filled the shell craters and brought to the surface crudely buried bodies and did nothing to cleanse the smell of death.

We bivouacked the next night in a grove of naked tree stumps beside a stream choked with the litter of war. From beneath the spread of our greatcoats, we smelt the comforting stench of pipe and cigarette smoke as we looked out at the flashes of shellfire that might have been mistaken for lightning that outlined the low-slung hills of the Somme.

Dawn gave birth to the colossal roar of artillery that seemed to erupt from the soul, it shook the ground, drove away dreams and rammed our heads and bodies deep into the grey mud. A continual stream of star-shells exploded above our heads, showering us with shrapnel. Shells from the big guns behind the German lines exploded on the road amongst the early morning traffic. Plumes of smoke and debris sprang up like giant mushrooms and fell to earth with a hiss, while downstream I watched as a shell exploded in a grove of trees that made the earth tremble and split open. It sucked and spat out tongues of flame with such ferocity that a clump of trees was uprooted and seconds later burst into flames. We were showered in hot ash and boiling sap that blinded our souls to a transient world made invisible in dense clouds of acrid smoke.

Fear spawned the word GAS. We fumbled at our belts, donned the gas masks and stared at each other wide-eyed through blurred glass, before flinging ourselves down to seek the solace of the soil.

Then chaos! Uncertainty! Plans conjured up in a blinding second, each idea considered then discarded. Dozens of them, unplanned, all culminating in the urge to retreat and get a second chance at life.

Suddenly, something displaced the seed of helplessness nurtured by the sounds of battle. It was a call to sanity born of the parade ground. We halted in our planned flight, held our ground and turned to hear the voice of Captain Wilkinson, who rose from a crouch and stood tall, with a patch over one eye and a pistol in his fist. His very figure seemed to throw out a challenge to the enemy and seemed to mock the starshells that exploded about his form into myriads of gigantic sparks and shrapnel. He stood like a statue of liberty, gauging the distance between us and the beleaguered allied trenches.

It was the Captain's orders that day to supply reinforcements and to lead us raw conscripts through a baptism of fire to relieve soldiers who for the past two months had lost 60,000 comrades, including 19,000 dead in an effort to gain a few hundred yards of useless territory.

FORM EXTENDED LINE! MOVE!

We scuttled to our positions on the left flank either side of our C.O. and lay flat, as long-range artillery fire began finding its range, forcing us to hug the ground like humpback lizards in an effort to make ourselves as small targets as possible, all the while fearful of the command that would see us forced from our burrows like terrified rabbits to face the machinegun fire that would surely come.

STAND BY!

We braced ourselves, did a last minute check on rifles, a hitch to an ammunition belt and patch straps, a nervous tug to ease the weight of the backpack.

ADVANCE!

The call came and went, forced its sound clearly above the sudden ear-splitting blasts of shells and the crack and whine of bullets, descending like the wings of a guardian and spreading its placating influence as the shouts of command extolled and urged us forward in cool precise military parade jargon, to keep uniform the extended line of attack.

The C.O. looked mean and invincible. He brandished his revolver as if it was an extension to his hand, the finger a muzzle that spurted sparks and smoke and a voice that could be heard even above the sound of gunfire. We followed his orders even though it meant leaving deceased comrades behind in the struggle. Like ghosts, minds and limbs separated from one another we moved on, driven not so much by fear but by an urge to survive.

Meanwhile, Ginger and I, as soon as there was a lull in the firing, darted from shell- hole to shell-hole, some of which were occupied by both dead German and British soldiers where hand-to-hand combat had taken place. In one we lay resting on the bodies of two Germans that was much more comfortable than lying on the bare ground.

We were caught in the open, running, when there was a sudden burst of machinegun and artillery fire directly overhead. Immediately we fell flat on our faces, frightened and surprised. On looking up, I watched a platoon take cover in a shell-hole and heard the cries of an officer shouting orders. There was a whoosh! and a blinding flash in front of me and a great column of flame and earth rose into the sky. Concussion hurled us backwards—and I watched as a helmet descended through the pall of smoke, like a round bird. It bounced as it struck the ground and rolled on its axis before coming to rest inches from my face.

Still reeling from the blast, we screamed at each other in relief as we were both still alive. Then, spurred on by the 'whit-whit' of hot lead, we sprinted for the cover of the shell-hole that still steamed and stank of cordite, scrambled up the mushroomed lip and rolled down the side to land on a cushion of warm and oily bodies. There was only one soldier still alive, but there wasn't much we could do to help him. We made him as comfortable as we could, found a pack of cigarettes and matches in his tunic pocket and left him smoking, propped up on a mangled pile of packs and webbing.

There was a lull in the fire as we drew closer to the Allied trenches, and I remember so well, looking around at the figures of the others as they ran then dropped to escape the firing. When they rose again some were left behind and remained like mounds of earth that were part of a graveyard.

The trenches that had been prepared with so much care and attention to detail were in a sorry state when those of us that had survived 'dropped in'—for that morning the trenches had been under attack. There were bodies everywhere, some lying still while others had dragged themselves or had been helped to the walls of the trench and were sitting, propped up, being attended to by their comrades-in-arms, waiting for the medics to stretcher them to the field hospital.

In November the weather broke in earnest, it did not stop raining for a month and that turned our trench into a river. We were supplied with scoops attached to long poles with which to bale out the water. After being tossed over the top the water simply percolated back into the trench. The object of the long handle was to enable you to toss the water over the top without the risk of being shot through the hand or arm by snipers. Some men purposely raised their arms higher than they should in the hope of being wounded, but of course they kept their heads down. I dug out the infernal lice from the seams of my clothes with a heated bayonet, while those on my flesh I pinched with my nails, but nothing helped really because there were millions to take their place.

A clandestine attack on our trench was carried out one night, but before the enemy could engage us, an alert guard sounded the alarm and fired a shot. Immediately a small battle took place and in the morning there were scores of the enemy lying dead within yards of our position.

We carried out a retaliatory attack during which we captured at heavy cost an enemy trench. We held it for less than a day before it was recaptured by the enemy, again with heavy losses. What a bunch of savages that war turned us into. We saw the most horrible sights of bloodshed and simply laughed. There seemed to be nothing but blood everywhere we went and on everything we touched. We were walking amongst the dead, day and night. It was as if human life was of no value. And so it went on day after day, a tit-for-tat, thrust and retreat after which not a foot of the enemy lines was taken.

There were no clouds in the sky that day. All the sounds of battle had ceased and I could swear I heard a birdcall. What was more, it was the day before our Company was to be 'stood down'. It was so pleasurable for Ginger and me to listen to the banter of the men, only hours away from the imagined pleasure that awaited them in the taverns and bordellos miles away from the carnage.

We smiled at each other and listened some more… then Ginger said something, propped his rifle against a sandbag, rose to his feet and stretched his arms and legs to ease his aching body. He looked down at me smiling… then dropped across me as I heard the crack of a rifle break the silence Those few seconds of careless pleasure cost Ginger his life from a sniper's bullet."

I spent the last few days in Paradise fishing with Bob in the

Hunyani and chatting with Ina in the kitchen; two people who more than anybody I had known had shaped my character and values.

How could I have known that in twenty-five years from then I would once again visit Paradise, but under vastly different circumstances.

Chapter Twenty

Hillwood Farm – Mwinilunga

I said goodbye to Fairbridge at the age of 17, in March 1956. My ambition had been to become a teacher, but Kingsley Fairbridge had decreed I should become a farmer instead. So, after a fond farewell, I left with a suitcase in hand that contained clothes more suited to a lad starting out in the banking business, including a suit and a strange shirt with detachable collars, both of which I never got to wear.

Other than a letter to my future employer, I had nothing to say who I was—no birth certificate, no passport, no letters—nothing but my memories and two keepsakes. One was a photograph of my dormitory inmates and me that was taken when I first arrived at the home, and the other a certificate of my First Class award for Elocution. I guess you could say I was starting off as a migrant again.

I was put on a train, much as I was put on a ship nine years before, and sent on a journey to a place called Hillside Farm near a village called Mwinilunga in the northwest corner of what was then Northern Rhodesia. The farm, thousands of acres in extent, bordered the Belgian Congo and Angola, and was within an hour's walk of the sources of two great African rivers, the Zambezi and the Congo.

I must confess that despite its importance and the fact that the source of the Zambezi originated on the farm, it left me quite unmoved. In eighteen months, which was the length of my stay on the farm, I visited the source twice, once out of curiosity because everybody spoke of it and once under sufferance when I was directed by the boss to show it to a visitor. After stumbling with me through the dense mosquito infested rain forest, to my surprise he all but fell on his knees to worship the tiny stream that trickled and burrowed its way through the mossy roots of a single tree to form a crystal-clear pool that drained across the leafy ground, on its way to becoming the mighty river.

I was never sure right from the outset whether Hillwood was a mission station or a well run prosperous business. It boasted a beautiful church, an old mission station on top of Kaleni Hill, and a thriving school called Sakeji where the sons and daughters of missionaries were taught. But more important was the huge trading store on the farm that sold everything except motorcars and traded in such diverse commodities as beeswax and honey that was exported to Europe. Farm products, including butter and cheese, were delivered twice a week to the Copperbelt and cattle on the hoof were driven to the railhead in the Belgian Congo and thence to the abattoir at Elizabethville. Even the money paid out in wages to the white staff and the hundred or more black workers found its way back to the farm's coffers via the trading store.

Kaleni Hill was the highest point on the farm where the original mission, a drab brick and mud huddle of buildings, still stood. It was built by Dr Walter Fisher back in the 1800s and was still in existence when I was there. It was run by my favourite of the sons, W.Singleton Fisher. A humble man, he was the only one of the family who gave me the time of day and was prepared to put up with an endless string of questions from a youngster who was far removed from the 'straight and narrow'.

What I remember most about the mission was the view from his office window that looked out over three countries, and the untidy pile of books that always littered his desk. I was only able to visit him on Saturday afternoons and when I did, I always found him hunched over his desk, scribbling words on sheets of paper and surrounded by open books. They included a signed leather-bound Bible that he told me had not only belonged to his father but had become his reason for translating the book into Lunda. The task thus far had taken him more than a decade and would still take him another two years to complete.

The home I lived in with the family was immense with all the rooms built around a garden alive with birds. A generator that supplied electricity for the homestead always came on at nightfall to my chagrin, because by that time I was expected to have finished dressing in my best clothes after a bath by candlelight.

Dinner was always a ceremonious affair that lasted a long time and was served by a waiter in white. He later served homegrown coffee with a dollop of fresh cream, in a lounge with bookshelves that covered two walls to the ceiling and a floor so polished it reflected not only the furniture but anyone moving on its surface.

I didn't spend much time in the lounge, in fact no longer than it took me to swallow the coffee. This was for no other reason but a feeling I always had that I was an intruder, because it was at that time that family business was discussed and an hour at least was spent by them discussing passages from the Bible.

In fact I spent as little time as I could in that house, preferring instead to take the time when I wasn't eating and sleeping to visit one of the farm's employees, an Australian god-fearing man, with a wife who seemed afraid to open her mouth except to breathe and was as sexless as a yard broom. She reminded me always, without wishing to be unkind, of Olive, Popeye the cartoon character's girlfriend, without the exaggerated mouth. He, on the other hand was a friendly religious person who got on with everybody except Paul, my boss's son, who, he said, had disliked him ever since a day that due to pressure of work he had ignored Wednesday's compulsory call to prayer in the farm church. I knew how he felt because I, too, had been guilty of the same offence and had experienced Paul's wrath at my unforgivable transgression.

The Australian (I can't remember his name) was the farm's mechanic and gunsmith. His was the responsibility of maintaining the farm's fleet of vehicles and the lucrative gun repair business. He was a very inventive sort and out at the back of the workshop in front of a high solid mound of earth, he had set up a contraption that enabled him to fire, at no danger to himself, any rifle to be found ranging from a 0.22, through the many shapes and sizes of flintlock rifles and shotguns, to the extremely heavy recoil .500 express elephant rifles.

I watched once as he set up his contraption to test-fire one of these heavier rifles. First, he would clamp the rifle in an adjustable cradle with adjustable springs to take the recoil. After placing a target on a stand in front of the mound of earth, he would spend a long time setting the sights of the rifle. When he was satisfied and ready to fire, he would attach the hook of a fishing trace to the trigger and retire to the workshop, then with a sea-fishing rod in his hands he leisurely wound in the line until it was taut. After making sure there was nobody in the vicinity, he wound on the reel until it pulled the trigger.

The financial returns from the gunsmith shop were huge, not only from the repairs to the flintlocks belonging to the hundreds of black hunters that frequented the shop, but the trading store profited immensely from the reciprocal purchases by the hunters not only of the rifles themselves but from gunpowder, wadding, caps and shot.

The countryside on Hillside Farm and in the neighbouring Congo and Angola was the most pristine and beautiful I had seen or will ever see. The huge forests that grew along the crystal-clear rivers were dense and green all year round, but what struck me most about these forests was the silence that prevailed the minute I stepped inside them. It was like walking into a cathedral, lofty and spiritual, with the whisper of voices each time a breeze stirred the canopy.

Once I spent time in the forest with a game-hunter, a husband to one of the daughters of Folyet Fisher. He had been requested by the 'locals' to reduce the population of monkeys that were raiding the shambas (gardens) of the farmers who grew cassava and plantains along the forest edges. Each request for the game-hunter's controlling skills came only as a last resort after the monkeys had learned to circumvent the traps the farmers had set. They were crude and designed to crush the animals to death beneath a fall of logs.

As usual, the forest was as quiet as a graveyard until the hunter instructed a gun-bearer to cut down a tree. The chop-chop-chop of the axe echoed through the forest but still there was no sight or sound of life. Suddenly, the tree gave a warning creak and it was then I heard the first alarm call of a monkey as the tree began falling, taking with it the branches of nearby trees on its way to the forest floor and crashing in a cloud of leaves and debris. The forest exploded into life and there were dazed monkeys everywhere, leaping, barking and screeching. Impassively, I watched the hunter run from tree to tree, firing into the canopy. With each shot a monkey fell, until the troop vanished and the forest was still again.

There was little time in which to spend my first wages, for my seven-day week began before dawn and ended at sundown. Within a week of my arrival I had learned the art of milking. With one young black assistant, who couldn't have been more than twelve years old, we milked on average 32 Jersey cows every day of the year. They produced enough cream, when mixed with the milk from dozens of indigenous cows, to produce 75 backbreaking pounds of butter a day.

God! I hated that job, almost as much as I loathed the flock of turkeys I fed on the whey. Stupid birds! Instead of shielding their chicks in a tropical downpour like any other self-respecting hen would do, they would leave them and scurry for cover, leaving me to pick up their drowned chicks. Horses, up to that time, I'd always admired until I came face to face with a crippled retired Belgian racehorse. It had a swollen knee but had been spared the bullet because it was still able to mount a mare and hence was used purely for stud purposes.

I led that same horse out to the pastures each day in the company of a massive Sussex bull. It was quite a long walk to the paddock leading these two animals one in each hand, then returning with them in the evenings. The bull posed few problems for I led it with a rope through its nose-ring and each evening it would come to me when I called, but the horse was a bastard. It purposely gave me a hard time and would only come if I offered it a handful of cubes, and even then it did its best to bite the hand that fed it. Everything seemed to go fine for a while until one morning the horse refused the halter and I had to ask for Paul's help. When I asked him what had caused the beast to play up, he said the animal had sensed my fear and the only way to overcome it was to exert my authority otherwise he would pass the job over to someone else. That was as good as saying that there was someone among his workers with more courage than I, so with that in mind I exerted my authority by taking the crop to it.

After that it seemed to behave itself, until one morning it broke free from my grasp and galloped ahead of me. The bull then turned and stood snorting, facing me, before the horse reared up, whinnied, and bore down on us. I shouted and screamed, waving my hands wildly, while the unperturbed bull stood at my side and watched, but somehow I knew that horse wasn't going to stop. I let go the bull's lead and fled, reaching a barbed-wire fence that I dived through just in time, ripping my clothes and flesh in the process. It was a revenge attack for sure, and there was no way I was going to take any more chances, so I swallowed my pride, succumbed to Paul's arrogance and handed the beast over to some unfortunate with more courage and less sense than I.

Now you could say it was a victory for the horse, but it wasn't really because one day it got the better of my replacement while he was leading it back one evening. It galloped away and spent the night hiding in the bush where it became prey to a lion. The lion itself was shot by the monkey-shooter who paraded the carcass with pride in the back of a bakkie (pick-up truck) I still remember feeling deeply sorry for the poor lion.

I was delighted one day when Paul called me aside and told me I was to be relieved of my mundane chores for three days. I was to repair a stockade and accompany the herders and a herd of cattle to the railhead and thence to abattoirs in Elizabethville in the Congo. The stockade was a permanent structure built from hardwood trees that were less prone to wood-rot and attacks by termites. Nevertheless, they succumbed to the ravages of elephants that used the poles as scratching posts and something foreign against which to vent their anger when in musth. The purpose of the stockade was for the protection of the cattle against predators such as lions and hyenas. It took two days to drive the cattle (I can't remember the exact distance) at a grazing pace to avoid weight loss in the exceptional heat.

I spent the night with the herders around a roaring fire that was designed to keep lions away from the stockade. The herders well knew of the habit the lions had of creeping up to the stockade under cover of darkness and urinating downwind, which would encourage the cattle in their panic to break through the stockade walls. But it was not lions that kept me awake that night but a pack of hyenas, their appetites whetted by the discarded bones from the herders' supper.

The rest of the drive was uneventful and after the cattle were loaded I fell asleep in the guard's van, only waking up when the trucks arrived at the abattoir. I hung around while the cattle were being slaughtered and late that evening I was driven to a hotel. After a heavy meal, I fell asleep in the lounge watching a dubbed version of the musical, *The Student Prince*. Early in the morning I left by taxi for the abattoir where I met up with the herders. After collecting the invoice and grading sheet, we left by train for Kolwezi, the railhead where I was met by Paul. To my surprise, for he was slow to praise, he congratulated me on a job well done.

The next few months were boring, for though I loved the bush, of necessity there had to be something else to occupy my spare time. I had begun to read a lot, mostly National Geographic magazines of which there were literally hundreds in the bookcase in the lounge. Such was my state of mind at the time that my only interest was in nature's 'soft porn', photographs of nubile tribeswomen, and the nude paintings of the 'grand masters'. Besides being rather mediocre masturbatory material, they did nothing to reassure me that I was anything but an adolescent. I called myself a man, but I failed every test of manhood. The test of Age—I was just seventeen; of Taste—I liked watered-down communion port and Portuguese cigarettes; of Purpose—I avoided Sunday evening services and hard work; of Size and Development—I was small, puny-chested, skinny-legged, with a mop of black hair; and finally, of Experience—I had never fought with a man and had yet to sleep with a mature woman or share the tales of my high-school conquests... Even worse the gunsmith's wife was beginning to look like Marilyn Monroe.

Yet through all this monotony there were certain incidents that come to mind that, though painful, were more interesting and help fill the voids in my memory. Take for instance the time I fell ill with what I believed to be a dose of flu', but what Paul's mother said was malaria because I had neglected to take my dose of Mepacrin. Whatever it was left my system so rundown that I developed a boil on my backside that had to be treated at a Jesuit mission hospital in the Congo. The mission doctor was away on his rounds that day so I was treated instead by his aide, an elderly Belgian lady who couldn't speak a word of English, and besides suffering from severe shakes had a very bad limp.

Then began one of the most painful ordeals of my life. She told me in Flemish and with hand-signs to pull down my trousers and lean against the wall of the surgery while she prepared an injection of penicillin—which in those days was as viscous as molasses. Looking back over my shoulder I watched her advance with the most lethal-looking hypodermic syringe, the sight of which I let out a moan and began to shake, this was followed by a muffled yell as she battled to insert the needle. When at last she had, she then proceeded to wrestle with the plunger. She gave up in the end and left the needle dangling from my arse as she hobbled to a table with the syringe that I could see to my horror was still half-full. I was in absolute agony when at last she returned with the unblocked syringe and seemingly without feeling reattached the syringe.

By this time my hands were wet against the wall and perspiration had soaked my shoes, but she felt nothing as she continued unsuccessfully to administer the dose.

It's difficult to believe but yes, again, the infernal machine blocked and again she had to detach the syringe, but this time she measured the remains of the dose and refilled a fresh syringe, which all takes time. By the time she resumed the task my arse was on fire and I had been reduced to nothing short of a trembling lunatic. When the ordeal was over, I hobbled from the surgery with a fear of injections that has stayed with me to this day.

It is said that adversity sometimes follows misfortune and in this case it did. Soon after my experience with the doctor's aide, an errant insect flew into my ear while I was pruning coffee bushes and created havoc by crawling around inside my ear and giving a buzz every so often that nearly drove me crazy. In desperation I filled my ear with water in the hope of flushing it out, to no avail. Either the insect was a good swimmer or was able to hold its breath for an inordinate length of time. That night, unable to sleep, I held my ear as close as I could to the glass of a paraffin lamp beside my bed in the hope of cooking the insect, but it didn't help.

In the morning I told Paul of my plight and with the buzz of the insect still in my ear we set off for the mission clinic. Again the doctor was out and I came face to face with the same assistant! God, no! I visualized the woman puncturing my eardrum, but thank God she was in a healing mood and soon the wretched insect was drowning in a kidney bowl. I was so relieved that, forgetting Paul's affiliations and remembering my recent ordeal, as we drove home I sang aloud a naughty ditty in honour of the nurse. Would you believe it, Paul laughed and even asked me to repeat it!

There was an old lady of ninety-two, who let a fart and away it flew,
Up the alley and down the lane, into a copper's window pane,
The copper took out a rusty gun and shot it bang-bang, and out the fart ran,
Up the alley and down the lane, and into the old lady's bum again.

As a treat on Christmas Day, after my daily chores ended with the turkeys all (minus one) having been fed, I was invited on a picnic by the family to a sacred lake called Chabasha.

It was an eerie place, deep in a stretch of forest and only accessible by an overgrown path that led to a clearing and a stretch of water fed by an underground spring and kept level with a tiny stream flowing out at one end. I joined the men in a walk around the perimeter, while the women sat and talked, their voices magnified within the dense walls of the jungle. We searched diligently for any sign of human presence but there was none, not a single human footprint to be found. Animal footprints were everywhere, especially elephant and buffalo.

"In fact," said the monkey-hunter, pointing to the huge spongy footprint of an elephant in the mud slowly filling with water, "they were here not minutes ago. You won't hear them, they move like two-ton shadows," and he added, "more silent than we do."

Each time he spoke, his words mingled with those of the women across the water and echoed around the clearing, adding to the spectral atmosphere. I remember quite clearly feeling relieved when leaving the lake. It wasn't the place that had scared me, I just found it depressing. Perhaps I would have felt differently had I seen a living creature, anything, but there wasn't so much as an insect and even the water seemed sterile.

Over lunch in the sun, for my and the Australian's benefit, Singleton Fisher repeated the legend of Chabasha. Way back at the beginning of time, there lived in the area of Mwinilunga, a chief who was revered by his subjects, so much so that his subjects offered their lives in return for his. After he was defeated in a battle with the Ngoni, a particularly bloodthirsty tribe, the beloved chief would have nothing of it and persuaded the enemy to accept a wager that should he survive a walk across the bottom of the lake from one side to the other so his tribe would be spared. Secure in the belief of his supernatural powers, the chief walked into the lake but never came out the other side and as a result, his tribe was put to the sword. It is said that his spirit continues to walk in the lake and in the spirits of his tribesman, and the animals too, that drink from the sacred waters. The locals believe the legend and have done so since before the first white men came. And why shouldn't they? There are those after all, that believe in the Immaculate Conception, life after death, and the parting of the Red Sea.

I was fired from the job in September 1957 after an altercation with the dairy assistant, who decided without asking to take the weekend off, leaving me to milk the cows single-handed. Everything would have been all right on the Monday.

Sure, I would have admonished him, and if he had given me any lip I might have docked his pay. But no, the fool had to laugh and get personal which made me see red, so I gave him a bloody good hiding.

I can't say I was sad to see the back of Hillwood. It wouldn't have lasted anyway. Sure, there were moments, but strangely enough it was religion and the style of living that wore me down. I think that living so close to people who were so different from Bob and Ina left its mark too.

Chapter Twenty-One

Lions Den 1957 – 1960

The town called Kalomo was in the southwest of Northern Rhodesia. I didn't know then but have subsequently learned that during the three years I lived in the South West Province it was the capital of the province. It was a town of little note except for a quaint corrugated-iron house on stilts, and a magistrate's house that was last occupied in 1907. For some reason it was kept closed and was never opened while I was in the area.

As well as these antiquities of a bygone era, the town boasted a hotel with an expansive bar, a post office, a couple of shops, a garage with manual petrol pumps, a few houses and a sports club built on top of a hill above the Kalomo river. The club as I recall was very popular amongst the farming community, not so much for its nine-course golf course and tennis courts, but more for the bar that, because it was some distance from the police station stayed open most nights well after the compulsory closing time. The same bar was the watering hole for the district's doctor, who sadly passed on one Old Year's Eve after he took a stroll down to the river and fell in. The remains of his clothes, torn to shreds by crocodiles, were caught on the hook of a local fisherman weeks later. Jimmy attended the funeral. There wasn't a dry eye at the graveside, he told me, and the wake lasted for days.

There was also a railway station in Kalomo that I pulled into one sweltering day in November 1957. A phone call from Hillwood to Fairbridge was all it had taken to land me with a new job, drawn from a substantive list my guardian had of farmers wanting farm assistants. What made the process economically simple was that the school would be minus the costs of having to re-consign me to another part of the country, because Kalomo was on the beaten track from Hillwood, only a few hundred miles back down the line. Jimmy, my new boss, collected me and my suitcase at Kalomo Station after I said goodbye to the sunburnt white man with his peaked cap, a green flag and a whistle.

Within an hour of my arrival, I learned first-hand of the temperament that drove Jimmy. It came to light in the dining room of the hotel. Having not eaten for sixteen hours, I said I was hungry so Jimmy stood me to a mixed-grill. The tomato sauce came in a plastic tomato-shaped dispenser with a long spout. I tried several times to squeeze the sauce from the dispenser without success. Jimmy tried too, but the spout was well and truly blocked. He signalled to the waiter to replace the tomato sauce. The waiter made for the kitchen that had curtains covering the entrance. Through a gap in the curtain, I watched him squeeze and suck on the blocked spout until it was cleared and then saw him spit the blockage into a sink. Jimmy also looked on, his face and neck turning scarlet like the wattle on a magobagobam (turkey), his chosen bemba (Bantu language spoken by the Bemba people) name, and I just knew that something terrible was about to happen when the waiter returned with the cleared dispenser and set it on the table.

Jesus! One minute the waiter was bowing politely as a sign of respect, before the next when he received a hefty slap from Jimmy that sent him flying across the room, the two plates of food following him in quick succession. The place was in a mess, there was food and shattered china everywhere, and Jimmy wasn't happy until he had lifted the waiter by his collar and the seat of his pants, dragged him through the foyer and threw him into the street. I waited helplessly in the foyer while Jimmy sought the owner of the hotel, but the poor man must have hidden in one of the rooms. Jimmy, still fuming, left the hotel and drove home muttering ceaselessly and blaming all the faults of the hotel service on "kaffirs" (derogatory term once used to describe a black man) the world at large, and a government that was capitulating to the demands of the black nationalists.

My tobacco farming career began in 'the deep-end' before I had even grasped the rudiments. I didn't start at the beginning that involved preparation of the seedbeds where the seeds were germinated and the young plants nurtured like babies in a nursery. When I arrived at the farm, the plants were mature enough to be transplanted into the fields that had already been prepared in fertilised ridges that waited for the early rains.

The rains began falling early that year, which was a good sign at first because it enabled the transplanting to be completed before the main rains came. The rains came and never stopped day and night for weeks. We couldn't get the tractors near the lands because the road to the lands ran through vleis (Afrikaans: marsh).

that became so waterlogged there was no passage through. We spent day after day, the labourers and I, up to our knees in mud, trying to drain the land. But it was futile, the tobacco plants began to drown and there was nothing to do but wait and sit it out.

Then one day, the skies began to clear and we were able to begin reaping the lugs and cutters (the bottommost leaves). Under normal circumstances, the leaf would have been cured slowly to achieve the required colour and texture, but because of the excessive damage from the heavy rains, we were forced to speed up the process. It was a complete disaster—the leaves from the bottom of the plant to the flowers were incurable due to an infestation called alternaria. It is a type of airborne virus that spreads very rapidly. It could be seen as a glow like sunset above the field in the evening, and by morning all the leaves would have turned orange, but as soon as heat was applied in the barns the leaves turned brown, making the leaves unsaleable.

Jimmy had to make a quick decision. Either plough the crop in and plant some other crop like watermelons or nyemba, a type of ration beans issued to farm labourers or mineworkers. Or alternatively, wait for a heavy hailstorm on the off-chance of a payout from his crop damage insurance, a long shot but under the circumstances an option at least.

Salvation came in the form of a phone call from one of his neighbours, who hearing of Jimmy's plight, offered him a bed of tobacco seedlings that were excess to requirement and were about to be ploughed in.

We worked day and night, replanting the crop. The weather remained kind for the rest of the season. Costs were covered but there was very little profit, if any. However, Jimmy had put enough money from the good years to cease the practise of renting and instead bought a virgin farm he named Lions Den. I will never forget the day Jimmy sent me to Lions Den. I'd never been to the farm before. It was halfway along the Great North Road between Kalomo and Livingstone, a distance of 60 kilometres to the turnoff at Zwimba and from there 30 kilometres along a typical farm road to a drift on a river that bordered the farm.

I set off on a Vespa scooter one Sunday afternoon in September with a spare set of clothes and enough food for a few days wrapped up in a blanket strapped to the pillion. The Great North Road in those days was a dirt road with corrugations and loose gravel that made riding on the small tyres of the Vespa pretty hazardous, especially on the corners where the gravel was so deep they were difficult to navigate without spills. That exercise became so predictable and boring I found it more comfortable to negotiate them on foot. To add to my problems it was getting dark, and the Vespa was dynamo-driven. That meant that speed was necessary to keep its lights bright enough for me to avoid colliding with animals, or indeed bright enough to light up the road-sign, that indicated the road I should take, which to my dismay was nothing more than a very minor road with grass growing between the tracks.

I remember asking myself if it wouldn't be better to spend the night in the bush on the side of the road, rather than try to complete the final 30 kilometres to the farm, or should I hide the bike in the bush, walk the distance and fetch it the next day? At the slow speed I would have to travel, the scooter lights would serve little purpose in lighting the way. Then, just as everything seemed pretty hopeless, the moon began rising through the trees and pretty soon there was enough light to show up the twin pale ribbons of track without me having to use the bike's lights except where the bush was dense.

I was feeling pretty good until something ran out of the shadows and hit the scooter side-on, leaving me sprawled in the road and the bike on its side on the verge. For a minute or two I didn't know what had hit me. I thought of bush-pig or steenbok, but it was neither. Of all things it was a porcupine, and a very furious one with rattling quills. It backed out of the shadows and took a stance beside the bike, and for some time prevented me from retrieving it by backing into me each time I got close. I tried throwing stones, but that only made it more angry. In the end there was nothing I could do but sit on the opposite side of the road and wait for it to calm down, which it did eventually then ambled off down the road as if nothing had happened.

But if I thought the porcupine had been a surprise I was in for a shock, when no more than a few hundred yards from Lions Den I rode up a steep rise and down a steep bank towards a river... Shit! I remembered too late, Jimmy's warning of the drift with the steep banks. I slammed on anchors and ended up with my heels dug in only a few feet from the water. Although in a panic, I remembered him telling me of the kraal on the far bank where his farm workers lived. I began shouting for help at the top of my voice, then with less vehemence in an effort to conserve what energy I needed to keep me from sliding into the river. Thank God! Somebody heard my cries and I heard voices, then the sound of splashes and just before I felt my legs begin to buckle help arrived to save me from plunging into what I had envisaged was deep water. Actually, the water level was ankle-deep which made me feel a bit of a fool. Because I'd had enough and wasn't in the mood to look for a suitable spot to lay my head, I slept the first night on Lions Den in an empty hut in the kraal, in the company of a cricket hidden in the eaves that kept me awake for most of the night.

Considering the poor start, I was proud of our first month or two's achievements, for in that time, I and my gang of twenty labourers stumped and cleared for the plough thirty acres of virgin bush.

Jimmy joined me some time later and together we prepared a campsite. Until the house and barns were built, we showered under a paraffin tin punctured with holes and slept beneath a roof of stars on camp beds inside a boma (pen for livestock) erected from gumpoles and sackcloth.. While he and his crew dug the foundations for the tobacco barns and house, my labourers and I moulded and fired thousands of bricks in readiness for the building. So hard did we toil, that before the bricks had cooled we had corded the wood and cleared the land in readiness for ploughing.

The rains were still months away and it was the time of the year when the night air was fresh and the days as hot as hell. The stars with their brightness enhanced the eerie calls of a pair of silver-backed jackals that lived on the high ridge above the site. Lying awake I would hear the crunch of chicken bones the jackal had found in the garbage hole beside the long-drop.

I got to know Jimmy pretty well as the months went by and I guess he got to know me too. He was a great teller of campfire stories that were either experiences of his past life or were stories that centred mostly around the conflict between the Boer and the British, and because he was fluent in both English and Afrikaans, it gave his stories the ring of truth. He used both languages in the same measure, ostensibly it seemed as an encouragement for me to learn his language, a kindness that was wasted, for I was typical of the English who are known to be poor learners of another language. However, I made it a point to pick up the African dialects simply because very few of the blacks on the farms in those days could speak a word of English.

But getting back to Jimmy's tales, one sticks out in my mind because in its humour it broke away from the mould of hostility that surrounded the tragedy of the Boer War.

A Boer commander had been on the run with his men from a British force for weeks. As a result they were unable to bathe and so wore the same khaki uniforms that in the end rotted and hung tattered and stinking from their bodies. On the other hand, the British soldiers chasing them had bathed and shaved every day and were resplendent in their freshly washed and ironed scarlet and white uniforms. One day the Boer commander captured a British officer and forced him to exchange clothing with him then sent him on his way back to his troops, with the words 'Voetsak (an expression of dismissal) you dirty Dutchman'.

Jimmy could also be very annoying. He was always trying to scare me and did once, very successfully. He followed me to the long-drop one night and waited in the bush outside. As I pushed aside the sackcloth that concealed the entrance, he coughed into a paraffin tin like a lion on the prowl. It wasn't the first time I had heard his party trick, but right then it was a lion I heard, not Jimmy. I shouted for help once or twice as I ran like hell to the camp and hid beside the bed. It was then I heard his laughter outside as he appeared carrying the empty paraffin tin that usually sat beside his bed.

I was fucking angry at first and in my rage swore at him, something I would never had dared do. There followed a shocked silence as I calmed down and waited for his response. I could sense his anger at being called a 'fucking bastard', and took advantage of the silence by pointing in my defence at his .303 propped up against the sackcloth wall beside his bed, its barrel gleaming in the light of the fire. "What if I had used your gun, Jimmy?" I asked, and without waiting for his reply I stripped, donned my pyjamas and lay down on my bed.

Jimmy never said a word, just turned away, lit a cigarette and stared out into the night. He never mentioned the incident the next day, which left me unsettled at first, but then as the day wore on he must have realised his mistake and by the end of it he was his same old self.

It was a great day the day the borehole was sunk and we no longer had to cart water from the river. It was Jimmy himself who had divined the water, using two lengths of 10gage wire held in his fists. The borehole was a good two hundred yards away from the site where the house was to be built. The pump fitted was one of the latest at the time and was driven by a Lister diesel engine that you could hear miles away. It had a flywheel so heavy that if you didn't remove the crank-handle in time it was capable of breaking your wrist, which is what happened to Roman, Jimmy's Hottentot mechanic who came with him from Rustenburg.

The flywheel was also used to drive a generator that supplied enough power with the aid of a roomful of batteries, to supply the house and barn lights but not sufficient to supply my outside room.

It took no more than five months to erect all the buildings. Jimmy reckoned it was a record and I knew that if we hadn't worked every day for five months, including weekends, it would never have been possible. It was only after the sixty acres of tobacco had been planted by the end of November that everybody was able to relax while the tobacco ripened. As soon as the house was built, Jimmy's wife moved in and our diet of bully beef and fried rice was something of the past, though I still slept in the storeroom despite the house having five bedrooms, and still took a bath in a galvanised tub.

I can understand why Jimmy was able to afford to buy Lions Den despite the past season having been a disaster. It had been part of the neighbouring farm and contained a large proportion of non-arable ground. Perhaps it was for this reason the former owner had sold it off cheaply. The farm was unfenced and because of this, there was an abundance of free roaming game that included kudu, hartebeest, and a large herd of resident sable that I came across quite unexpectedly while I was taking a stroll along a ridge of high ground early one Sunday morning.

I was e-Enchanted by the view of a green vlei dotted with what I took to be boulders and I stopped for a smoke. To my surprise one of the 'boulders' rose to its feet and shook off a shower of dew. Intrigued, I decided to get closer, little by little and keeping to cover, I made my way down the ridge at a crouch, in line with a large termite mound with a dead tree lying at its base. For a while I lost sight of the animal as I crept closer. Then on reaching the tree, I rested my arms on a dead branch and searched the area where I was sure the animal had been. All of a sudden I heard a snort to my left. Without moving my head I rolled my eyes in the direction of the sound, and there, not twenty feet away, stood a sable bull looking straight at me. Its black coat and mane and beautifully curved horns sparkled in the early morning light. I stared at him with heart thumping so loud I was sure he could hear. He stared at me, nostrils flared seeking my scent, ears flapping, then dipped his head and snorted, then eyed me once more until seemingly satisfied that I wasn't a threat and turned side-on to face the rest of the herd lying in the grass. I stood in awe as one by one they rose to their feet, each shaking and showering the grass with diamonds.

I stood absolutely still, as a female with calf at foot, left the group and wandered towards the dead tree. She stood so close I could almost touch her. Then, on making out my form the cow shied away, startling the rest of the herd and in seconds they had disappeared like ghosts into the bush.

There wasn't a time, in my first year on Lions Den, when on a walk through the bush I didn't come across game. There were even six pairs of Oribi that grazed never far from the back of the house. They were my favourite amongst the antelope; wide-eyed and dainty with long graceful necks, pointed elfin ears and small straight horns.

Kudu, plentiful as they were, took a liking to the flowers of the tobacco plants. I could never understand why they were persecuted for doing this, after all it was part of the process to remove the flowers (topping it was called), to give weight to the plucked leaf. Granted, some leaves were damaged as the beasts moved around the field but the damage was never enough to warrant shooting them. It was just as easy, I would argue, to leave one labourer to guard the field at night and chase them off rather than shoot them, but unfortunately Jimmy perceived them not for their magnificence, but rather as a source of the tastiest biltong.

When I look back on the wholesale slaughter of game that took place once a year in the Luangwa/Chisomo area east of Lions Den, in the supposed interest of foot-and-mouth disease control, I understand why the black tribesmen of the time must have looked upon us as plunderers, and rightly so. There is no forgetting or forgiving what took place after Jimmy and his family descended on that wild and beautiful area. For a whole week, Roman and I followed the hunters with our tractors and trailers and a gang of labourers who loaded the carcasses and delivered them to the campsite where they were skinned and then butchered by the womenfolk.

The less palatable meats that came from old animals, waterbuck, zebra, giraffe, warthogs and suchlike were cut into large strips, salted, and put in the sun to dry before being packed into grain-bags to be transported to the farm to be used as ration meat for the workers.

The choice carcasses were kept for the white hunters, the butchering of which fell under the control of Jimmy's wife whose pinafore was forever splattered with blood. She seemed to relish more than the other women having her arms bloodied to the elbows as she prepared tons of boerewors (spiced sausage) and biltong (dried game or beef meat) that was hung in the shade of portable driers.

What a tragedy that was, the tons and tons of animals sacrificed on an altar of blood lust and pretence, for it was widely known even then that foot-and-mouth was passed on mainly by buffalo. The most senseless of all was that neither Jimmy nor any one of his family had to fear foot-and-mouth because none of them ran cattle.

The first crop on Lions Den turned out to be a fairly good one after a poor start, when Jimmy in an inventive mood, decided to attempt what he thought would be a radical departure from the proven method of curing tobacco and reduce the labour needed to cure the crop from six to one. Needless to say, it didn't work. The modifications proved to be theoretically and practically a disaster, notwithstanding three days lost when the labourers stood idly by instead of reaping, while we battled to reintroduce the time-proven system. In short, Jimmy was one of those men who listened to no one and made arguing a pastime, but worst of all would never admit a mistake.

If he taught me one thing though, it was that efficiency and mutual respect in the workforce did not occur automatically because one was white. "You're too soft," he said to me one day after I laid a complaint of impertinence and disobedience against one of the workers.

"What would you have me do?" he asked, "I can beat the hell out of him, but where will that leave you? You have to earn their respect and obedience and if you feel you are losing control, it's quite simple, choose one preferably bigger than yourself, make out as if he has disobeyed an order and while he is still unsure as to your intentions, lay into him. But whatever you do, don't start with a punch in the face, their skulls are like concrete. A good kick in the belly or balls, because most of them are riddled with bilharzias (parasitic infection), is usually sufficient to lay him on his back, but don't give him a chance to recover, that's the key. If there's a stick handy use it, if not use your fist, but now's the time to go for his face, it always looks better with some blood. Whatever you do don't stop until he cries for mercy and even then give him a few more kicks for luck. And when it's all over with, you will find for the next few months they will fall over each other to do your bidding."

"And if I lose?" I asked.

"You mustn't" he answered, "for if you do, you may just as well pack your suitcase."

It didn't sound good to me. In fact, it appeared downright stupid and besides I was and still am a bit of coward when it comes to fisticuffs. So I practised my own powers of persuasion and psychology, blended with a little competitive spirit to obtain the maximum effort from the labourers. If I thought they were purposely slacking, I thought nothing of taking a badza (long handled hoe) or axe in my hand and joining the gang. I was young and strong and kept up with the best, and in doing so showed them that theirs was not a menial task since I, the boss, considered it worthy of their efforts. I laughed and joked with the forerunners while chiding in a diplomatic manner those who were slow.

To further prove Jimmy wrong, I introduced him to the

advantages of an mgwaza, or piecework system, where each labourer was allocated a task that was designed to last eight hours. If the task was completed in say four hours, the labourer not only earned his full daily wage but was given the balance of four hours to do with as he chose. The system was so successful; I was able to apply it to almost all farm chores, so that with time everybody, including Jimmy, was happy.

I had thought I knew all there was to know concerning the psyche of my farm workers until one day I was given a rude awakening that left me shaken.

The farm compound was preparing for a grand annual social event that prompted my workers to approach me with a request that I thought to be reasonable as everybody had worked hard all year. I approached Jimmy with the request, which was that they be allowed to triple the output of barns reaped on the Friday so as to give them the day off on Monday. Jimmy thought about it long and hard and at last agreed.

You never heard such celebration that Friday morning and everybody set to work with a will, me included, because it meant that I too could take the break. We worked like Trojans from sun-up to sundown and well into the night when the tobacco had to be tied by the light of lanterns. God! I was tired by the time we were finished, but it was a pleasant tiredness and I went to sleep looking forward to the next day. Saturday came and went, then Sunday. Come Monday, I planned a lie-in, then a long walk around the farm with a pack of sandwiches and a bottle of tea.

I was still asleep when the gong was struck I didn't take any notice at first thinking that somebody was playing the fool, until I heard Jimmy shouting to Roman to hitch up the trailer. Quickly I scrambled into my clothes, convinced the Jimmy had forgotten the arrangement. I met up with him at the door of my room. "What's going on, Jimmy, we've given them the day off remember?"

"I know," he said, "but surely you didn't think we could afford to give them all three days off, besides," he said with a grin "we got one extra barn reaped for nothing."

"They aren't going to like it Jimmy, we gave our word."

"Don't worry," he said, "I knew they wouldn't be happy so I spread the word yesterday and they came to their senses when I threatened to dock a day's pay. I always tell you, you've got to be one step ahead of them all the time. Besides, they've had a good two full days and if they work as hard as they did on Friday they'll finish reaping one barn before midday, then they can enjoy the rest of the day off."

It was a sullen crew that set off for the lands that day, there was no cheering them up and they were impossible to handle. Halfway through the morning they turned on me after I rebuked one for purposely reaping unripe leaf. It all happened so fast and there were so many I didn't stand a chance. I didn't fight back, I knew that would have been foolish. Besides I was terrified, so I lay in the furrow and let them beat me until they had vented their anger. I thought at first they were digging my grave when I saw hands digging into the furrow of sand before my eyes. It was then that I wet myself and suffered the indignity of having my head covered in soil, which was how they left me while they completed the day's reaping. When they were finished the boss-boy came to help brush me off, but I was so suffused with anger and hatred that I pushed him away and pointed my finger at them.

"You fucking imbwa!" I screamed, "I will remember what you've done, you'll get no more help from me... and from now on you are my enemy!"

I didn't tell Jimmy about the incident, but he got to hear of it through Roman a few days later. Jimmy only added to the misery I felt by suggesting I lay a charge of assault with the local police, which only made me even angrier and resulted in the inevitable confrontation when I accused him of breaking his word.

"I want you to go and lay a charge of assault with the police," Jimmy said.

"No, I won't," I replied, "it was all your fault Jimmy, you broke your word, which is something you have told me never to do, especially where they are concerned. No, I'll get my own back, my way, or pack my suitcase and leave."

Jimmy took no notice and a few days later at roll-call, after he had found out from Roman as to who the main culprits were, he singled them out and on the pretext of giving them a task sent them unawares to the grading shed that was locked behind them. Jimmy and Roman got stuck into them with such savagery that the screams and sounds of the beatings could be heard far beyond the walls of the grading shed. I was told by Roman that it resembled a butcher's shop after Jimmy and he had laid into the alleged ringleaders with mattepis (sticks for hanging tobacco leaves). Jimmy gave them a week's sick leave after the beating then paid them off.

Jimmy was right. For the next few months the workers did my bidding. In July 1960, I received my National Service call-up papers, and in August I too was paid off and left with a travel voucher for Brady Barracks in Bulawayo.

En route, I stopped off in Livingstone and went to the bank to withdraw a portion of three years' wages, which would have amounted to £350. Imagine my surprise to find there was no account in my name and later to find that Jimmy's assurance that each month my salary was deposited into my account was a lie. Worse still after I reported the theft to my guardian, he believed Jimmy before me, that I had spent my salary through a works account, that included a guitar that I had thought was a Christmas present, and clothes that I thought came with the job. Last, but not least, the balance of money owed by him to me was absorbed by a minor accident I had in the line of duty on the farm with the farm's jeep. The jeep I remember well, because it had no brakes and no windscreen and was held together with luck and a piece of wire.

My time at Brady Barracks was short, no more than a month. A medical doctor discharged me after deciding my feet were not suited to the rigours of forced marches in army boots.

Perhaps then was the time I should have quit farming and joined the railways, which at that time was considered by man to be the 'bottom of the dung heap' and the 'last chance' for the unemployed. However my guardian, unwavered by my complaint at not having been paid for the past three years, decided I should return to Lions Den and give it another chance. I did, only to find my job had been given to some other unfortunate. I put up a token resistance by seeking the advice of a retired lawyer who lived on a farm outside Kalomo. He approached Jimmy on my behalf, only to be chased from the farm by an infuriated, shotgun-wielding Jimmy who insisted I had been paid my dues. Fortunately, my would-be benefactor was a kind man who insisted on paying my rail-fare back to Fairbridge, where despite my protestations my guardian decided that farming was still my last hope.

After a week spent in the Rejects Cottage, I found myself once more on the overnight train and bound this time for Salisbury, where I was met by Harold, a short, ginger-haired, arthritic farmer, dressed not in khaki as I had visualized, but smartly in a suit and red tie.

Chapter Twenty-Two

Inversnaid Farm 1960 – 1962

The farm was situated near the village of Melfort, 40 kilometres southeast of Salisbury on the main road to Marandellas in an area well known for the large number of pedigree cattle breeders. Harold was not one of these however, but a tobacco grower who had a pathological dislike for smokers and smoking, referring to those under the spell of the noxious weed as weak and ill-mannered.

Although I wasn't a smoker at the time, I found his insults aimed at the smoking fraternity hypocritical, very boring and irritating, especially in the presence of Audrey, his wife's auburn-haired, attractive, high-spirited and often flirty younger sister. She was a smoker who in order to keep the peace kept her smoking to the verandah, unless Harold had visitors who smoked, in which case she ignored her self- imposed restraint and joined him and his friends in the lounge.

I remember well an argument between the two that began in the kitchen before breakfast and ended with Harold leaving the table in a rage after Audrey had accused him of hypocrisy. It wasn't always like that, for when they weren't arguing over politics and business they appeared to be friends, but I couldn't help wondering sometimes if perhaps Harold felt threatened by her. She was a very capable lady who was head of a longstanding firm of auditors. I was very fond of her, not only for the way she stood up to Harold but also her commiserations for me having to live with him.

I met his wife Sylvia in her rose garden the day I arrived, before he drove me around to meet his manager. She was in her late forties, little more than average height, 5ft6ins perhaps, with a body that illustrated to perfection her slim straight shoulders, lush breasts, rounded hips and buttocks packed smoothly in a tight white skirt that revealed when she turned away, what I could have sworn were tight indented panty lines. She was quite beautiful, with dark brown curly hair and eyes large enough to emphasize the wet black centres in surrounding blue. Most endearing of all were the faint crow's feet that appeared in a smile that portrayed a mature prettiness.

I would quite happily have spent the whole afternoon with her, rather than her husband and his manager Frank, a man I disliked from the moment we met. I had and still have a pet aversion to men who find it difficult to look me in the eye, and even more so a rude and possessive husband, who snatched a cup of tea from his wife without so much as a thank-you and later stared daggers at her and me as we exchanged pleasantries. He was tall and strong, with hands like hams but lacked the genuineness of a firm grip, and even as we spoke a few meaningless words I knew that soon we would clash.

Thelma, Frank's wife, sat opposite me in their lounge that gave me the chance without it being too obvious, to study her good looks and lithe figure. She was a genuine blonde with a fringe and a sweep of hair tied back in a short ponytail. We locked eyes often in the course of conversation and if Frank's attention was diverted she smiled shyly and fidgeted with the gap in her divided skirt, in an unsuccessful attempt to hide the V of a semi-transparent half-slip that gaped interestingly each time she crossed her legs.

I liked Thelma from the time we met, and in time to come, when Frank wasn't around, I spent as much spare time as I could making friends and helping her with her two responsibilities. These included the supervision of the farm's trading store and the farm's flock of chickens that were housed in movable runs on the lawn outside Frank's house.

It was at supper that evening that I noticed the extent of

Harold's arthritis. The swollen joints in his hands resembled the joints in the claws of a bird of prey, and because he was hirsute, the long fair hairs on the back of his hands only served to accentuate his ailment. Mealtimes with them would never be pleasant times for me. I felt uncomfortable for him and sorry for Silvia, because of his battle with simple things like handling a knife and fork or a glass of water that he had to grasp in both hands. It was already dark when we moved to the verandah for coffee and a get-to-know-you conversation that included me giving a brief synopsis of my disastrous experiences as a farmer, ignoring of course any indication of my true feelings for farming and farmers.

Over a liqueur followed by coffee, Harold related the history of the farm stretching back thirty years to the times when the road from Salisbury had been a dirt road and post was delivered once a week by a postman on horseback.

"There was a sense of comradeship amongst us farmers back then," he said with a sigh. "We shared information and techniques, which was a godsend for the likes of me, a 25-year-old and fresh out from Wales. Social life too was pleasant then, there was always somebody celebrating something, and once or twice a month in the in-season, we gathered together on different farms for a guinea fowl shoot, using beaters with sticks to drive the birds to the guns. There are few of the old farmers left now and even those have drifted apart through politics."

Harold was a brilliant farmer. He stuck rigidly to the past, not because he was afraid of trying new things, but because he was secure in the knowledge that the past, for the present, was the way to go. It was a case of oxen-versus-mechanical power, and to prove this point he owned but one small tractor that was used solely in the domestic vegetable and flower gardens with the odd carting job thrown in. For the rest, teams of oxen were used to plough, harrow, till and sow. The only task oxen were unable to do was plant and reap tobacco, and the only task a tractor could do that an oxen couldn't do was to reap maize—and that didn't amount to anything because it was cheaper to reap by hand rather than use a combine, which in those days was an ugly-looking piece of metal on wheels that was forever breaking down and required a team of specialists to keep it operational.

I shared Harold's sentiments when it came to animal-versus-machine. Perhaps we were both romantics, or did it take soul to appreciate the grand and exhilarating sight of a span of oxen dragging an 8-furrow Dragoon plough, their backs bent like bows, ripping and turning a swathe of land eight paces wide, at a cost covered by nature plus a few Pounds for the mukoken (leader of the span) and the whip-hand? So much controlled power, and their supposed equal, a fuel-guzzling, smoking monster driven by a driver who earned three times as much as his counterpart, who controlled all with a crack of a whip and a voice calling orders in a language understood only by him and the oxen.

Part of my responsibilities was to watch over the welfare of the oxen by tending to their wounds, and to make sure there were always replacements that were trained to the yoke by an old man they called Pingudza. He also named each animal according to its temperament, shape of horn or colour pattern. I remember one in particular with odd shaped horns. The one horn had grown up and out in a regal arc, the other arced in a down curve as though it had been twisted so that the tip of the horn had to be sawn off to avoid it growing into the cheek. This malformation gave the animal a sly, mean look and shaped its bad-tempered character, but because of its great strength, Pingudza had persevered with the brute and named it Hasha, after Harold. The teams were a credit to Pingudza's patience and wisdom. His was an occupation taught him by his father in the fields of his youth. Unlike the tractor drivers who were a dime-a-dozen with a calling that was simply a job.

I had very little to do with the tobacco crop once it had been re-ridged and cultivated. When the plants were tall enough to tickle the bellies of the beasts, the oxen were withdrawn from the fields. Then the monotonous tasks of suckering, topping and pest control were taken over by labourers, until such time the crop was ready to reap and it became once more the task of the oxen to return to the fields and resume the task of transporting the crop to the barns for curing.

Thank goodness it was not my job to supervise the reaping of the crop as I had done in the past, that was left to Frank and his boss-boys. Mine was the joy of building haystacks and preparing silage for the coming winter months.

I was in my element then, and rejoiced at the thought of not having to spend day after day watching over a bunch of colour-blind humans, whilst shouting out the same phrase over and over: "Regera tanha mbishi mdoda, tanha wakaibva mazanhi cheti"— don't reap green leaves men, reap ripe leaves only— until I was hoarse. While I took a break from the chant, some idiot or two would forget my instruction, by accident or to test my patience, and reap green leaves that were un-curable and worthless.

But above all this was the pleasure of not having to work in the company of Frank, who disliked me not only for my platonic friendship with Thelma, but because of an incident in which I caught one of his boss-boys, a fellow called Rice, stealing a sack of brown sugar and a sack of mtemba (dried fish) from the farm ration store. It was an incident that saw Frank castigated by Harold for allowing Rice the use of his key to the store. On the other hand, for my diligence for a short while at least I was the apple of Harold's eye.

Christmas came and went and on New Year's Day I celebrated my twenty-second birthday. Frank and Thelma joined us and for that day at least, Frank and I shed our differences. Harold too appeared to be in good spirits, and I got to know why after he invited Frank and me to join him on a trip around the farm.

We stopped at a stream that ran through a steep valley that cut through the middle of the farm. I could sense the excitement in Harold's voice when he pointed out the site for a dam that he said, after discussions with the Department of Conservation and Extension, would have the capacity to irrigate 30 acres of tobacco and 20 acres of maize in a dry year, and appreciably more in a normal season. "It is my intention," he continued, "to breed and harvest fish to supplement the labour rations, plant some trees and make it into a picnic spot for friends to enjoy, but most of all it will make us self-sufficient in times of drought when the rivers run dry. It's going to cost a lot in overtime and effort because it must be completed before the start of the rains in November."

Harold and I, with scores of labourers and teams of oxen, worked on nothing but the dam for eight months. It was a huge construction with an earth-wall that, if I remember, stretched for a hundred yards or more between two rocky outcrops either side of the valley.

For the first month, the sound of explosions rocked the valley every evening. The next day it echoed with the shouts of men, the ring and clatter of picks and shovels as scores of labourers, in shifts, picked and shovelled their way through piles of shattered rock. The rock was tossed into heaps before being loaded onto an ox-drawn trailer that had been manufactured by Frank from the chassis of an old 5-ton lorry reclaimed from the scrapheap. It was then carted to the dam site where it was bonded with concrete to form the slipway and a buttress against the waves that would one day beat against the earth-wall.

In awe, I watched as trek chains were fastened around boulders that had been landmarks for centuries, before each lost its identity beneath tons of earth after they were dragged down the hillside by a team of oxen to form the foundations for the dam wall.

Then came the time when the blast of dynamite and the sound of steel against rock and the shouts of orders ceased. A calm settled over the site, broken only by the timeworn melodious cry of the driver, the crack of his whip, the clack of horn striking horn and the bellow of discontented double teams of oxen, straining against the drag of huge dam scoops. Reinforced blades dug deep and scraped up thousands of tons of virgin earth and gravel that formed the wall. Each scoop increased the capacity of the dam and formed a basin before the wall that would be deep enough to hide the hull of a trawler. With that scene of peace, still to this day comes to me the songs of the women, echoing through the valley as they planted the wall with the roots of grass that held the soil together.

It was more than a month before the rains came and during that time the stream that once flowed through the valley had widened and settled the foundations. When the rains did come it took weeks for the water to foam down the slipway and by that time the high-water mark was established for certain. Within days a pump-house was built, two pumps were installed, and a network of asbestos pipes was laid to carry the water to the lands.

As I look back on what was without doubt the greatest achievement in my farming career, one man stands out in my memory taller than the rest: Munhriripiri—the man with the hot mouth—the Welshman who dreamed the dream and faced with me the numbing cold of winter and the choking August winds of dust. No matter the weather or his disability, Harold was always there, issuing orders, seated on his shooting stick, ever alert as he limped over the rough terrain from one site to another.

With the completion of the dam came normality. If I had missed anything during the past gruelling months, it had been the companionship of Thelma, especially on Saturday afternoons when it had been my habit to hang around with her and chat while I watched her feed the fowls and turn the eggs in the incubator.

She always looked so pretty those afternoons, in her crisp cotton blouse and divided skirt. I can be forgiven for believing that she did herself up especially for me, because most other times she wore her hair in a ponytail and wore drab slacks that did nothing for her, or me, except when she leant over and overtly displayed a strip of flesh and the waistband of a pair of underpants.

I caught her off-guard one afternoon. When she saw me coming, she left off what she was doing and rushed into her house. She appeared a short while later looking like the Thelma of my fantasies, wearing a split skirt and a fresh cotton blouse. Instead of the ponytail she normally wore, she had let her hair down to her shoulders, with a narrow scarlet scarf covering her forehead and tied at the back beneath the blonde waves. She looked so fetching and desirable that I was tempted to reach out and welcome her with a hug, but thought better of it when she interrupted my train of thought by telling me how much she had missed my company and asked if I would help her in the farm store pricing some merchandise that had arrived that morning.

Being Saturday the store shut early, which pleased me because it meant we would be alone. Frank, as always, would be in the workshop slogging his guts out to impress the boss; while right at that moment his wife's arm and thigh were brushing mine and her lips were only inches away as we dug together in the box of merchandise.

What happened that afternoon wasn't the result of some accidental encounter that stemmed from a mutual friendship. Not a bit of it, and I make no apologies in acknowledging that hidden for months, no, better still since the first time we met, behind the veneer of friendship lay a desire so powerful that there were days and nights when I could think of nothing but Thelma.

Meanwhile, it hadn't been easy for me, living under the same roof as Sylvia all this time, starved of sex and the company of a woman. The sounds of her bathing in the bathroom, so conveniently close that I heard the splashes as she washed her body and the sound of her rubbing against the enamel of the bath. And it wasn't easy not to stop and stare when I passed her bedroom with the door ajar to see her lying stretched out like Cleopatra in a satin nightgown. So close I could smell the scent of talcum powder and Lily of the Valley... the same scent I had smelt one day on a pair of knickers and a bra she had left on her bed while she was out picking flowers...

But this was different, Thelma was here beside me feeling, as it turned out, the same as I did. Everything slipped into place when I fetched a stepladder so she could reach the top shelf. As I passed her the goods, she stacked them, unaware that I could see up her skirt to her small firm bottom, its shadowed division visible through the taut white nylon with its opaque strip of gusset. She turned on the ladder to descend and in doing so her skirt rode up and I caught a mind-blowing glimpse of her pants sandwiched tightly into a mound between her thighs.

The atmosphere was electric and I felt its pull when she moved away from the ladder. She stood so close I could literally taste her desire. She must have whispered something because I saw her lips move, but any sound there might have been I couldn't hear until I pulled her to my chest. I felt her ribs flatten against mine and I heard the words "Take me," as our lips met in a flare of action. The last thing I noticed, while I was still sane, was the reflection of light on the countertop before we both stepped back to free our arms to tear off clothing. I was ripping buttons off my shirt as she tore at her blouse and bra, freeing her tiny breasts with nipples that stood out like little fingers. I tore off my shorts and underpants, kicking and stamping on them to free my feet, then watched eagerly as she threw her skirt and slip behind her. Leaving her pants on, she leaned back against the counter, removed her sandals and unabashed, turned her beautiful bottom to me. I was on the edge then, the ache so intense I could feel it tugging at my groin, and oh God! I could sense the impending eruption as she crossed to a shelf behind the counter to retrieve a blanket that she spread on the floor between us. She lay down, looked up at my erection and I was after her then, kneeling, pulling at her pants, dragging them down over her hips before dropping feverishly onto her. We drove hard at each other, mouth to mouth, tongues entwined, groins rubbing in passion. She whimpered when I touched her clitoris, cried out and wept, and whispered, "Fuck me," as it slid in so smoothly… The second time was slow and easy, in fact I made a game of it. I took her panties and after spreading them carefully over her breasts, sucked the marine taste of her from her nipples.

I was so in love and lust that work took second place. It became nothing more than a 'cooling off period' between trysts that became so uninhibited and driven by lust, that I couldn't have given a damn had we been caught 'in the act'. We very nearly were on two occasions and each time by Sylvia. Once when she came to enquire from Thelma about eggs, and found her behind the incubator while my hand was down her slacks caressing her bottom. Fortunately, she couldn't see because the incubator was in the way. The second time was when Frank was away and she caught me sneaking back into the house late at night.

Then one day I sensed a change in Thelma's attitude. Instead of making love, we fucked because we both needed to and after we were finished she told me it was over. She gave me some sick story about being in love with her husband, but I knew it was because we had been caught out. It suddenly dawned on me that Silvia may have hinted of the affair to Harold, or perhaps Frank was aware of it all along and might have relayed his suspicions to Harold.

Between the three of them, they made the decision to rid themselves of the affair and any possible consequences, by finding a reason, any reason, to fire me. A month later Harold found a reason to do just that.

Ostensibly, I lost the job not because of any philandering, but through the carelessness of one of the mower-men who attached the wrong ox to the mower. It just so happened (or was it ordained?) that I should have decided to take a turn on the mower that day (something I seldom did, unless bored), and ended with the oxen bolting in fright with me clinging to the seat. To avoid falling onto the blade of the mower, I flung myself backwards off the seat and left the galloping oxen and mower to plough through a field of maize before it was smashed beyond repair against a rock.

It was my fault as supervisor, that the incorrect ox was used and there laid the reason, according to Harold, for my dismissal. I remember so well standing before him in his office while he admonished me. I felt the anger inside, but did I fight for my rights? Not a damn! I stood before him like an errant schoolboy and accepted his insults without saying a word. Once he came close to revealing what I believed to be the real reason for my dismissal when he mentioned a complaint he had received from Frank regarding the attention I continually paid to Thelma. He quickly switched the subject to a scurrilous attack on my unsuitability as a guest in his house, accusing me of putting pressure on the house-servant by leaving my bedroom untidy, not washing the bath, my table manners, and my lack of respect for his wife.

And what did I do through all this crap? I stood there fuming inside, looking down on him sitting in his chair, spectacles perched on the end of his nose, listening to his insults, I could have easily have reached across his desk and lifted him up by the throat and hurled him through the window. But instead of swearing at him, telling him to stick his job up his arse and storming out and slamming the door behind me, I reached out for the cheque, thanked him for it, stuffed it in my pocket, turned and walked out of the office without a word.

I remember so well the rage as I stuffed what I had, which was no more than I had arrived with two years ago, into my suitcase. I passed Sylvia on my way out. She said something, but I didn't hear it. I should have said goodbye but I didn't. I met Harold at the door with an envelope in his hand. "It's your testimonial," he said. I was about to say 'fuck you', but I didn't, instead I glared at him and walked right past without a word.

I began to slow down as my temper cooled and stopped just once to look back at the farmhouse. You know, it was then, right at that very moment, that I severed my ties with Fairbridge! I didn't contact my guardian to let him know I had lost another job, there was no way I was going back to the Rejects Cottage to endure the humiliation that came with having to hang around until my guardian handed me over to some other farmer to do with me as he chose.

No, hell! This was a new somebody, sitting by the roadside thumbing a lift to another world.

Chapter Twenty-Three

Hartley, and a Different Kind of Life 1962 – 1964

I reached Gadzema, a small village ten miles east of Hartley late that evening, tired and footsore. I slept that night in a strange bed, in a strange room at the rear of a trading store owned by an old Greek called Passaportis. In the months to come I got to know the old man and his wife fairly well. He had settled in the area in 1905 about the same time the Giant Mine, situated about a mile away, produced its first ounce of gold.

One of the old man's customers coincidentally, was a local farmer by the name of Duvenage, who in 1949 had invited my brother John to spend a holiday at his farm. For the remainder of his schooldays John spent every holiday on the farm and left school to become a 'slave' (the typical Fairbridge story).

While working for the 'slavers', John and Old man Passaportis became firm friends, so was it any wonder that after dropping in that evening to enquire after John's whereabouts and on learning we were brothers, the old man insisted that I spend the night.

It was the old man's attractive daughter, with an unpronounceable name, who delivered me to John's doorstep the next morning. Now, I hadn't seen John for coming on six years, but it was she who he hugged and kissed before he even noticed me. When he did, he shook my hand casually like a friend does a friend who was last seen yesterday! All the same, it was so good to see him again and (would you believe it?) because he only had the one bed, we slept in the same bed together for the next two months.

I have written at length about my emotional and sensual self-education, making little attempt if any to describe my mind up to this time. Actually, I'm not sure I had one.

I had absorbed quite a lot of information about ideas and attitudes from what I had read and from people, but had yet to develop a mind or intelligence by means of which I could assess let alone conceive an idea of my own. Until one morning whilst sitting on the bank of the Beri beside a pretty little waterfall, I looked back on the last six years. I had nothing to show for them materially. In fact, I had grown poorer and the suitcase that contained all my worldly possessions was lighter than when I had left Fairbridge.

Suddenly, in the depths of despair, the seeds of my mind shook loose, a plant grew, and I came to a decision! Tomorrow I would go to Hartley to look for work. To hell with farming! I screamed at the top of my voice.

The excitement was still there when John got home. He was sceptical at first then warmed to the idea, even suggesting that he ask Tom, his boss, to phone around the businesses in Hartley to search for vacancies. I jumped at the idea. John, true to his word, spoke to his boss who came to the farm a few days later to give me some good news.

It was the first time I had met Tom. He was a tall, broad-shouldered giant who despite being Afrikaans spoke fluent English. He looked to be in his early forties, and was prematurely bald except for a thin straggle of fine fair hair that lay flat on his scalp like mown hay. He said there was a vacancy going in the hardware and timber yard of a newly built departmental store called Maitlands and had spoken to the owner, Colonel Hopcroft, who had arranged an interview for me the following morning.

I got there on time, riding a bicycle that John once used before he was given company transport. It had been years since I had ridden a bicycle, but after a wobbly start and a few spills in the loose sand on the farm road, I was off down the strip road in a race with black cyclists who too were on their way to

Hartley to begin a day's work. I must admit I felt conspicuous at first, being the only white I imagined to have ever been seen on a bicycle on a road frequented mostly by white farmers. They hooted politely and slowed down giving me time to pull off the tarmac strip onto the loose verges, unlike the travelling salesmen in search of the fast buck who, contemptuous of cyclists, drove at speed in heavily laden station wagons that swayed on and off the strips, throwing up clouds of dust and stones. In time I got to know them all, especially the kids with their parents on their way to school, who got to know me so well they hung out of the windows and cheered or jeered depending on the mood.

Something in my dusty appearance must have appealed to the Colonel, for as I was later to find out most interviews with him lasted hours, even days, while mine lasted no more than ten minutes from the time we met until my introduction to John Flynn, the hardware department manager.

The job was mindless and boring for the first month. There were two other youngsters fresh out from school that worked with me like syncopating robots, loading and offloading trucks of timber, steel, and cement. We didn't have to think for ourselves, the customers didn't come to us. Orders were placed at the counter manned by Richard, nicknamed Dicky, an ex-RAF pilot. He was a pleasant enough fellow who insisted that the till was 'out of bounds' to everyone, including John Flynn who he was quick to point out had made him responsible for any shortfalls at the end of each day. The system worked fine when business was slow but on busy days when there were queues. I often left the shop in the evening with a 'war' going on between the two of them, across a battlefield littered with invoices paid from the till and scraps of paper relating to requests for change and sundry payments to the other department.

Slowly but surely I began to gain confidence and it wasn't long before John Flynn considered me competent enough to take my place beside Dicky and attend to customers in the front of the shop. Dicky taught me how to work out the quantities of materials needed to build farm structures and because of my past experience in farming, customers began to turn to me in increasing numbers, seeking advice on pesticides and fertilizers. While the seeds of the mind scattered, Maitlands boomed and I with it.

In the first two months I had saved enough to open a bank account, which made me very proud. I bought a Norman Nippy on tick from old man Passaportis in place of the bicycle. It cut down the time travelling to work from an hour to about 15 minutes. You could say it was an extravagant purchase and as it turned out it was, because it wasn't long afterwards that due to pressure of work and longer hours (the price of climbing the corporate ladder) I moved into town, which took some getting used to after the peace and sanctity of the farm.

Hartley, named after Henry Hartley an early hunter and prospector, was a small town with a white population of about 600, most of whom worked in the David Whitehead textile factory a few miles out of town.

I couldn't afford to live in the town's hotel, so in the end had to settle for a boarding house run by an obnoxious elderly couple, Jack and Mary. Mary, judging from a wedding photograph that hung in her living room, had once been an extremely attractive bride but bore no resemblance to the stooped arthritic figure who met me at the door and shuffled around the house in bed-slippers, pointing out the areas in the house I was restricted to. On the other hand, Jack, the short, stocky, bald-headed bridegroom in the photograph, had changed very little in looks and still suffered from a superiority complex that the camera had failed to hide. He was an irritant, like an itch in the arse, always finding fault with the people he worked with, especially the management of David Whiteheads that he referred to as a bunch of idiots and who constantly refused to recognise his superior knowledge.

I can be forgiven after all his bluster, for believing at first that he was a head of department or suchlike, until I found out that he was a fitter and turner in the workshop. After that I ignored him and we rarely spoke for the two years I shared the digs with three other young people. One was a nerdy bank-teller with a Ford *Prefect* who I believed and rightly so, though he always denied it, was having an affair with a middle-aged librarian who lived in a block of flats in the same street. The other two were an engaged Irish couple from Cork and close friends of Jack and Mary. I can't remember their names but whenever I think of them, the phrase 'opposites attract' comes to mind. Never was this more pertinent than in the case of these two, for she was not only extremely attractive and talkative but was delightfully immodest when it came to crossing and uncrossing her legs— so different to her fiancé, a dour amorphous carpenter with the personality of a block of wood.

I was reminded often by my landlady, when I appeared a little thankless and as if I should be grateful, that the room I rented belonged to none other than their son, a divorced travelling salesman. I was unfortunate enough to meet him on several occasions when he popped in to either borrow money from his doting parents or cadge a few meals and doss down on the sofa in the lounge. I was told by those that knew him that he was a philanderer of note, which surprised me because like his father he was certainly nothing to look at. But, as the saying goes, there's no accounting for taste.

For all that, I thanked God for the weekends that I still spent with John on the Beri. John meanwhile had bought a second-hand Land Rover, the old model with its petrol tank beneath the driver's seat and the fuel pump beneath the bonnet, it ceased functioning twice on the way back from the showroom due to a bad connection that wasn't pointed out to him by the salesman.

Anyway, it seemed to have righted itself when he came to the boarding house to show me with pride his latest purchase and invite me to spend a weekend on the farm. On the way out of town we stopped off at the pub for a few drinks to celebrate. It was a mistake because by closing time we were both well over the limit and well on the way to a never forgotten experience.

It was only a few miles out on the Gadzema road when the fuel pump stopped working and we ground to a halt. It took a long time for us to sober up sufficiently to look for the cause. Thank God John had a torch with him, not that it helped too much. I can vaguely remember both of us searching blindly and unsteadily for the lever that would release the bonnet but there was none. We fell into a fit of swearing, cursing foully the manufacturers who had failed to fit the lever and the salesman who John swore had never explained to him how to release the bonnet. Suddenly there was silence and in my befuddled state I was sure I could hear him thinking. "Shit! Now I remember," he shouted, "the fucking clamps are on top," and sure enough there they were, all four of them, sticking up on top of the mudguards for all but a blind drunk to see. After successfully lifting the bonnet we still had trouble finding the rod to keep it upright, but that wasn't too much of a problem because I held it up however shakily, while John tinkered in the engine.

To this day I don't know how he in his state, found the source of the problem, but just maybe his sodden brain leaked the message through that twice that day he had experienced the same problem after the nut that held a lead to the terminal had fallen off. He had simply bound the lead with a piece of copper wire and he did the same again and soon we were on our way, but hadn't gone far when the same thing happened, again, and again.

Then I came up with a 'brilliant' solution! It entailed me lying on the mudguard while I held the lead with my fingers to the terminal of the fuel pump, the bonnet tied up with a piece of wire to the windscreen. John drove, leaning as far as he could out the window to try to see as much of the road ahead as he could—which wasn't much. As a consequence he hit every bump in the road, and each time this happened I was thrown up and down and ate mouthfuls of dust and grit that came up past the engine. It was as we neared the turnoff to Mount Carmel that the engine died altogether, not through the fault of the pump but because it had nothing to pump— we had run out of petrol!

Well, there was nothing left to do but ditch the vehicle and walk the last few miles to the farm, but then my 'scientific' brain swung into action when I noticed there was still an inch or two of fuel in the tank below the outlet pipe. That prompted the idea to fill the tank with rocks that I estimated would raise the level of fuel sufficiently to get us home... I won't bore the reader with John's remarks on the long, unsteady walk to the Beri.

You might well ask what the reason is for including this bizarre incident. Well, I'll tell you. In the 70-odd years given me thus far, I have spent far less of them than I would have liked to have had with John, so every little memory becomes that much more important.

Huey, the 'new' man came to Maitlands, and into my life like the heat rash that I used to get after a day's ploughing in the sweltering heat of a summer's day. It wasn't there when I got up in the morning, but halfway through the day I'd develop an itch and that evening in the bath discover a scarlet patch around my balls.

I hadn't been told of his coming, in fact nobody knew that the short tubby man in the navy-blue safari-suit, driving a Thames utility van, was to take the place of John Flynn who was about to take over the reins from the ageing colonel.

Never to this day have I met a man like Huey. In the space

of a month he managed to turn the department upside down with reforms that made no sense to me, even less to him, and endorsed the feeling that it wasn't his brains or intellect that had got him the job. But be that as it may, Huey, to his credit was above all things a 'cat with nine lives', who survived a daily onslaught of self-made errors that would have prompted even the hardiest to throw in the towel. How did he do it? I would ask myself. The answer lay in his ability to shift blame.

There was an incident for example when Huey, for a reason that never came to light, shortcut the system and placed one of the youngsters in the yard in the difficult position of either carrying out his order or, in the interest of correctness, ignoring it. He chose the latter and Huey, in his inimitable style of cajoling argument, had the poor youngster believe that it was indeed he who was at fault. Dick and I were appalled when the lad apologised for his indiscretion and in the interest of justice tried to persuade him to seek an audience with John Flynn, but it never happened. The next day the youngster resigned and, with Huey's blessing, received a month's pay in-lieu.

Yet, despite his deviousness, I developed a soft spot for Huey, for he was forever seeking to improve our conditions at work. From the time that he persuaded Management to pay us overtime and had our leave extended, Dicky and I took it upon ourselves to protect him from his own errors and played him at his own game. From then on, Huey flourished and accepted all the acclaim for which we were responsible, but that didn't matter at all, so long as the ship remained on an even keel.

It was months before I met Huey's family. Up until then he hardly ever mentioned them. He spoke fleetingly of his two sons that he delivered to and collected from school every day and a wife called Rita who didn't drive, but other than that they were a complete mystery until the day he invited me to a party for family and friends at his house.

He lived as it turned out, opposite the tennis courts of the town's sports-club that Dicky and I sometimes visited for a drink after work, and was to my surprise only a short walk from the boarding house. Not having been given a time, I decided to leave it for eight, unaware that being a Saturday, the party, or should I say the drinking, had already begun at two o clock that afternoon.

It was the voice of Elvis Presley mingled with the sound of splashing and laughter that led me to a driveway littered with cars and teenagers smooching and smoking in the shadows. The front door was wide open so I walked straight in and followed the strains of 'Flaming Star' to an empty lounge and a pair of glass doors. They led out onto a paved area bathed in a surreal yellow light that was supposed to repel insects, but instead had lured a well-oiled mixture of the sexes, leaning on each other in an attempt to remain upright while shuffling to the wails of Frankie Lane.

Nobody noticed me as I sidled past a table littered with the remains of a buffet in search of Huey. I found him on a bench beside the pool in what seemed intimate conversation with a very attractive, bikini-clad lady with prodigious nipples. Contrary to my nefarious thoughts she turned out to be none other than June, his sister-in-law.

What a party that was! It ended just short of an orgy, during which I saw a topless Rita pushed into the pool by June, who dived in after her and in turn was chased around by Rita before she was trapped against the side and had her bra ripped off. Rita waved the piece of cloth triumphantly above her head as she climbed out, so close to me, I could almost touch her chilled nipples large as acorns, and a pair of sodden nylon panties glued to her loins like a second skin.

Huey persuaded me to stay to the end, and after the last car had pulled out of the drive, I wandered around the lounge looking at pictures and a showcase filled with ornaments and family photos while he busied himself in the kitchen making coffee.

Rita, still very much in my mind, looked good in the family pictures with Huey and the sons, but by herself she looked stunning with all the expressions of an actress at an audition. I could tell that in most cases the photos had been staged, the way she flirted with the camera, making the most of her full round breasts, hips and thighs crammed into skin-tight toreador pants. I envisioned her naked rising from the pool.

I moved away smartly on hearing the faint sound from the kitchen of tea being poured and female laughter. I was at the far side of the room pretending to admire a hanging picture when Huey arrived carrying a tray with three cups. By his side was Rita bearing a plate of biscuits and looking most desirable and sexy in a transparent negligěe and pink shorty pyjamas.

For the best part of an hour, I listened politely to the couple's theories on the importance of open relationships that included sexually-loaded incidents that had occurred in their own marriage. All the time out of the corner of my eye I peeped dry-mouthed, and felt myself stirring, as she constantly tugged at the fold of her gown, pulling it back over her knees so that it lay across her lower thighs. I pretended not to notice when one of the fingers of the hand holding her skirt began to play up and down the skin above her knee, each time progressing a little higher till it reached a point when she lifted the hem, momentarily flashing a pink V before she carried it down to cover her knee.

Despite the presence of her husband I enjoyed her flirting, convinced in my mind that that was all it was. How could I be so vain as to think for one minute that this beautiful woman would have been interested in someone like me? Sure, there had been Thelma, but with her it had been different. It had happened as it turned out, because of the lack of interest shown in her by her husband. I was certainly no stud, any female could see that. Rita had teased me probably because she had sensed my innate shyness, that was all, and she probably did it to all the men.

A few days later, while Huey was away for the day on business, he phoned and asked me to collect an order from the local chemist and deliver it to his house.

It was a 10-minute brisk walk to his house in the heat of summer. When I arrived all hot and sweating, Rita met me at the door, looking all fresh and pretty in a skirt and a blouse with the top buttons undone. I looked past her into the shadowy hallway as she took the parcel from me and after thanking me, invited me in for a cool drink. I declined at first but without waiting for further dissent she disappeared inside, leaving me with no other choice but to follow.

It was cool inside and I felt a little twinge of something as she paused in front of a wall mirror to primp her hair and smile at my reflection. She left me seated on the sofa in the lounge while she went off to the kitchen, returning a short while later with a glass fizzing with lemonade. I took the drink from her and murmured an almost indiscernible thank-you as she sat down facing me, so close I could feel her knee against mine.

I became aware of a not unpleasant and familiar musky smell when she moved closer, almost without me knowing, and removed the glass from my trembling hands. At the same time her hand crept round and began fondling the hair on my neck, her warm fingers slid beneath my shirt-collar and sent pleasant shockwaves hurrying down my spine. As she leaned across me to place the glass on a stool, I could not prevent my eyes from taking in the fullness of her breasts and the intoxicating glimpse of bare flesh in the dip of her blouse.

I felt her hand on my thigh, the soft warm touch mingled with her muskiness roused my passion to new heights. The hand on my neck drew me closer to her ruby lips. I put up a show of resistance when she pressed her mouth to mine but undeterred by my mulishness, she spread her lips and thrust her tongue between my teeth. I found myself accepting the soft smooth slither of flesh and sought to capture it with my own. Suddenly I was matching her pressure by kissing her so hard it became almost painful as our teeth ground together like millstones… we paused in our passion to breathe in and exhale each other's ecstasy. Even as I felt her hand slide up my thigh and come to rest with a gentle squeeze on my erection, my own hand found the bare, smooth flesh of her arm.

Unlike the mutually instantaneous and explosive coupling I had experienced with Thelma in the farm store, Rita led me instead to a bedroom, where a rumpled bed from which she must have recently arisen still carried the smell of talc and her. We sat down facing each other, waiting for either one of us to make the first move. She continued looking at me without much expression, before leaning back on the palms of her hands. I then leaned forward and kissed her, nervously, and nervously I kissed her again. I worked an arm around her waist and pressed against her awkwardly because of the way we were sitting.

I think she had had enough of my awkwardness, because instead of pressing back she clung to me and let herself fall back, carrying me with her. At the same time she lifted her legs, displaying a long expanse of thigh as she stretched out comfortably, making no effort to push her skirt down. My impulse was to put my hand between her legs, but I thought better of it and reached for her breasts instead. I must have spent minutes to (and finally she had to help) untangle my hands from a net of slip and bra straps.

Rita was patient through all this and except for the help she gave in removing her clothes, she lay back quite inert, eyes closed, as I removed the last remaining article and rolled on top of her in a gesture of authority that gave me a brief illusion of being in charge of her white and throbbing body.

I can't say it was much of a success, for even when I was inside her I seemed unable to excite her, though she pretended

I had, and at the climax I wasn't really with her or myself. It was like a dream turned bad.

One Monday morning, without warning, Huey didn't pitch up for work. There was no reply from his home phone so Dicky sent the truck driver around to the house. Huey's car was in the drive, he reported, but there didn't appear to be anybody at home. We phoned the school. Yes, the boys were there, so Huey must have dropped them off. So where the hell was he or Rita for that matter?

He pitched up a few hours later looking really upset and went straight upstairs to John Flynn's office. By this time the whole shop was abuzz with speculation. It was only at closing time that we were told that Rita and Huey had parted company. I dropped in on Huey and the boys after work and I spent the evening with them. It was only after the boys had gone to bed that he gave me the whole story.

On Saturday he had gone fishing with the boys. Rita, apparently suffering from a headache, decided to stay at home. "When I got back," he said, "I found them in my bed."

Right then I wished I hadn't gone around because I had to listen to him telling me how he had suspected his wife was being unfaithful. "It wouldn't have been so bad, George," he whispered, head in hands, "if they had fucked at his house or even in the classroom, but to do it here, in my house and in my fucking bed, no, that's unforgivable."

I had no answers. Even an apology would have sounded hollow. I can't say I felt any remorse when I left him sitting alone in the lounge, but the same cannot be said about the guilt I felt for the two boys.

I never saw Rita again. The story goes that she 'lived in sin' with the schoolteacher, until the scandal cost him his job. He skipped the town one night, leaving Rita with no option but to move in with a divorcee, a pleasant lady I knew, who it was said eventually brought Huey and Rita back together.

It was a promise of a hefty bonus made by one Jack McIntosh, and for no other reason, that I was persuaded to return to farming. My move coincided with my brother's move from the Beri to a tobacco farm at a place called Selous, not far down the road from Hartley. It was a good move as it turned out, for over the next few years John made a small fortune.

My move while not being as profitable as John's, gave me the opportunity to earn the bonus I had been promised but, as is the way of the world, just as things were coming right and my sights were set for the next season, I blundered in a costly calculation. I tried to cover up my mistake by shifting blame and in doing so fell out with Jack. I deserved to lose the job and I know now that had I accepted the mistake and apologised, I might have at most lost no more than a small percentage of my bonus. Instead, I lost everything. I was in the doldrums after my dismissal, for jobs were hard to come by because the new season was well underway and farmers had already taken on the season's labour. I turned in desperation, as I had in the past, to my brother.

After obtaining his phone number and address from Tom, I phoned John that same evening. The following morning I bought a car with the last of my last season's bonus, packed it with my possessions (or what the more affluent may have termed junk but to me was a treasure trove). These included amongst other things: two paintings by unknown artists; an antique collapsible screen (purchased from a deceased estate after being assured it once stood in one of the many bedrooms in a stately home in England), and a brass coal-bucket embossed with the figures of two men crouched around a brazier smoking pipes (a piece that was given to me for free by the same person who sold me the screen).

I arrived at the farm on a sunny September morning after a bumpy drive over corrugated gravel roads in my overloaded Baby Austin A30.

Looking across an open stretch of veld to where the house stood, I saw someone sitting on the verandah. I jumped out of the car, grabbed a suitcase, yelling, "Hey, John, I'm here." I thought it strange that John didn't get up and come to meet me, and I continued up the road, wondering if perhaps he was upset with me. The man on the porch waved, without rising, I waved back and lowered my head to complete the walk. When I arrived at the verandah's edge, it wasn't John at all of course, but a slight man with shifty eyes and receding hair.

I was disappointed. "Where's Mr Bowley?" I asked brusquely. "Have I come to the right place?"

"John's with the boss," he replied genially, which caught me off-guard considering my curtness, "and you must be George the brother. You don't look alike, but you speak the same."

"Yes" I said abashed, "can you please tell me where they've gone?"

"To the barns I think," he said, pointing to where the road continued past the house. "Just follow the road, it's about a mile down, but why don't you hang on, he'll be back just now." He smiled and stuck out his hand. "By the way, my name's Chris Groenewald, call me Chris if you like."

Groenewald—I had heard the name and it came to me in a flash, he was the manager who took over from John when he left the Beri. What the hell was he doing here? I wondered.

I decided to wait for John to arrive. I didn't unload my car, because I had a sinking feeling that the way Chris showed me through the house was as if he was living there. And I was right, there were three bedrooms in the house and each was lived in.

I spent three days with John, not in his house but in an empty one-bedroom cottage on the property, which pleased me because I spent as little time as possible in the company of the Groenewald family. There were three others besides Chris: a wife who seemed to sit around all day and a son who I disliked intensely. He took advantage of John's generosity by making a pig of himself at every meal, especially breakfast when he insisted on never less than three eggs covered in a revolting mix of tomato sauce and jam. Thank goodness the daughter—and the love of John's life—was a surprisingly pretty and quiet girl who brought some propriety to an otherwise dysfunctional family.

I learned from John that Chris had worked for Tom for less than a year and whereas I was feeling the shame and emptiness that came with living off my brother, it didn't seem to worry Chris. In fact, the one time I broached the subject, he shrugged his shoulders saying, "I'm in no hurry to find one." The deliverance from my situation came quite unexpectedly on the evening of the third day, when I received a call from none other than Tom. He had tracked me down after hearing of my dismissal (the rivers of gossip ran deep in Hartley) and had words with Jack, my former employer, who must have said some good things because before I put down the phone I was offered a job as Tom's assistant on Mount Carmel.

That night we celebrated my good fortune and I, inexperienced in the art of drinking, spent most of the night hugging a toilet bowl. I rose 'from the dead' feeling really ill with a thumping head and aching limbs, having spent what remained of the night unconscious on the sofa in the living room. I vaguely remember feeling an invasion of fresh air that brought me to my senses in time to see the outline of what turned out to be John as he opened the front door and left for work.

I was in a hurry to get on the road but at the same time I didn't want to wake up the parasites. I dressed as fast and as quietly as I could which wasn't easy—in fact I remember distinctly trying to put my underpants on over my shorts, before finally creeping along the well-worn route to the bathroom, that still smelt of vomit. I took a pee, aiming the stream high up in the bowl to lessen the sound and after patting my face with cold water, that had me feeling a whole lot better, I crept out of the house and left behind the memories of me as 'the last of the great drinkers'.

After I had packed the car, I went off to look for John. I found him sitting so deep in thought that I was almost breathing down his neck before he became aware of my presence. We had a long talk. I knew he wouldn't take kindly to what I had to say about his guests, but I felt I owed it to him so I said it anyway, though I was careful to exclude the daughter as much as possible from my observations.

We may not have left on the best of terms, but I did promise him that one day I would repay his kindness. That time came, but that was in another time, another place, and when we were not so young.

Chapter Twenty-Four

Mount Carmel 1964

Tom, with the preferred name Nyati (buffalo) by all those who feared and served him, came from a family of Transvaal farmers with roots stretching back to the Voortrekkers (Afrikaans/Dutch: pioneers). He was a slave driver for six days of the week and on the Sabbath a Lay Preacher in the Dutch Reformed Church.

There were aspects of him I admired: the down-to-earth way he would get grease on his hands and face and on his spacious khaki overall when wrestling on his back with the nuts and bolts of the caterpillar tracks that were so heavy it took six men to lift them from the runners of the Oliver tractor; the majestic manner he strode through the lands with a sjambok (heavy leather whip) in his hand, head-and-shoulders above the rest, with a smile for everyone—even the boy who carried water for the workers; and the humble way he would unhesitatingly don his overalls and grab a hoe or axe and join his men in the task at hand.

It is strange how one can be drawn to remember of a man the simplest of things? Like the almost lazy, idiosyncratic way he did up his boots without tying the laces in a knot, preferring instead to tuck the loose ends in the top of his boots, or the way he pared his fingernails with a penknife.

But on Sundays he was a different man. He objected to his children playing tennis in the garden and if they did he confiscated bats and balls. He wore a black suit and white tie and looked hot and uncomfortable when filling his Ford Fairlane with petrol for the trip to church, and was always in a bad temper after the midday meal.

Unlike Tom, I enjoyed my Sundays and an afternoon ramble along the banks of the Beri—especially in the winter when the water was low and clear and the bed was split into small streams separated by rocks and reed-beds. It didn't look as grand as it did in flood, but it was quieter and much more beautiful, and vastly different when water was scarce. It was then that swempie (Francolin) and pheasants were plentiful along the river, as were duiker (common antelope), and the reed-beds themselves were alive with guinea fowl. There was always fresh spoor to be seen in the mud and I knew of a spot where I was sure to see the dragon footprints of a leguaan (monitor lizzard) peppered with the remains of crab shells and fish scales.

The house John had lived in was empty, but never once on my walks did I miss the chance of walking around it, remembering it as it was in the time I stayed there with him. While peering through the windows, I would see in my mind's eye the two of us and hear from somewhere the sounds of our voices.

I liked the old Hottentot from the moment we met. His age could have been anywhere between 60 and 100, but no less I reckoned than the artefacts (the reader may remember) that Bob Murdock had gathered from the site of the old kraal on Paradise. He was tall and thin, with legs like knobkerries and a body as sinewy and dry as biltong. His deep-set far-seeing eyes were shielded from the elements by his high cheekbones set in a wrinkled sphere. His face was hairless, even his eyebrows and lashes had worn away, and what little hair remained clung like lichen to his skull. Because of the ochre colour of his skin Tom called him 'Hotnot'—a derogatory name for a Hottentot. The blacks, in a similar vein but with a xenophobic twist because he was a foreigner, disparagingly called him Chimandionrepi, or Bushman, while I, who couldn't pronounce his name, called him 'Madala', a respectful term for 'old'. Tom, I was told, had inherited the old man from his father, together with the family farm in the Northern Transvaal. Tom had sold the farm before emigrating, like so many visionary Afrikaners, to Rhodesia—and coincidentally as it turned out, at the same time I left England for Africa.

It was Madala's job to look after the herd of cattle from which once a fortnight he selected a beast for slaughter. It was always either a barren cow or one that had passed its breeding usefulness. I was nervous the first time, in fact I didn't want to do it but was forced to because Tom was away for that day, so he left it up to me to do the shooting. He didn't even ask me if I could handle a rifle, I suppose he didn't think he needed to, he simply thrust the single-shot Schlezinger.22 and two bullets in my hand. "An extra one in case you miss," he said with a chuckle and drove off.

That afternoon Madala drove the small herd into the kraal beside the slaughterhouse. All the workers and their families were there waiting for their fortnightly food ration, when I arrived carrying the rifle. I'd dreaded this moment all day and it didn't help when the crowd of expectant onlookers drew silent as I drew the bolt back and slid a bullet into the breach. It wasn't like shooting a buck, these animals were only six feet away, so close I could smell the sweat on their hides and the snot streaming from their nostrils. Madala and I were the only ones in the kraal. The animals knew and trusted him so they calmed down as he walked among them and pointed out to me the one to be shot. It was an old barren cow with a shrivelled udder and knock-knees, a trusted friend that had outlived its purpose.

Madala sensed my nervousness as did the crowd that had gathered to witness the spectacle. I could hear the banter as, uncertain of where to place the shot, I continually raised and lowered the rifle, until Madala rescued me from my predicament by surreptitiously pointing to a spot on his forehead. I took aim at a spot an inch above the whorl of hair below the boss—a sharp crack and the beast fell as though pole-axed. Immediately

Madala dropped to his knees and slit the throat of the poor beast.

A cheer rose from the crowd, followed by murmurs of respect as I ejected the spent case. With a pretence at innocuousness, I shouldered the rifle and strode away, leaving the crowd with the misguided belief that what I had done had been as natural as breathing.

I was with Madala the day Alfred died. He was a driver, a KoreKore tribesman of whom the missionaries had Christianised vast numbers.

He was a damn good driver too, but a flagrant religious braggart who swore he was blessed with a lack of fear, until I caught a puffadder one day and asked him to hold it, whereupon he took off and wouldn't come near unless I got rid of the snake. He was also terrified of Tom's fox terrier and when I pointed this out to him, he admitted he did have an inborn aversion to snakes and dogs. Hardly a day went by that I wouldn't find him preaching to his flock of workers. He seemed to draw all his inspiration from a tattered notebook he carried in his pocket. It was given to him he said, by his father, an evangelist. From this book he was able with some difficulty, to make out a few monosyllabic sentences that held little meaning in the unacademic atmosphere of Mount Carmel. I, unlike Tom who disliked Alfred's eccentric behaviour, tolerated it even though at times we had words when his preaching upset the flow of work. There were times when I was sure Tom might lose it and thrash the man with his sjambok, but each time Alfred stood up to him and if in the process, as often happened, Tom in a fit of temper threw his hat on the ground, Alfred would simply pick it up and hand it back.

I believe that it was their religious beliefs, tempered with Alfred's skills as a tractor driver that saved the one from committing murder and the other ending up in a grave. Alfred was the only tractor driver I had ever come across that could plough an opening furrow, without the aid of markers, which was so straight and uniform in depth it might have been drawn with a ruler.

So what was the argument between the two that prompted his untimely death?

I heard the tractor drive in at sunset. I was sitting in my living room listening to the soft play of my radio. It was so quiet I even heard the discs of the plough strike the concrete on the floor of the garage as the driver lowered the three-point hitch on the tractor. Then I heard their voices, a mumble at first rising to an argument. Tom was shouting, then they were both shouting. There was a strange noise, then silence. I thought it was all over when I stepped out of the bath and dried myself.

It was sometime later that I heard a vehicle arrive, then another, and the sound of voices. Curious to know what was happening I stepped outside the cottage and walked across to the garage. The lights were on and from where I stood in the shadows I could see two uniformed policemen. One of them was stooped over a body I knew was Alfred, and a few feet away Tom, watched over by the other policeman, was slumped against the rear wheel of the tractor, sobbing like a baby, rubbing his hands back and forth through his hair.

Behind me from the direction of the house, I heard Tom's wife weeping. I turned, the lights were on in the house and I could see her standing, very alone, in the doorway of the kitchen. I wanted to be with her but instinct told me it was better not to get involved unless I was asked. I don't know how many times I woke up that night to the sound of voices, male and female, slamming car doors, and the clatter of stone against steel as cars accelerated down the drive, the lights from their headlamps lighting up the walls in the bedroom, driving the sleep from my befuddled brain. The next few days I remember as being a bit of a nightmare. A pall of gloom hung over the farm. Fortunately, Tom's brother Paul came to stay to help me run things while Tom was preparing for what I was not sure was either a trial or an inquest. Thank God, I was not ordered to attend, instead I was questioned by the police. In fact, I remember a feeling of being caught 'between a rock and a hard place' when I was asked pointedly what I thought was the relationship between Alfred and Tom.

I had no option but to tell the truth for I knew there was a strong possibility that there would be others who would be asked the same question. Besides, it had been too obvious to deny the ill feeling that existed between the two, but I played it down as best I could, for in the back of my mind I was aware of the debt of gratitude I owed to Tom for having helped me out when times were bad.

I never got to find out what had prompted Tom to commit murder. Not once in the short space of time before I left his employ did he mention the incident. I don't know what the verdict was; I'm not even sure whether it went to trial.

I heard later through the grapevine, that he sold the farm and moved to an isolated area that bordered the Mhondoro tribal trust land. It proved to be true for it was there we met five years later at the height of the Chimurenga (Shona: revolutionary struggle) after our Call-sign received an order to proceed to a farmstead that was under attack. It was all over when we arrived to find that Tom had single-handedly fought off the attackers.

He hadn't changed much, a little more haggard perhaps and he still wore his boots with the laces tucked in the tops. I wasn't surprised to find he was living alone, for like most of the farmers living in isolated areas, he had moved his family out of the line of fire to live with relatives in Salisbury.

Fearing another attack, we spent the night at the farmhouse and at first light carried out a 360-degree search of the farm. Late that afternoon we came across tracks that led back across the Mhondoro border and followed them until they vanished in a range of kopjes. That was the last time I saw or heard of Tom.

Thirty years have passed since then. There are few white farmers left in Rhodesia since Independence, but I'm pretty sure he would have left before then because individuals like him would have been high on the Wanted list.

Chapter Twenty-Five

A Country in Trouble

It is important to digress at this stage. I must set aside for the moment the trials and tribulations of my life. In the scheme of things they were relatively unimportant when compared with the shadow of darkness that was creeping across the political front.

Rhodesia had been a self-governing colony since 12th September 1923. After this date, Britain's interests remained purely commercial. She retained through the British South Africa Company the ownership of 1.6 million hectares of land, controlled the railways, and held the mineral rights, which were later bought by the Rhodesian government for £2,000,000.

In 1961, a referendum was held to decide a new constitution and the majority voted in favour of acceptance. Rhodesia was then, ostensibly to any right-minded politician, independent.

The Federation,* Britain's great experiment that had been spawned by Winston Churchill's government by men who still believed in the concept of the Empire, was followed by those who did not, and looked on as the Empire crumbled in Africa. The Federation, after a lifespan of ten years, was formally disbanded on the 31st of December 1963.

Britain refused to grant Independence based on the 1961 Constitution and so began years of haggling with the likes of Harold Wilson, who made it clear that 'one man one vote' was the only basis on which he would grant Independence. So Ian Smith, who had already stated that this would not happen in

*The Federation was set up in 1953 to combine three southern African territories – the self-governing British colony of Southern Rhodesia and the British protectorates of Northern Rhodesia and Nyasaland. It was Disbanded in 1963

his lifetime, held a referendum as to whether Rhodesia should declare its Independence Unilaterally (otherwise known as UDI). The white populace voted 10-1 in favour.

I voted for the first time in that referendum after years of trying to get on the Voters Roll. Each time in the past I had been refused because I had no birth certificate or documentation to prove who I was, but now that every white vote was needed it was made easy.

Speculation was rife around the world that Rhodesia would declare UDI, and if they did, would Britain send troops to crush the rebellion? The British government ruled out that option which left the way clear and on Armistice Day, 11th November 1965, Rhodesia declared her Independence unilaterally.

Harold Wilson said that the rebellion would be over in weeks, and introduced trade sanctions that included an oil embargo that was enforced by a flotilla of warships with the power to stop and search ships entering the port of Beira on the Mozambique coast. Despite these punitive sanctions, Rhodesia's economy grew, outstripping Britain's. And why? you might ask. Well, the reasons were relatively simple. We tightened our belts, ration cards were introduced to control the sale of fuel, and above all, we produced goods that hitherto had all been imported, even down to weapons and vehicles of war. But the honeymoon was over when South Africa withdrew a lot of her support and Mozambique fell to Frelimo so our borders were open to terrorists.

Within a few months of UDI, the terrorist infiltrations began. The first group was trained mostly at the Nanking Military College in Peking and split up into three after entering the country. Two of the groups had orders to blow up the Beira-Umtali pipeline and kill as many white farmers as possible, but they were caught before they could carry out their orders. The other group infiltrated 250 kilometres into Rhodesia but they were apprehended at the Hunyani River on the outskirts of

Sinoia. In the battle that ensued, seven of them were killed. The contact on the 29th April 1965 had been nothing more than a fiasco for the terrorists, but it had been the deepest penetration into Rhodesia to date. For ZANU it heralded the beginning of their War of Liberation, their Chimurenga Day, and it was the start of a bitter war that would last for another 14 years.

For many, the real war began a few weeks later when a white farmer and his wife became the first victims when they were attacked on their farm, 25 kilometres from Hartley. "Then Mummy and Daddy lay down and went to sleep on the floor," their four-year-old son told the police.

Chapter Twenty-Six

Sherwood 1965 – August 1966

Sanctions had put an end to the once profitable tobacco industry and the market had become a cloak-and-dagger affair. The once bustling auction floors where buyers from all around the world had congregated were no more and the sing-song chant of the auctioneers had fallen silent. The crop was bought from the grower at arranged prices and sold by phone to invisible buyers, or was bartered for cars and other equipment with which to fight a war that was on the increase.

Due to a vastly diminished export base, quotas based on a farm's past production record were put in place that curtailed expansion of the acreage grown in the country.

Instead, farmers were encouraged to diversify into other crops such as cotton for which there was great demand, as up until that time most yarns had been imported. The beef industry expanded too, as did the crops of cereal grains, all of which found ready markets among the countries in Africa that were, ironically, sympathetic towards Rhodesia enemies.

It was for that reason that after leaving Tom, I broke with the past and took up mixed farming instead with a company named Rhodesia Tobacco and Ranching Company. It was a Limited Company comprising two enterprises.

At the headquarters on Sherwood Estate at Norton, I was given the post of assistant to the Estate Manager, Jack. He was a slightly built, wiry Englishman in his fifties, who was christened Mubvakure (foreigner) by the labourers because like many colonial Englishmen, he refused to learn a foreign dialect, believing it to be incumbent on the conquered to learn his language. He was one of the few I knew who couldn't speak Fanakalo, a bastardised mixture of English, Afrikaans, Sindebele, Chishona, and Swahili. It was introduced by the early settlers to negate them from having to learn the many dialects spoken in the tribal trust lands. He communicated instead in a mix of 'Pidgeon English' and a series of arm and hand movements that even I more often than not, failed to understand.

It wasn't only his lack of spoken communication that Jack had to contend with. His wife Hazel suffered from the same failing. As a consequence and because her voice sounded nasal and aristocratic, I nicknamed her 'Queen Mother'. She was a lot taller than Jack and occasionally pretty, depending on how I saw her at the time. I often wondered if I could find her attractive...

I could!

Sometimes I imagined what it would be like to be her lover when we walked our dogs before sunset while Jack stayed at home and read the paper. I'd let her walk ahead so the sun played tricks and I would guess at the enticements beneath her light cotton dress each time she moved from light into shadow. But there was another who I believed may have seen her in the same light. His name was Robert, a close friend of the family. I came across them both one afternoon swimming in the concrete reservoir that supplied water to the houses on Sherwood. She was wearing a two-piece bathing suit and because I was hidden behind a bush I was able to study with impunity her small pointed breasts, lithe thighs and firm buttocks and to my dismay, the incongruousness of Robert's erection in his tight blue trunks, the sight of which changed the complexion on things for me. The 'Queen Mother' suddenly appeared to me as decidedly 'unpretty' and I was cured very quickly of any carnal thoughts.

It was busy times on Sherwood, the rains were not far off and it had become my responsibility amongst other things, to prepare the farm roads.

The state of the roads, Jack oft remarked, was what gave visitors the impression of a well-run establishment. He was very proud of the roads on the farm, especially the main road that ran through the estate and the turnoff that led off to the grand homestead with its acres of manicured lawns and gardens. The camber had to be just right and the drainage ditches deep and angled so that even after the heaviest of storms there were no puddles or muddy patches left in its wake.

It was late in the afternoon and I had one last stretch of road to grade. I had spent the day on the Galleon tractor-drawn grader and my body ached from the vibration, and my arms likewise as I wrestled with the two wheels that controlled the level and bite of the grader blade.

Everything seemed to be going well, when suddenly the blade caught a hidden tree-root and the next moment the machine up-ended. I screamed to the driver to stop, but he didn't hear me above the roar of the tractor. The next minute I found myself clinging for dear life to the wheel and being dragged along the ground. Fortunately, the bolt that held the grader tow-bar to the tractor snapped and the grader came to a stop, pinning me beneath an axle. I wasn't in any real pain, but I remember feeling thoroughly pissed off when the tractor driver (who as it turned out thought he had killed me) fled the scene, leaving it up to a pedestrian to seek help for me.

Other than a few bruises and a sore stomach I thought I had got off lightly, until I woke up with a fright to find I was bleeding from the backside. I was rushed to hospital where I was found to be suffering from a damaged spleen and was also diagnosed with a dose of bilharzia. I couldn't have been in hospital for any length of time because I can't remember the stitches being removed or, for that matter, the face or name of the surgeon who performed the operation. Unlike the time I had my appendix removed in the Gatooma Hospital by a

Doctor Robertson, who had a sense of humour and placed a bunch of arum lilies in my arms as I was coming-to from the anaesthetic.

It was soon after my experience with the grader that I was sent to the company's Insindi ranch to assist in drought operations. The ranch was situated in the Lowveldt near a small town called Gwanda.

Jack had been to the ranch a few times and his description of it formed in my mind's eye, the picture of another country, so vast he said that it had taken him ten days on foot to circumvent its border. It was a true wilderness of sweet-grass plains and baobabs, where thousands of cattle grazed with herds of antelope and they drank together from the Umzingwane River that had its source in the Matopos Hills 130 miles northwest of Gwanda.

Alan Tredgold was the manager of the ranch. Jack's description of him reminded me very much of my Uncle Bob of Paradise. I gathered that he had the same build and disposition, though unlike Bob who as you will recall was of humble stock; Alan was the son of Sir Robert Tredgold, the former Federal Chief Justice.

It wasn't the country I had imagined it to be from Jack's description when I arrived there in October 1965, for it was gripped in a drought that was the worst in recorded history.

The bush had become a desert. Grass had been cropped to the roots and even the trees that normally provided nourishment to the browsers had been stripped of leaves, except for the tallest branches that only giraffe could reach. The antelope and cattle stood around in groups, too weak to flee, framed in the dust of whirlwinds that swirled across the landscape sucking in and spitting out clouds of dust and the ash of veldt fires. Most distressing was the sight and smell of a rotting carcass in a dried-up waterhole where the clay had been trampled and scarred by the hoofs and pads of desperate animals.

Alan took me to the Umzingwane to show me the extent of the drought. The once sparkling river that had last flowed two years ago was reduced to a necklace of muddy pools inhabited by scores of hippo. They jostled and fought for a position in the shallow muddy water while waiting impatiently for the relative coolness of darkness. Further upriver he showed me a weir he had built decades before. The water level of the dam he explained, had never dropped significantly over the years, but now all that remained for me to see was a few gallons of churned up, discoloured liquid, heavy with bird feathers, rotted oxygen weed and the excrement of multitudes of thirsty animals.

While there was little that could be done for the game, the cattle were kept alive with salt and urea licks that activated the rumen and gave them the appetite to consume the bark and wood of branches that we stripped from trees. Twelve hours a day every day these were fed into a tractor-driven hammer-mill, reducing the branches, into a coarse meal that was sprayed with a mixture of protein and molasses to make it palatable. It was weeks of hard work, but for me the aches and pains were made easier with the knowledge that I was helping in keeping the herds alive.

Inevitably there were losses, but in order to keep them to a minimum, the weakest of the beasts were delivered in cattle trucks to Sherwood, where Jack had erected acres of pens. In these pens the animals were fed a high protein mix of corn and cob, and within sixty days they were transformed from skeletons into beasts so heavy they had lost the urge to joust with each other. They lay around like swollen barrels until the trucks arrived and drove them to the abattoirs in Salisbury.

I was there for a month before there was a build up of clouds on the horizon. Alan said it had been like that for the last year, each time the clouds had drawn closer the wind had shifted and the clouds dispersed, as if the Devil himself had driven them away.

But this time the wind remained true and just as we were finishing for the day, there came a rumbling of thunder and the clouds that I had pretended not to notice all day for fear they would vanish were now directly above. They had amassed into a single dark blanket that covered Insindi from horizon to horizon. I felt that familiar chilly breeze and the mingling smell of parched earth and water as the first drops fell like silver bullets in puffs of dust. The patter became a roar as the clouds opened up and in seconds I was drenched to the skin. I looked down at my feet and watched the earth change colour as little rivulets formed a puddle that soon covered my ankles. Soon I was in the centre of a river and its flotilla of leaves and grass that rose and fell as each depression was filled and overflowed. The storm lasted until there was water everywhere. The cattle close by to where we had been working shook themselves off in showers of spray and commenced licking at their hides. The parched land drank heavily, and no sooner had the clouds given way to the setting sun, the flooded dongas (steep sided gully) and my clothes were almost dry again by the time we headed home. That night the rains returned in a series of soaking showers that lasted until morning. It was still drizzling when Alan and I set off in his Land Rover at daybreak to see what effect the rains had had on the Umzingwani. It must have rained heavily at the river's source too, for the water had risen and was flowing once more in a muddy stream that brought relief to the hippo.

It rained heavily for days. A few cows were lost through bloat, caused through the salt and urea licks that had crumbled in the rain and allowed the beasts to eat, rather than lick, at the blocks thereby increasing their intake to dangerous levels. It was a horrible death for the poor beasts when their stomachs swelled like balloons. Alan was able to save a few by piecing their hides with a knife that allowed the gas to escape in a nauseous explosion of air.

Within days the veld began its restoration and by the time I left Insindi the colours of drought had been transformed into a haze of green. The weavers were building their nests in trees adorned with fresh leaves and the nights were filled with the sound of bullfrogs calling to each other in the vleis.

I am going to backtrack a little to the time I was between jobs after having left Mount Carmel. I have not purposely ignored that period, but thinking back after a lapse in memory—which is common at my age— I remember catching up with my brother on a farm called Esmeralda on the outskirts of Norton. John had lost his prosperous job at Selous when his generous boss sold his farm before taking the 'chicken-run' (a disingenuous term for those that left the country for fear of the future) back to South Africa. His present boss was a fellow by the name of Martin Skea who together with his charming wife Vera and their four offspring became my firm friends, and it was Martin who was instrumental in getting me the job at Sherwood.

Christmas was only a few weeks away when I arrived back at Sherwood and Jack, having heard of the work that had gone on at Insindi, gave me a week off.

I shared the time with John and the Skea family on Esmeralda. It was school holidays, the kids were home, and because the terrorist threat was confined to the borders a million miles away nobody seemed to give them much thought. The papers were full of news of 'talks about talks', and while the politicians practised their deceit, John reaped and cured tobacco as if there was no such thing as sanctions while I enjoyed hours of fun and laughter with my newfound friends in their rambling farmhouse.

Martin was optimistically biased about the future, which was understandable I suppose, as he was a founding member of the Rhodesian Front. As such, he was on first-name terms with Ian Smith and other members of the ruling party, in particular P.K.

van der Byl, the eccentric Minister of Defence, or 'PK' as he was affectionately known by the public and his adoring troops. Martin admired his devil-may-care attitude that bordered on the comic.

What Rhodesians could forget the day he was interviewed for television at the scene of a skirmish, dressed in shorts that displayed a large expanse of white skinny leg and a captured A-K slung over his shoulder? The stunned silence when a British journalist asked what his troops would do if faced with a British invasion force, and his reply in his frightfully English old-boy accent, "We will shoot them."

. Martin and Vera were convinced that by Christmas, Britain and the Government would have settled their differences and UDI had been merely a tool to show 'we mean business'. Besides he said, public opinion in Britain would swing our way soon, for after all, were they not our kith and kin? It was a well known fact he pointed out, that not less than 64% of the country's available manpower had served in the First World War and when the world was plunged into war for the second time, the Rhodesians once again rushed to Britain's aid. Rhodesia had supplied more troops per head of its population to the British war-effort, he said, than did any other country in the Empire. He was right, but unfortunately the new government in place in Britain were not concerned with the emotions of the past. They were determined at all costs to complete the de-colonisation process through majority rule in Rhodesia. It wasn't for want of trying that Ian Smith sought to bridge the impasse by installing Abel Muzorewa as Rhodesia's first black Prime Minister, with him as Deputy. But it was too late, for by that time ZANU and ZIPRA, led by Joshua Nkomo and Robert Mugabe, had smelt the scent of victory even though that was still years away.

Chapter Twenty-Seven

The Redhead

There was no doubt that politics was on every person's mind—young and old. It was like a fever and 'I Hate Harold' Stickers were selling like hot cakes, as was the hit-single of John Edmonds the folk singer:

We're all Rhodesians, we'll fight through thick and thin,
We'll keep our land a free land, stop the enemy coming in,
We'll keep them north of the Zambezi, till that river's running dry,
And this mighty land will prosper for Rhodesians never die.

Young men with the exuberance and fearless courage of youth, joined the elite brotherhoods of the RLI (Rhodesian Light Infantry) and the RSAS (Rhodesian Special Air Services). And there were those such as the Selous Scouts or 'pseudo terrs', with their secret chain of command, who were hardly ever seen but were known to be there somewhere in the bush. They lived on anything nature could supply, killing swiftly and silently before melting into cover. Then there were the bulk of the troops, ordinary soldiers like my brother, the enlisted ones that came packaged in platoons and battalions, the 'Black Boots' the mainstay, the uniformed, conventional force with a code of dress.

There were those like me who worked the land and banded together to form PATU (Police Anti Terrorist Units), sticks of six who were commandeered to hunt the terrorist on his own turf and provide back-up for the security forces, while the veterans of previous wars and others patrolled the villages and towns as Police Reservists. The womenfolk manned the radios and provided the link between the men on the ground. Each had their place in the scheme of things with no one more important than the other. Soon after my week's leave on Esmeralda, John left the farm and farming and went to Mashaba to begin a career as an asbestos miner. It was the last I was to see of him for a number of years.

His move, whether through chance or fate, coincided with me toying with the idea of making a move myself, but I put the idea on hold because there was a more important event that was about to take place that unbeknown to me at the time, would change my life for good.

The event was a variety show that Vera had been chosen to produce to raise bar funds for the Norton Country Club. (The show was free and lasted for as long as it took the thirsty patrons to down enough drink to reach the target set by the committee). Vera persuaded me to take part and because what little talent I had lay in my singing, I agreed to do so provided she could find an instrumentalist who could accompany me at rehearsals.

"I have somebody in mind," she said with a wink. "I'll take you to meet her on Friday. There's a concert on at the Dudley Hall Junior School and she'll be there."

She was there all right—and even amongst all the fine-looking women at the concert, I noticed her first and looked nowhere else! There was some irony in Vera having been the agent of our meeting, for I must confess that she, who I had always thought to be so pretty, now looked a little less so next to Pat.

Pat was beautiful—a goddess with flaming red hair that seemed to gather all the available light in the hall. It drew my attention to her clear and regular face and eyes that showed a hint of interest when she rose to shake my hand. Everything about her—her looks, her eyes, and her body in the ruffled white blouse and tight blue slacks— inspired emotions quite beyond anything I had ever felt before.

Pat was a divorcee with two young children. I was too inhibited by her beauty to make the first move, even after the hours I spent rehearsing with her in her house in the village and the times she visited me in my cottage on Sherwood, where she experienced as a town girl what it would be like to live on a farm. I wondered what went through her mind when she was forced to use a long-drop instead of a waterborne toilet; build a fire to heat up water in the Rhodesian boiler to take a bath; iron clothes with an iron filled with hot coals and cook a meal on the Dover woodstove in the kitchen.

I was tormented by all these things and it was this primitive mode of life that helped me decide to move, coupled with the idea that I should take a step up in life. Marriage, I visualized, required a certain level of social standing that came with the responsibilities of a manager, rather than those of a lowly farm assistant.

So what up until then had been no more than an idea at the time John made his move into mining, suddenly it became a reality. Our agreed marriage was only two months away when I was offered and accepted the job of managing a farm called Farraline.

I was over the moon and it was time to celebrate, so what better way than for the two of us to take time off and reflect, make plans, and do what all lovers do! We had little money between the two of us and the chance of a honeymoon in October wasn't on as I had no more than a weekend before moving on to the farm, so we decided to take a trip to Bulawayo by train.

I so much wanted to show my future bride the home where I had grown up and introduce her to my guardian, the housemothers, and anybody else who might know me. I even thought of asking my guardian for the names and addresses of any relatives I might have, or the possibility of obtaining a birth certificate—there were so many questions I wanted answers to.

But I was unable to show off Pat to anybody, nor was I able to have any questions answered. I could not show her the dormitory that I slept in, nor the chapel where I was confirmed, the dining rooms, or the gym where I had suffered the pain of initiations. I had so much wanted to show her the great hangars and, because it was still so fresh in my mind and I had nothing to hide from the one I loved more than life itself, the hidden places where girls and boys had once exchanged kisses… for Fairbridge had died almost two years before; her records destroyed! Nothing remained but the headmaster's house that appeared to have been taken over by squatters. Fairbridge had disappeared like it had never existed!

But love is patient and understanding. We spent that night and the next in a hotel where I experienced the true meaning and passion of love.

Chapter Twenty-Eight

Farraline 1966–August 1967

It was a smaller farm, half the size of Sherwood, but much more picturesque. Its only tobacco quota was ten acres of Turkish tobacco, used as a mixture in toasted cigarettes and the manufacture of cigars. It was a totally different process from that of Virginia tobacco. It was air-cured and didn't require the huge set-up used in the production of flue-cured tobacco. However unlike its counterpart, it was sold through co-operatives to selective buyers who bargained for the crop, and hence one could never be sure of the price it would bring.

The main crop grown on the farm was maize, the price for which was set by government. An attempt had been made by my predecessor to grow cotton but there wasn't sufficient arable land to make it viable, so between me and my new boss, Mr Palmer, we decided to grow Canadian Wonder beans instead, for which like maize, the price was set.

There was no bonus attached to my salary of £20 per month (which was £5 more than I had earned on Sherwood) but it didn't worry me, for at last I had the power to hire and fire and do things my way without having to answer to anybody except Mr Palmer. He must have had some faith in me because soon after I moved in, he and his wife left for an extended visit to America to spend time with his daughter who, I got to learn was the owner of Farraline.

I loved that farm and everything on it—from the tiny two bedroom cottage with its rustic furniture, to the corrugated iron tank that was filled from a borehole that produced water as pure as the purest spring water. There was a tiny leak in the outlet pipe that I could have fixed in minutes, but I chose to leave because in the heat of the day I would stand at the kitchen door and watch flocks of birds drink and splash in the puddle formed by the leak, while ever wary of the leguaan that lurked not far off in the lush green shrubbery of an anthill. The anthill stood on the path that led to a huddle of the mud-huts of the farm workers, each surrounded by beds of rape and the raised mounds of pumpkins and sweet potatoes.

In the garden out front, there grew a grove of sweet-scented msasa (a tree with fragrant green flowers) in which a colony of bush squirrels had made their homes. They were little chirpy animals that warned me of the presence of any strangers who passed by on the footpath that led to and from Mondoro, the tribal trust land that formed the western boundary. It was a lonely existence for me when Pat was away, but made pleasant in the knowledge that each day was a step closer to the time we would be together. Meanwhile, there was much to keep me busy. Fields had to be ploughed and harrowed and already I had prepared and sown the first of the tobacco seedling beds in case of early rains. After having painted the cottage inside and out and removed excess furniture to make room for Pat's, I employed two women to scrub the floors and carpets until there was no sign of the previous occupants or their wild parties.

But before Pat and the children were to move in, there was still the question of security. It wasn't the lack of locks on the doors that worried me for that was normal. Nobody locked their doors in the houses on the farms in those days—burglars were only 'fantasy beings' that lived between the pages of novels—and any uninvited muenzi (Shona: guest) or stranger caught wandering around the farm by my labourers would either be manhandled and sent packing, or would be brought before me. In which case I would either hand them back to the mob, depending on how I felt, or charge them with trespassing.

What did worry me however, were the ill-mannered

students from a neighbouring African agricultural college called Chibero. They either couldn't read or purposely defied the 'No Trespassing' sign I had erected to stop them making annoying footpaths. After circumventing the well-worn path to the tribal trust land bordering the farm instead they cut through my fields, passing so close to the cottage that often I would wake up to the sound of their drunken voices passing by the bedroom window.

It didn't take long for things to come to a head. One Saturday afternoon while hunting for guinea fowl, I came across a small herd of very thin cattle from the tribal trust lands grazing on my land along the path used by the students, who rather than climb through my fence they had pulled it down to gain access. Blind with rage, I chased the cattle back across the boundary and repaired the fence as best I could, all the time swearing vengeance on the students. Had they been in the vicinity and feeling the way I felt, they would most certainly have felt the wind of a bullet pass their ears. I was tempted to lay in wait for the students who I was sure would return at nightfall, but commonsense prevailed.

Despite meeting up with a group of them one Sunday—when they smiled at me patronizingly, letting me know through their actions that at any rate they had no respect for the white man—I kept my cool. I decided to confront the head staff of Chibero on the Monday and if that was unsuccessful lay a charge of trespassing with the local Police.

To my surprise the head of Chibero took a sympathetic view and promised to lecture the students. He even went as far as offering to fund the erection of a stile on my boundary fence!

So ended a feud that may well have ended in me being arrested for murder, had it not been for a measure of diplomacy that up to that stage in my life had been markedly absent.

Pat and I were married in October at the Registry Office in Salisbury. Pat's brother-in-law and her daughter Evelyn witnessed the simple ceremony. I was so filled with hidden emotion that I remember distinctly wishing I could have given her a more befitting ceremony, with a few flowers perhaps and a few more familiar happy faces.

It was surprising how swiftly Pat and the kids settled into farm life. However, since the children were entirely different in character, they squabbled like cats and dogs, so much so that I was forced to build a rondavel (a hut with a thatched roof) in the garden to house Arnold, rather than have them share a bedroom in the cottage.

It is right that, at this moment, I proceed no further with the story and take time to reflect on the fears that must surely affect not only me but any man, young or old, who is forced by love and circumstance to face the reality of marrying into a ready-made family. I have always got on with children, but that isn't the issue, despite it being one of the reasons other than love, that Pat accepted my hand in marriage.

Neither Arnold nor Evelyn looked upon me as a replacement for their father. I was grateful for that, because now and again one of them would let slip a remark that, if my intentions had been to be more than a friend, I would have felt a hurt that may well have caused a rift in my relationship with them. It was hard enough for Pat and me to put up with their nonsense when the two of them had come home from being on holiday with their father in South Africa. For a while they were unmanageable after weeks of being spoilt and having their minds poisoned by their father. Despite this, I was surprised that never once did I hear Pat talk ill of him in front of her children.

It was Pat's passivity and tolerance and my hopelessness as a disciplinarian, that others who knew me might have construed stemmed from my age and upbringing, that there came the day when I may have failed as a stepfather. I made no effort to intervene when Arnold was persuaded by his father to return with him to South Africa.

He came back to us a few years later after a fallout with his father. I thought it might be the start of a new beginning after he married and seemed to settle down. Then, before the war began in earnest, he did the only right thing he ever did and that was to move again back down south.

I have, through emotion and not intentionally, taken a step into the future, which perhaps I shouldn't have, because I must now with an apology draw the reader's attention immediately back to the past, to a time that Pat became pregnant and, as a family, we faced a *catastrophic* drought on Farraline.

I had dry-planted everything with the early rains that fell in the first week of November, but by the end of December no more rain had fallen and the 70 acres of maize that had looked so promising simply sprouted and shrivelled away.

In desperation I re-planted and together we prayed for rain. I remember so well the two of us lying on our backs on the lawn outside the cottage, watching the clouds build up and drift away. "I never gave clouds a thought up till now," Pat had whispered, "they were just things that floated past. I didn't know the difference between cumulus and cirrus or that there were people like you and I that needed the rain so badly they prayed for it." I would look at her and force a smile, and inwardly curse myself for having lured her away from a comfortable town life to the harsh reality of Farraline.

Despite our prayers it didn't get any better, for when the rain did come it was just enough to dampen the soil, which caused the seed to germinate, but after the hot winds had driven the clouds away, they dried up what little moisture there was the plants wilted and turned the colour of shrivelled onions.

For days on end I avoided going to the lands for fear of witnessing the inevitable and concentrated all my energy into saving the crop of Turkish by watering by hand once a week with water from the borehole.

Then one night we woke to the sound of thunder!

Everything was still; even the crickets had ceased their chirping. Through the window as the curtains stirred, I smelt the smell of the drought-bound earth as the first drops rattled on the corrugated-iron roof. In seconds, the rattle became a metallic roar so loud I could barely hear the cries of delight from Pat as we both leapt from the bed and stood by the window to watch the lightning light up the garden, reflecting the masasa trees and raindrops slanting down like streaks of steel. The storm soon settled down to a gentle rain that lasted for days with intermittent spells of sunshine that gave us the chance to sow the ten acres of beans and wait for the tobacco to ripen.

Those were balmy days in March and April, watching the crops grow, and I felt and watched the infant move in Pat's womb. I marvelled at the way she had made the transition from town to country girl without so much as a sigh of regret. Times had not been easy for her, what with the drought and a thousand other things foreign to city life. She had had to contend with not least of all the Cyclops owl that appeared on her pillow one night when she was undressing for bed, or the leguaan that crawled into the kitchen while she was cooking.

I heard her scream above the clatter of pans and thinking the worst rushed to the scene and bumped into her. "There's a crocodile in the kitchen!" she shouted, waving and pointing with a broom to where a terrified, hissing leguaan was trying to escape through the door. It couldn't because she was standing in the way, which forced the two-metre-long lizard to attempt climbing the wall, and it couldn't do that because its claws and tail kept sliding on the linoleum floor. It was all over in minutes and after the indignant reptile had scuttled away we were left staring at each other, laughing to the point of hysteria.

It was just right I thought, for my first attempt at hunting bush pig by night. There was a scattering of drifting clouds that allowed intermittent periods of darkness and moonlight that would make stalking easy and, because the breeze was blowing steadily in one direction across the maize lands, it meant that provided I kept downwind the pig would not catch my scent or hear the sound of my footsteps above the rustle of grass.

For weeks bush pigs had plundered my lands under cover of darkness. They were serious pests and wasteful feeders, destroying as much as they ate and breaking down maize stalks in a wide swathe. They would take a mouthful of cob here and there and leave the uneaten cobs to rot or become forage for termites. I'd spent hours hunting the pigs by day, often on hands and knees in the dense bush dividing the two fields, with nothing to show for my labours but a shirt full of grass seeds, bruised knees, and on one occasion I was attacked by hornets. So after several failures, I decided the only way was to hunt them by night whilst they were feeding. But in order to do this, it would mean that Pat would have to go with me and sit in the car while I hunted, for with farm attacks on the increase and the children at boarding school, it was out of the question to leave her alone at night in the house.

It was an hour before midnight when I woke her up and we set off, me in shorts and shirt with a pocketful of cartridges, and she looking very vulnerable in a pair of my gumboots, wearing a swollen pink nightdress that would have fitted her beautifully eight months before.

I drove without lights to the lands so as to avoid alarming my quarry and parked on the ploughed strip of fireguard that separated the two lands. After wrapping a rug around her shoulders and with assurances that everything would be fine, I kissed her goodbye. It was beautifully still when I closed the car door and made my way up the side of the land, keeping to the shadows and stopping now and again to listen. I hadn't gone far when I heard the soft grunts and rustles of a sounder of bush pigs that were about to cross the fireguard to enter the maize land. I crouched and watched as a huge boar who was undoubtedly the leader stepped into the moonlight and raised its long narrow head to test the breeze, its short sharp tusks grey and pointed in the moonlight. In a second, it bounded forward and was lost in the maize, followed by the rest of the sounder that slipped across my vision like shadows. I could hear them crashing through the maize like a herd of goats. There was a sudden silence that lasted for perhaps a minute or two before they began to feed and the night was filled with the sound of snapping stalks, grunts and grinding teeth. I gave them time to settle in their foraging before I flicked off the safety catch and prepared to move into a furrow that I estimated would lead me to the centre of the sound.

It was as I put my foot into a furrow that a cloud moved across the moon and the world was momentarily plunged into darkness. At the same time I heard a strange flapping sound coming towards me. I melted into the maize and waited for what I now knew to be the sound of gumboots. Behind me I could hear the foraging pigs, and in front nothing but darkness, thick and silent, that began to lift like a stage curtain as moonlight fingered the darkness with silvery streaks. My tongue turned to straw as Pat emerged from the shadows in all her beauty and heart-stopping womanliness, unspoilt by the synthesized incongruity of the gumboots.

I didn't know whether to laugh or cry as I stepped out into the open and gathered her in my arms. I should have been angry at her sudden appearance. Our agreement was that she sit in the car until the hunt was over, but the loneliness and the night noises had frightened her into seeking my company. That invoked in me a feeling of guilt for having left her alone, and stupidity for my decision to hunt at a time that no sane person should.

I went to the lands the following late afternoon, to see what damage had been done by the bush pigs the night before. While I was there I took a path that meandered through the dense strip of veld that separated the two lands.

I hadn't gone more than twenty paces when I heard a soft 'pad-pad' and peering through the bushes, I saw the biggest baboon I had ever seen sashaying down the path, head roaming from side to side. I ducked down and moved ahead very carefully until I could get a clear shot. The bullet couldn't have missed him by far for I saw the dust and leaves fly where it had struck the ground. But the old man neither started nor looked back. He just stepped off the path and walked towards a termite mound that had a bald top and a base surrounded by a mantle of thick shrub. I wasn't more than 50 yards away when I fired again but he took no notice of the bullet flying past his ear. He climbed to the summit of the mound and sat down looking at me. I fired once more and this time the bullet ricocheted off the sun-baked surface. Unperturbed, the old fellow ignored me and looked around at the veldt before rising to his feet, turning his back on me and walking quietly away.

The season on Farraline proved to be the worst financially I had encountered thus far. With no market due to sanctions, the tobacco crop which was estimated to be worth not less that three shillings a pound was sold privately for less than a shilling a pound. The maize, that in a fair season would have yielded 30 bags an acre but attributable to the severe drought and the bush-pig infestation yielded less than 15 bags to the acre, proved disastrous.

It was for this reason that I saw no future in farming.

Chapter Twenty-Nine

The Fractional Years September 1967-June 1970

It was in the *Rhodesia Farmer* that I came across the advert for a counter-hand for a company called Engineering and Milling situated in a small town called Sinoia that lay in the northwest district of Lomagundi on the road to Kariba and the Zambian Border. Sinoia is the town that I wrote of earlier where seven insurgents were killed during in the battle that sparked the start of the Chimurenga.

The transition from Farraline and its wild free life to the monotony of clerking was, as I experienced in my time at Maitlands, filled with irritation and petty accuracy. Even more soul-destroying was the horrible little block of flats above a supermarket with walls so thin we could hear the newly married couple next door making love, that because of economic restraints we were forced to live in for at least six months before I was able to afford the move to a more pleasant semi-detached garden flat. The company was split into three entities: a garage with workshop; an engineering department that sold everything from hardware to tractor spares and farm implements; and a milling and stock-feeds department to which I belonged. It stocked a range of dried canteen feeds, animal stock-feeds, and milled products that were supplied to shops and supermarkets and the mines at Alaska and Mangula.

Competition was fierce among the suppliers, so much so that in my first year it was decided I should spend most of my time travelling between mines and farms, putting together contracts with the mines for ration goods and instituting livestock feeding programmes with the farmer. My company transport was an Isuzu Elf two-ton truck with which I covered an area that stretched 100 kilometres north-west to Karoi and beyond to the turn-off to the Kariba Dam, east to Doma and west to the farms along and beyond the Hunyani Hills as far as the Sanyati River.

On average, I did my best to visit my customers once a month, especially the farms that were isolated and accessible only to infrequent visits by the RMS, better known as the Road Motor Service that was established by the railways back in 1927 after an outbreak of East Coast Fever had decimated the animal-hauled transport system. The RMS became a lifeline that operated along routes where railways did not exist and whose work involved hauling goods, livestock, and indeed people to and from the nearest railheads.

It was farmers such as these that I looked forward to visiting, not so much for the business they generated, but more from an affinity that I shared with them having also experienced the loneliness of isolation.

I had passed the overgrown turn-off to the farm many times on the lonely back road to Karoi, but because the name of the farm on the plough-disc sign was illegible, I had hitherto hesitated to take it for fear it might lead to nowhere. However, on a whim I decided one day to take the road. I had travelled perhaps 10 miles or so when the road forked. I chose the fork that bore the imprints of a bicycle. The road soon degenerated into a rutted bush track that got steadily worse and I was ready to turn back when the road forked yet again. I must have taken the wrong fork, for the track ended at a deserted huddle of a few old huts, some fallen in, some all twisted and cockeyed. I stepped down from the truck and walked across to a mound of earth covered in couch grass and khaki weed that hid a hole with the mouth covered with a platform of ant-eaten logs. Nearby I found the remains of a windlass with a length of sisal rope and the remains of a rusted bucket still attached to the drum. I inched to the edge of the hole, dropped a stone inside, and heard the splash of water deep down. Just the sound brought me to the realization that had I driven over the mound of earth the truck and I would now be in the hole!

I'd had enough of driving blindly around the bush. All I wanted to do was to turn around and head back to the main road, but it wasn't that easy. Soon I realized I was lost after I drove around in circles and ended at last before a concertina gate stretched across the track. The gate was not in use and hadn't been for some time but in desperation I cut the wire that bound it to a fence and drove through. I was overjoyed to find that the track met up with a smooth gravel road that ran alongside a field of ripening sorghum, alive with flocks of quelea.

What turned out to be the family's slate-roofed house and outbuildings appeared like a mirage at the end of the road after I had passed through an orchard of orange trees. They must have heard me coming because the farmer, his wife and three daughters were there to meet me when I pulled up in the drive outside their front door. I was greeted like the proverbial 'prodigal son', which had me feeling a little uneasy at first, until I learned I was the first white man to have visited the farm since an RMS driver with a cattle-truck had collected cattle a few months before.

The farmer couldn't believe that the road I had used had not been reclaimed by nature and was still navigable, for he had last driven on it years previously when it was impassable after heavy rains. That had prompted him to forgo that road and cut another that linked up with an existing all-weather back road to Karoi. I spent an afternoon with Hendrik, who was of Dutch descent. He surprised me the more I got to know him, for never once did I hear him speak a word of Afrikaans. He spoke Zezuru fluently, which made him well known among the KoreKore, who he understood well. By speaking their language, I could see by their attentiveness when he spoke and their reverence to him that he had entered into the spirit of the black people.

He was a tall man in his sixties, over six feet, with a hooked nose and the eyes of an eagle. He was taciturn and lacked friends among the local Afrikaans farmers, but he seemed to like me and spoke often of his past when we were alone together.

Most of the farmers I spoke to on my trips knew about him, but because he kept to himself and was never seen at the Dutch Reformed Church, they were suspicious of his leanings. Because most were customers of mine and as I relied for a living on their patronage, I pleaded ignorance rather than say anything in his defence. Perhaps I should have done when they unwittingly and out of spite spoke ill of him. How wrong they were, and I gleaned a certain comfort in the knowledge that I, who had met him only recently, knew him better as somebody who rather than speak about his farm and family, spoke of them as a man does of loved and familiar things.

There were many diverse characters that I added to the client base in the course of my travels. I met rich farmers, who teased with empty promises then beat me down despairingly with demands of discounts they knew to be beyond my reach. Then, like throwing alms to a beggar, rewarded me if I was lucky, with an order for a ton or two of stock-food if the truckloads they had ordered from the millers in Salisbury failed to arrive on time. At the other end of the scale, I knew a poor farmer with hard times gnawing at his bootstraps, who rather than pay for a ton of discounted Rumevite off the back of my truck to maintain his herd through the harsh winter months, gave the money to the church instead, rather than face the wrath of the dominee.

I made friends of many of the farmers, even those who didn't buy a thing from me but rewarded me nonetheless with their company and were an inspiration. Take Ronnie Struthers and his wife for instance, who were as poor as church mice and lived in a tiny two-roomed thatched cottage. It had rough-plastered whitewashed walls and a cement floor painted with red stoep paint that she had polished with such vigour that it reflected the sparse furniture on its shiny surface. Two windows, one fixed and one opening, were 'kept alive' with two pretty curtains, and beneath each of them was a wooden shelf on which were placed bowls of fresh cut flowers. The kitchen, with a corrugated-iron roof, though separate from the house was no less neat. It had a wood stove, a paraffin fridge, and a china sink with chrome taps that were fed with steaming hot water from the Rhodesian boiler that stood outside on a brick plinth, seen through the single window framed by two colourful curtains.

The two were in their middle thirties and had lived on the farm for the past ten years. While others his age had made their money growing tobacco, his dream had been to breed Aberdeen Angus cattle. Cattle breeding was a slow process then, especially when one started as he did with a bull and a handful of cows. It took dedication and self-sacrifice to build up the herd to the stage that he was able to make a modest living from the sale of the progeny. However, it was not long after we met that everything came together and he was rewarded for his efforts when one of his young bulls was awarded Champion status at the Salisbury Agricultural Show. Things never looked back for him after that and his stock was in such demand that I arrived at his farm one day to find he had demolished the cottage and was putting the finishing touches to a modern electrified house with an enclosed veranda.

His was a success story that combined with the wisdom of Steve van Niekerk, my wife's brother, became the unwitting catalyst for a career change at a crucial point in my life.

Steve was Managing Director of a branch of Massey Ferguson, the world-renowned tractor and implement manufacturers that served the whole of that part of the country that stretched from Sinoia to the Zambian border.

It was Steve I am sure, who had had a good word to say on my behalf to Bill Plumb, my employer, when I applied for the job. Steve had also organised our accommodation and the collection of our furniture from the railway station. More importantly, as one of the catalysts I have mentioned, he persuaded me I was not cut out to be a salesman for I lacked the merciless cutthroat ability and natural inclination to slant the truth. He implied I would do better to lose myself in one of the larger corporations, "where," he confided during a tongue-loosening session in the bar of the golf-club after a game of golf, "it pays from experience to look busy even when you're not and keep your mouth shut until such time you have gained the knowledge to argue without looking foolish."

So I heeded his advice, studied, and passed a crash course in Bookkeeping, which gave me the confidence to apply for an advertised post as assistant accountant in a pulp and paper mill back in Norton.

Chapter Thirty

The Papermaker July 1970-May 1971

I was accepted without an interview, which surprised me at first for my experience of Accountancy was entirely theoretical—until I discovered that the person who had placed the advert was a close friend of Pat's sister Gladys and her husband Ron. He was head of the Electricity Supply Commission that controlled the distribution of Kariba's hydroelectric power, and would soon become a key figure in negotiating the power requirement for the mill's huge expansion plans.

My appointment stirred up resentment amongst the office staff, especially those girls whose service and experience that however it be construed, had been expediently overlooked and passed over for the likes of me. I had no qualification other than the old adage 'It's not what you know but who' and for this reason placed me fraudulently in a world where I trusted I would not be noticed until such time I was able to cope.

But I wasn't, and within the first month I was so out of my depth that, rather than conceal any further inadequacies, I approached the Company Secretary one evening after everybody had left the office to hand in the letter of resignation that I had prepared during the lunch break. He must have sensed what the letter was because he didn't even bother to open it. Instead, he handed it back and suggested I think about it overnight then meet with him in the morning before the start of business.

I remember thinking long and hard that night. A family man had to think, especially someone like me who up to then had lived on the outside, ex-farmer and salesman with nothing to show for it, and at any moment he might find his wife, child, house, everything snatched out from under him. Suddenly it became clear as to what I should do...There were three of us seated around the table, the Managing Director, Paget, the Secretary, and me with my resignation hidden in my pocket. It took a lot of convincing on my part and a lot of understanding, but after a stern proviso from the M.D. I was placed on strict probation for three months.

There were five of us trainees. I was the oldest; the others were just out of school. They had five years to qualify as recognised papermakers with the chance of climbing the corporate ladder. I didn't have that time, I had just 90 days to prove to somebody that I was someone, so for three months I ate, drank and dreamed the paper machine.

Because we lived so close to the mill there were nights I hardly slept, being kept awake by the omnipotent sounds of its machinery and the hiss of escaping steam. I would never have got through those first few months were it not for the rough, tough, hard-drinking, swearing, and quarrelling motley crew of expatriate papermakers. They included one Jimmy Malcolm, a quite brilliant Scottish papermaker who taught me all I knew about the trade. If it hadn't been for his constant clashes with management in his search for perfection, Jimmy would have made a damn good Production Manager and boss, which wouldn't have been such a bad move for me.

Nevertheless, I will remember him as the instrument for my letter of congratulations from Paget on completion of the three months, which was followed by a substantial increase in salary, my first since leaving school.

Chapter Thirty-One

The Sanction Busters

By the middle of 1971, the foundations for the new paper and pulp machines were nearing completion. No sooner had the concrete floors been laid and cured when the machinery and parts began to arrive in lorry-load after lorry-load. All the machinery looked new, but in fact both plants had been dismantled somewhere in the middle of England under the nose of the very government that had instituted sanctions. They were then transported to Germany where they were reconditioned and test-run before being dismantled and shipped under false documentation to the Portuguese port of Beira. I have wondered what words were bandied around in the halls of Whitehall after the British MI6 agents resident in the country had assured their government that the rebellion would be over in weeks. They had to make a turnaround and explain to their masters the sudden appearance of a British manufactured pulp and plant mill that would not only make the country self-sufficient in pulp but would save millions in foreign currency.

Rhodesian businessmen had become masters at busting United Nations sanctions and trade with her neighbours as well as the West. They flourished to the extent that between 1969-1974, Rhodesia's economic growth outstripped Britain's. What essentials and luxuries they could not acquire by devious means, they manufactured or produced their own. In doing so they made themselves self-sufficient, an attribute that helped immensely when the war got into top gear and they were able to manufacture their own weapons to overcome procurement problems. What British goods had become unobtainable, they could get French, Japanese, and West German substitutes that were better anyway. Fuel would always pose a problem but along with everybody else I managed on a strict ration of fuel. In my case it was, as I remember, four gallons a month, so instead of using my car for emergency callouts to breakdowns I used a Vespa scooter instead.

Chapter Thirty-Two

My Friend Ugo

After both plants were erected, I was assigned to the pulp plant to assist in its commissioning by an extremely intelligent chemical engineer called Ugo Testa. Perhaps he found in me without quite realising it, was that what changes easily will change again. The chameleon mind of an inquisitive young man is a mind without convictions. Hence, Ugo, who had very deep convictions on many matters, found me open to instruction and with much to give.

That was one basis for our friendship. Another was that my presence at the commissioning seemed to lighten his work for him. Not that I helped him directly or anything like that, but my keenness to learn and withstand his castigations without resentment seemed to reassure him that I took them all in the spirit they were given.

He was not so middle-aged at 42 as to lack a fondness for recreation. That became the subject of a discussion we had one day in his office while waiting for the fitting crew to make an alteration before a dummy run. Our conversation led to my years as a farmer and what I did in my spare time. His ears pricked up when I spoke of pig hunting and game bird shooting for the pot, and before we were finished I had offered to take him hunting for pheasant on Farraline.

I knew Farraline was still owned by the Palmers but had lain fallow since I had left. Ralph gave me permission as I knew he would, with two provisions: firstly, I was only to hunt game birds by day and secondly, it was incumbent upon me to notify Chibero College of any intention to hunt after dark for springhares that the old man considered vermin.

These hunting forays gave me the chance to experience the contrasting side to Ugo's vocal Italian temper and his difficult-to-please character. He changed and assumed the personality of a wild-eyed young boy each time he caught sight and gave chase at breakneck speed when the eyes of a springhare were caught in the glare of the headlights. As the vehicle's bouncing lights mimicked the animal's gait, I clung to the edges of the seat and croaked out a dry-mouthed warning as stumps and rocks leaped out like predators from the darkness into the light. It was a relief when he jammed on brakes, leaped from the car in a cloud of dust and knelt in the beam to draw a bead on the blinking eyes. Then came the echoing crack of the rifle, his cry of delight as the animal slumped or the stream of Italian expletives that followed a miss.

He was as laid-back on the hunt as he was in his home, where the subject of work and its problems were conversationally taboo and where he was able at the same time to divorce himself from the heavy-smoking, hard-swearing perfectionist that he left behind on the factory floor. There he was 'one of the boys' and as such was unpopular with the management staff, who I got the feeling were jealous and felt threatened by his wisdom and experience.

It might appear to anybody reading these last few paragraphs that in my friend Ugo I could find no wrong. Well let me dispel that notion, we had our differences but I believe that makes a friendship stable, for what is true friendship without healthy debate and argument? And argue we did, about everything except the intricacies of pulp and papermaking. I was careful to avoid that, for fear of appearing stupid in the eyes of somebody who could work out mathematical equations far faster on a slide-rule than I could on a calculator. Ugo was able to tell by the smell of the pulp blowing from the digester what the Ph was to a decimal point without taking a sample to the lab for testing.

Yet for all his knowledge and skills, Ugo was never one for rules and systems. He didn't theorise about anything. "It doesn't help," he would say, "for you to know the theory behind pulp making or indeed what goes in to making a perfect pulp. There are far too many variables. Rather stick to the basics and produce something that, no matter how unattractive it might look, meets the physical standards set out by the user. It will be experience and instinct that will point the way and give you the time to make the adjustments necessary to correct a fault, but before anything else you must know the plant and how it breathes. Remember, I am here for only a short space of time therefore, if I am to hand the plant over to you I must be satisfied you will manage." And I managed, because of Ugo's commitment to teach and my fortunate ability to grasp what I was taught.

There followed a period of uncertainty for me. After Ugo's departure to South Africa (where he resumed control of Usutu Pulp in Swaziland, a plant he had commissioned a few years before going to Rhodesia) Paget, who had always backed me and saw me as the natural successor to Ugo, was replaced as M.D. and retired to a little village in Kent.

The uncertainty I speak of had its beginnings well before Ugo left. In fact, I'd always felt that the resentment among my fellow workers seemed to stem from my friendship with him. There were those who viewed my rise through the ranks as nepotism, taking no account of a 2-year course in Pulp Technology that I completed in one-and-a-half years and for which I received a diploma. It was a hard slog not easily forgotten, that kept me up after work until the early hours of every day, weekends included. My family suffered from my determination to achieve my goal of becoming the first Pulp Plant Manager. However, Paget's replacement M.D., being young, inexperienced and easily swayed, listened to his close associates and social climbers. He looked past me and installed one of two engineers as manager with me as his assistant. Bill was a pleasant enough fellow in his middle sixties who I got on with pretty well to begin with while he drained me of my knowledge. Then, as the months passed and he gained confidence, he put forward a plan for a system he was convinced would revolutionise the industry. I could see his theory but practically I knew it to be impossible cost-wise.

He ignored me of course, and went ahead after the M.D. approved his plans. We battled for weeks without even a modicum of success. Eventually it was scrapped, poor Bill returned to his post as engineer and the M.D. had no choice but to promote me as temporary manager until the post was filled. Then suddenly the wheel of fortune turned full circle, the M.D. lost his job and was replaced by a far older and wiser man by the name of John Scholes, who promoted me instantly to Pulp Plant Manager. Another year drew to a close. I can't remember what year it was, but by then I knew every inch of the plant. Each time I stepped out of the office, I had only to sniff the air and listen to know that everything was rosy and looking up at the control room I was bound to see my friend Daniel, the Assistant Manager.

It had been a long hard haul. Now was the time to begin in earnest a search for my family.

Chapter Thirty-Three

Whisky Hotel 1974 – 1978

It had been near enough one year since three white land inspectors, Gerald Hawksworth and his two companions, were ambushed near Mount Darwin in the northeast of the country. As the only survivor, Gerald was captured and force-marched for 1600 km through Rhodesia and Mozambique to a flea-ridden jail in Tanzania. I remember seeing pictures of his bullet-ridden companions on television, followed by an advertisement urging men of all ages to register under the Defence Manpower Act. So I registered and it wasn't long before I received my acknowledgement and number—044973H.

The war had reached a critical point and the storm clouds were gathering. Mozambique had changed hands and ZANLA had moved their headquarters from Zambia to Mozambique, where Samora Machel and Frelimo offered them sanctuary and base facilities. ZANLA were pushing their forces in ever-increasing numbers across the thick bush and rugged terrain of Rhodesia's eastern border.

The Police Reserve up to that time had performed a quasi-police role that included protecting the country's infrastructure and tourists, who unmindful of the country's position continued to visit and were the reason for my first assignment as a police reservist. I had to ride 'shotgun' on a bakkie, armed with a machinegun, leading a convoy of tourists from the border at Beit Bridge to the Bubye River and back, twice a day every day for two weeks. I got to know every rock and tree on that flat boring stretch of road. A month later found me and four others guarding the Lundi River Bridge, way out in the back of beyond with nothing to pass the time but watch a pod of hippo and a few crocodiles basking on the riverbank.

It was a change from working at the mill, but it lacked the excitement I was looking for, I had yet to fire a shot in anger and taste the real war, and left me in envy of those of my friends who had. It was for that reason that in early 1974, I joined the Police Field Reserve. After extensive training and selection by a staff core that—strange to say that consisted mostly of a mix of imported ex-British Army combatants and a few Americans, all lured by money and a wish to enjoy the colonial lifestyle—I became one of a stick (platoon) of six, with the call-sign Whisky Hotel.

Everything was running smoothly at work, so well in fact that mine had become mostly a trouble shooting and managerial role. Daniel had become so adept that the only time he called on me for assistance was to prepare the twice-monthly maintenance programme and monthly production report.

Call-ups had been set at two weeks in every month. It was a simple procedure. Whisky Hotel, led by our leader Maurice an ex-policeman with fantastic map reading and radio-procedure skills, assembled in the afternoon on the day before departure at the local Police Station where we were issued with ammunition and rat-packs (food rations). The next few hours were spent preparing ourselves for the bush. At this stage not even Maurice knew where the next two weeks would be spent. It could be anywhere and we would only find out at the end of the following day after a day spent re-training at a sprawling base on the outskirts of Mazoe, 38 kilometres north of Salisbury. God! I hated that place of trench latrines, ice-cold showers, and pre-dawn exercises when in winter it was so cold one's hand froze to the barrel of a rifle and the wind cut through like a knife.

That same morning we were given our posting and if we were lucky we were sent to a base like Sipolilo that I knew in my youth. We covered an area the size of Wales, never stopping except to eat and sleep in ambush positions that were set up on tracks or pathways that linked the kraals. Contacts with the enemy in situations like these were few and far between. It was more like a game of cat-and-mouse but we knew they were there. Sometimes I was sure, or imagined I could hear them moving in the dense bush, especially along the rivers where they preferred to travel. No doubt we were seen by them many times but fortunately for us, and being the quality of soldiers most of them were, they would have been hesitant to give away their positions. Most of them, judging from intelligence reports, were loathe to feel the sting of a K-Car (Kill Car– the Allouette helicopter with 16mm cannons) that could be deployed in minutes, or even worse, a kill hungry platoon of the RLI (Rhodesian Light Infrantry).

Mushumbi Pools – August 1974

In the Zambesi Valley where the Angwa and Hunyani rivers meet there is a place called Mushumbi Pools. It was an area of unsurpassed wild beauty and peace.

I can't remember how far it was from Oscar Base at Sipolilo, to the tiny brick hut that stood at the confluence of the two rivers. At the time, we didn't measure distances on roads such as the one that led to Mushumbi in miles or kilometres, but by the time it took the Landrover to traverse the road without milestones, over the escarpment formed by part of the Mvuradonha mountains. It went down into the hot and humid Zambezi valley that stretched in a carpet of dense forest all the way to the Zambezi River, on the border with Mozambique and Zambia.

It had once been the main infiltration route for terrorist incursions, but since the collapse of Portuguese rule in Mozambique it had become less popular with Mugabe's ZANLA. Preference was given to Rhodesia's eastern border with its extensive tea and fruit estates, inhabited by a large population of workers who willingly or otherwise supplied the terrorists with food and shelter. Nevertheless, the route despite its inhospitable nature was still used by Joshua Nkomo's ZIPRA forces based in Zambia.

Our mission on that trip was more of an intelligence gathering nature. Our instructions were to avoid contact with the enemy and look for signs of aiding and abetting by the few remaining Tonga tribesman that chose to remain in the valley. The majority had fled south from the Zambezi to settle along the minor tributaries such as the Kadzi and Hunyani, leaving the valley to the small herds of elephant that showed their existence by the occasional heaps of dung we came across during our drives deep into the forests.

It was a rough and potholed road that led to the army base on the Zambezi, 50-odd kilometres away according to the map, and along what was known as the border track that passed close by a deserted mission station right on the border. It had been closed down and its staff deported after it was found they had been aiding the enemy. The road ended at a disused airfield that had been used for forays against the enemy bases across the border and was now used as a drop-off and collection point for the Call-sign units patrolling the valley.

There was one thing about the track that stuck in my mind, more in fact than the unpleasantness of patrolling it on foot in the heat of the day, when flies descended in swarms to suck the sweat from the skin and the tsetse fly stung through a drill-shirt like it was tissue paper. More noticeable to me was the absence of game along the track, despite the isolation and quietness. In fact, one might have seen more wild life in the backyard of a house in the middle of Salisbury than I saw after many foot patrols and drives along that track. It came up often in the course of conversation and the consensus was that the herds and prides had migrated west to Mana Pools and Chiwore to escape the war. This turned out to be wishful thinking when

I learned from a Selous Scout that the game in the valley and surrounding areas had been shot out so as to deprive the insurgents of meat in the long trek through the valley. If that was the case it only added to the realisation of what man is reduced to in order to win a war.

As our two-week stint drew to a close we had begun to think the war had passed us by, until one day we received a call on the Small Means from Special Branch at the army base on the Zambezi. The order was simple but at the same time offered us a change from the mundane. We were to proceed to the mission and RV (rendezvous) with an Army Stick and take delivery of a starving terrorist, who had been found wandering the bush with an AK47 but not a single round of ammunition.

It was my first look at a genuine terr and the first time I had held an AK47— neither were in good condition. The terr had been scratched to ribbons by jesse and buffalo thorn and was so emaciated that he could barely stand. After we had loaded him handcuffed into the Land Rover, he was so weak he lay on the floor of the vehicle like a dead body—and stank like one. He was a target for myriads of flies that crawled in and out of his nostrils and eye sockets. I guess, because I was new to the war, I felt a measure of pity for the poor bastard and swatted the flies with my hat. When that proved futile I covered his face with a piece of oil rag used to clean rifles.

It wasn't the end of the day's drama. On the journey back we had stopped for a smoke-break in a patch of dense cover, when suddenly we heard the noise of a vehicle and the sound of voices coming down the track. We took up ambush positions and waited with bated breath as a truck containing a detail of SAP (South African Police) passed by without them seeing us. Fortunately, Maurice, having been a Chief Inspector in the police for many years before changing his vocation, recognised who they were. I shudder to think what might have happened had they with their bird's-eye view from the back of the truck, seen us and took us for insurgents!

It must have played on Maurice's mind for after having delivered the dehydrated terr into the hands of Special Branch he reported the incident to the Sunray of the base. He suggested we drop in at the SAP base that was situated on the Angwa River on our way back to Mushumbi and report it to their commander. As it turned out, because it was our last day at Mushumbi, Maurice dropped the matter and we took a drive to the 'petrified forest' instead. It was a little-known area close to the Angwa River where in the past millennia something happened that had turned the trees to stone. Many of them were still standing like stone statues without leaves, and those that had fallen bore stone bark and growth rings worn smooth by time. I searched for a souvenir and found a small branch that was so dense and heavy it took two of us to load it into the vehicle. As we toiled, swarms of tsetse flies descended from the live growing trees and stung with such fury we were forced to flee.

Tande – 1977

Whisky Hotel spent the next year of operations in the TTLs (Tribal Trust Lands) of the Tande area north of Sipolilo, between the Rukure and Hunyani rivers. Our orders on each call-up were to patrol by day and set up blindfolds (ambushes) by night on the paths leading to and from the kraals in the area. A curfew was in force throughout the country so that anyone moving at night was fair game.

On one call-up we had set up a blindfold on the outskirts of a kraal where we had stumbled upon evidence of a mass feeding of the enemy. It was quite incredible! We found the fresh spoor of at least 50 or more terrorists in a clearing on the outskirts of a village, the area littered with freshly chewed meat bones and an empty cigarette packet printed in Portuguese. Maurice radioed through to Base to report our find and since we were convinced the terrs (terrorists) were sleeping at the kraal, he requested a dawn sweep of the kraal by the Fire Force based at Sipolilo. Excitement was high in the camp as we visualized a kill and Whisky Hotel being 'mentioned in dispatches'. We slept that night on a gomo (hill) that had a panoramic view of the kraal and the surrounding countryside. As the first signs of dawn crept over the countryside the radio crackled to life and a voice from the Comm-Ops relay team, situated somewhere in a range of gomos to the north, began confirming with the sticks taking part in the operation their loc-stats and state of readiness.

It was to be a simple operation that it was envisaged would take less than an hour, a little more perhaps if indeed there were any enemy in the kraal and they decided to take a stand. That would turn the operation into a firefight, in which case it could last a lot longer.

The plan was for a sweep-line comprising a few platoons of regular troops from Sipolilo to sweep the kraal and surrounding bush and drive the enemy towards a number of hidden PATU (Police anti-terrorist Unit) sticks or 'stops' as they were commonly called, there to cover the strategic escape routes. All the forces including PATU and Whisky Hotel came under orders of an airborne commander ensconced in the cockpit of a K-Car with a 20 millimetre cannon and with the call-sign Leader-1.

The sweep-line emerged from the tree line and into the open country below our position just as dawn broke, because of the camouflage it was difficult at first to make out the full extent of the sweep-line. Then as the sun rose clear of the horizon, I could see the combat caps and the rifle muzzles of the crouching troops as they halted to reform the sweep-line that stretched across the belt of open country to the foothills of the gomos that housed Comm-Ops.

Then came what all had waited to hear—the whirr of a rotor

and the clack of blades beating the wind as the chopper rose like a dragonfly above the men, who rose as one and moved off at pace while the chopper rose and dipped in a dance of death. Over the Small Means we heard 'His Master's Voice', cool and collected, issuing orders to the platoon leaders on the ground, before the helicopter banked, broke away, and swooped low over the kraal.

Everything happened like a film on fast-forward as a group of figures fled from the huddle of huts straight into the path of the sweep-line which then opened fire. At the first shot, the gang 'bomb-shelled' into pairs and fled away from the line of advancing troops, disappearing into the long grass. I watched in awe as the troops moved on, firing into any patch of undergrowth that might conceal the enemy. From the direction of the kraal we heard the sound of an AK on automatic, followed by the countering explosions of cannon fire from the K-Car hidden from sight behind the far side of the gomo we were on. Then suddenly it appeared, swooping from behind the gomo and over the sweep-line. I could hear 'His Master's Voice' and the pop-pop-pop of FN fire as the nose of the K-Car dipped and pointed in the direction of a fleeing terr being chased in a cloud of dust and cannon. The chopper then rose and hovered fleetingly above a body in the grass before it turned about to follow the sweep-line and disappear into the distance, leaving behind spirals of smoke from burning huts.

It was well towards nightfall before mopping-up operations were complete and the bodies removed, leaving Special Branch and Army Intelligence to do what they did best. Was the operation a success? I like to think it was even though the Sit-Rep reported three terrs and six mujibas (local boys who acted as the guerrillas' eyes and ears) dead and one captured, far less than we had anticipated. To crown it all we weren't mentioned in the Sit-Rep other than a reference to 'a Field Reserve Stick that reported the sighting'.

In the last month of the same year, Whisky Hotel disbanded. The leader succumbed to pressure of work, two others called it a day and decided to patrol closer to home. That left three of us with no option but to volunteer our services for the final stint of the year. That was a big mistake...

Mangwende TTL – 1977: The Death of a Village Idiot

The three of us were teamed up with three inexperienced residents of Norton. It was their first deployment into an operational area and they were justifiably nervous at the prospect of a two-week stint in a 'protected village' in what had once been a heavily populated area where intimidation was rife and villagers were murdered wholesale on the pretext of them being 'sell-outs'. The security forces and INTAF (Internal Affairs) were losing control in Mangwend and in order to stem the tide, protected villages were erected. Thousands of villagers were uprooted and moved into such villages for their protection and to avoid them giving aid to the terrorists (there were many such villages spread throughout the country).

The village fell under the jurisdiction of INTAF and it was from the C.O. that we took our orders, which were to patrol the village and enforce a dusk-to-dawn curfew. The administrative heart of the village consisted of brick barracks, the C.O.'s quarters, a mess and a jail protected by sandbag walls and a surrounding bank of bulldozed soil.

The C.O. much to my surprise was none other than a work colleague, Mike, a wild womanising Scotsman with a brilliant analytical brain and who, for some reason, disliked men of colour. That left me perplexed at his decision to join INTAF rather than take a role to suit his personality.

He had strange ideas as to how the war should be fought, ideas that conflicted with mine and yet shouldn't have done, for the war had shifted from a shoot-to-kill and no-questions-asked attitude to one that was encouraged by INTAF that involved 'winning the hearts and minds of the people', starting with the thousands in his care.

The village was mortared one night by the terrs. Fortunately, they must have been amateurs because the bomb landed harmlessly inside the perimeter of the village, leaving no more damage than a direct hit on a maize granary. There was much excitement when the bomb fell. I must confess, having never been under attack before, that my first instinct was to vacate the barracks, which I presumed was the target, and run with my companions to join the Guard Force (INTAF Armed Unit). They had taken up defence positions amongst the huts closest to the bank of soil that surrounded the buildings and were laying down a curtain of such intense and frightening fire that on second thoughts I decided with my stick, to stay close to the bank to avoid being caught in any crossfire. Besides, I had no idea where the attack was coming from. It lasted less than five minutes before it petered out and in that time our stick between us, had fired not a single round.

My introduction to combat, since I had not fought back, so far to say the least had been casual. Over the next few days Mike, who had been furious at our indecision, put forward a defence plan of action. It was put to the test when a few days later, just before nightfall, the village was stonked (fired upon) again.

This time the terrs took advantage of the fading light and were more accurate. They hit a couple of huts within the village, causing a few injuries. I was mildly frightened at first until I realised the fire was not directed at where we were, but at the high volume of fire from the Guard Force who were some distance away. This prompted me, in a fit of bravado, to let loose two magazines in quick succession into the trees where I believed the terrs were hidden. Suddenly everything was quiet. I glanced across at the Guard Force positions and caught a movement. I watched amazed as one of the Guard

Force personnel, armed with a rocket grenade stuck to the end of his rifle, climbed on top of a henhouse and fired. The result wasn't what I expected. The structure gave way on the recoil and the man disappeared in a shower of white powder. He emerged from the ruins of the henhouse covered in feathers and chicken shit to shrieks of laughter and crude jokes that took the edge off the seriousness and marked the end of the attack.

Mike, in the meantime, had radioed for assistance, but by the time it arrived the gooks (enemy fighters) had disappeared into the surrounding hills.

Mike took the raids very badly, so much so he became quite paranoid and insisted we patrol the village in pairs on a shift basis. He made it clear that any of the villagers found outside their huts during the curfew between eight at night and six in the morning, were to be shot if they tried to run away or, if captured, be brought in for interrogation. A few days before the end of our stint, Mike and a few drinking buddies decided to take a shift patrolling the village at night. It was around ten when they found a young man wandering into the village from the bush. At breakfast the following morning, Mike recounted the events of the previous night. "We captured a gook last night, pissed out of his bracket. We interrogated him all night but couldn't get anything out of him. If you want to see what a gook looks like go to the jail."

I wasn't prepared for what I saw. I had expected to see something similar to what I had seen in the Valley, but the gook he spoke of was nude and bloody, lying dead in a pool of water.

Later that day a distraught villager reported the absence of his mentally challenged son.

Chapter Thirty-Four

Norton 1978

The war had moved close to home.

I was away on call-up when terrs were found to be resident in Ngoni, the black township adjoining Norton.

Pat was awakened by the sound of gunfire one night followed by the blast of a rifle grenade. The grenade removed the arm and part of the shoulder of a work colleague, Dick Venter, who was part of a stick sent to investigate. In the same contact two black policemen were killed before the enemy dispersed into the surrounding farms. In the same period our neighbour Denise Quincy, a young mother with children, the wife of Keith Ballantyne, a workmate, and 57 other passengers were murdered when the Rhodesian Airways Viscount en route from Kariba was brought down by ZIPRA.

In the same year I learned what it is to hate.

ZIPRA (Zimbabwe Peoples Revolutionary Army) murdered a mother and a 13-year-old girl I had shared the stage with only weeks before in a variety show to raise funds for Dudley Hall School. My stick was among the first on the scene after the father arrived within minutes of the attack to find the bullet-ridden bodies of his wife and daughter at the back door of their farmhouse. A second daughter aged five was still alive and despite her terrible wounds she survived to live a life in a wheelchair.

The police arrived soon after and carted away the gardener who we had come across after the shooting, mowing the lawn outside the house as if nothing had happened. I remember being restrained before I had the chance to put a bullet through the bastard's head.

The war had lost its patriotic romanticism and I changed with it. Scenes that in the past would have left me uncomfortable and pitying, no longer had the same effect. I became one of a stick named Alpha Lima—four men touched by the unforgiving nature of the Chimurenga.

I realized how different I had become on my first stint with Alpha Lima after we stopped a bus in Mhondoro TTL to search for arms.

We found a woman who had a dead baby tied to her back, its body had been gutted and the cavity stuffed with grenades. I felt little pity as Pfupi twisted her nipples while Chipo and I held her down on the dusty floor of the kia (dwelling) and Jimmy poured water onto a piece of cloth covering her nose and mouth. At first she held her breath but soon she could no longer do so and began breathing in water until I could hear it gurgling in her lungs. At the point of drowning, Jimmy allowed her to breathe again as she vomited up gallons of water. Pfupi grilled her some more when she was able to speak but without success, so the cloth was replaced and soon the water was flooded in her mouth and nose and between her legs. I felt nothing when Jimmy dragged in the girl's brother, who began screaming at the sight of his sister lying motionless on the floor and broke down and told Pfupi all he knew. The information proved worthless and resulted in a 'lemon' so we returned after a day or two, and because neither the brother nor his sister were at home, I joined in as we burned down their kia in front of the mother and father.

Both Pfupi and Chipo had lost their families through atrocities committed by ZANLA. Phupi was the son of a headman in his village who had been branded a 'sell-out'. He had hidden while the rest of his family, including his brothers and sisters, were locked in their kia and the roof set alight. He listened to their screams as they were burned alive.

Chipo was amongst 400 hundred male and female children

who had been abducted by ZIPRA and taken across the Botswana border for training in Zambia. Less than 100 were returned after pleas from the parents and pressure from overseas agencies. He was one of those that was returned and, in reprisal, his parents were tried as 'sell-outs' then axed to death.

Jimmy, being a schoolteacher, was exempt from military service at the time the war began. Rather than join the Territorial Army after resigning from teaching, he was employed in the private sector and joined PATU as a regular of Alpha Lima. Then as the war progressed and the whites began emigrating in ever-increasing numbers, the stick of six grew smaller and would have disbanded had I not arrived on the scene to make up a stick of four.

The war was so close to home by now that it no longer became necessary for Smithfield training before deployment. What training was necessary was then carried out on the rifle range in the hills near Kent Estate.

Norton itself now possessed its own relay station. It was housed in a brick tower high up on a hill only a few kilometres from the village, and had communications with all the satellite police stations and each and every Army, PATU and Police Reserve stick operating in the TTLs around Mashonaland.

The 'kills' were mounting, as were the killings of civilians. In June ZANLA murdered nine British missionaries and four young children including a three-week-old baby. It was pictures like these and other atrocities in the newspapers and on television that unsettled me even more and had me dreaming of retribution.

The time came, as it was bound to come, when I killed and stood over the body of an unarmed mujibas dressed in black.

What little remorse I may have felt at his death was overshadowed by a sense of achievement when I found in the messenger boy's pocket a letter from a Political Commissar addressed to a ZANLA Section Commander operating from a kraal in Mhondoro. The letter, I like to believe, proved to be of some importance, for no sooner had Jimmy shackle-coded the contents over the Small Means to Base, within hours not days as would normally have been the case, we found ourselves as part of a combined army and PATU operation that made a sweep of the specified village. It was an action that saw five gooks and an unspecified number of recruits killed after a long chase that ended in a kopje near Fort Martin that lay on the border of the TTL. We didn't take part in the chase, but we heard afterwards that the group had been so indoctrinated with political garbage that, though surrounded, they refused to surrender and shouted out political slogans as one by one they were picked off at random. When it was all done and we had RV'd at the contact position, we sat around with the other sticks waiting for the bodies to be loaded onto a truck. I laughed with the others as a soldier stuffed a lit cigarette in the mouth of one of the dead gooks. He pressed the body's chest a few times that made the ash glow and the smoke spiral and said jokingly: "Enjoy your last smoke, floppy."

Wherever I found myself in the country over the two-week call-ups I would endeavour to write home, provided I could get to a police or army base to post the letter. There wasn't much to write about as we had been told we were not to divulge the nature or form of the operations we were on. I have read some of my letters since. Strange, isn't it, how separation made it so easy for me to lay bare my thoughts and feelings of love for my wife, feelings that were there constantly but I confess were not shown when they should have been.

Mhondoro Ambush – July 1978

It was one of those call-ups that so far had been a dream. We were in the western side of Mhondoro patrolling along the edge of a dried-up riverbed that didn't show on the map, but we were sure was one of the many tiny tributaries of the Umfuli that held water at the height of the rainy season then dried up as soon as the rains ceased.

The first week had been completely uneventful, the countryside we had passed through had been largely uninhabited and water was scarce. That had been the only problem and cost us a 5-kilometre walk off the chosen track at night to fill our water bottles. It would have been easy to disclose our presence by keeping to the Umfuli, but Jimmy had purposely kept clear of the river to avoid compromising Alpha Lima on its way to Rocky Ridge, a tiny village in the Chiota TTL with a shopping centre where it was widely known the terrs did their shopping.

The dried riverbed had been an option because there had always been the possibility we might find water by digging into a depression or beneath a boulder that offered permanent shade. We couldn't have been too far from the Umfuli for the bush along the bank had become so dense that it became impossible to move through, , but rather than move away from the river and take a route through less dense bush, without thinking we took the easy option and walked along the open riverbed thick with sand.

Chipo was leading the way, suddenly he shouted a warning and dropped on his stomach and fired into the undergrowth. Bullets were ricocheting through the trees with a high pitched zinging sound and the whit-whit of bullets kicking up the sand at my feet. The air was full of noise and the smell of oil and cordite as I dropped and in a panic buried my face in the sand—I heard Jimmy screaming orders above the crash of rifles. Suddenly I was back on the range. I looked to my right at my buddy Pfupi, firing at the invisible enemy, took his cue as I gained composure and fired with purpose into every shadow within my arc of fire. It was terrifying, expecting at any moment to feel the bite of a bullet. I felt the sting of sand and stones as a bullet struck the ground inches from my face.

Suddenly the firing ceased and I heard Jimmy's order to take cover. We rose and scrambled to the dense river- bank and as we lay prone in the shadows I felt a trickle of blood where a stone had struck my face—'why am I not hit? I thought and with it came the realisation that by rights we should all be dead.

We lay prone in the shadows, guns pointed, waiting for another attack but it never came. We did a 360 of the ambush site and found eight ambush positions with the telltale signs of cartridge cases that numbered a few hundred. It was a miracle we survived and I can only thank God the gooks were such poor shots.

Chapter Thirty-Five

I Return to Paradise July 1978

It was hot as hell the day the order came through over the Small Means. Alpha Lima was halfway through a stint in the Mount Darwin area, stuck on the top of a gomo above a kraal that was reputed to be feeding the enemy. For seven days we had seen nothing. Either we had been compromised or the report of the feeding had been logged some time ago and we were there as an afterthought. Whatever it was, Jimmy—always one for action—wasn't happy until the call came through and we were ordered to RV for pick-up. It was a Friday afternoon when we arrived at JOC Mount Darwin.

Saturday morning and JOC Darwin was abuzz. In a portioned-off corner of the Ops room, two policewomen, with earphones attached to their foreheads, were busy making sense of the jargon that issued forth from the Big Means, the TR48 high-frequency radio that linked JOC Darwin with tactical headquarters in Salisbury. It was a continuous 24-hour operation that would see the women replaced by men of the Signal Corps who would man the Means until dawn. This day was different from other Saturdays when normally the base was manned by a skeleton staff. Sunray, the commander of JOC Darwin was on emergency call only, which meant he could play undisturbed a game or two of tennis with the local farmers followed by sundowners. It was different this day because Sunray was preparing for a major offensive and when we arrived he was in consultation behind locked doors with his subordinates. Around 10 a.m., Jimmy was amongst a roomful of PATU Call-signs being briefed on an operation that would involve not only the Police but also the Army and Air Force.

"It was big!" Jimmy said, when he briefed us that afternoon, not only for the number of gooks involved but also among them were two Section Commanders belonging to both ZANLA and ZIPRA.

It was only when Jimmy spelled out the extent of the operation and where it was to take place that it hit me like a bombshell—it was either on or close to Paradise! Uncle Bob's farm from 27 years ago, but the kraal name was different, which made me feel a little easier. Perhaps it was across the Hunyani. But no, it couldn't be because the river we were to follow to our proposed ambush position was the Mupingi. It had to be! Jimmy had spelled it phonetically in his notebook: Mike-Uniform-Papa-India-November-Golf- India.

Nah! Surely it was too much of a coincidence and besides, a lot happens in 27 years. The chances of the two still being alive were pretty slim, they would have to be in their late nineties at least. So I just sort of shook my head and put it out of my mind, which wasn't difficult for there was much to do.

The operation, to start with a sweep of the kraal, was timed for first light on Monday morning when it was estimated the enemy would be at their most vulnerable after a weekend of feasting and drinking.

But right at this time it was a case of 'hurry up and wait', everyone that was to take part sat around in the shade in groups each to his kind.

"I'd hate to be on the receiving end of this lot," said Jimmy, looking around and nodding at two platoons of the 2nd Battalion Rhodesia Regiment. They were dressed as one in camouflage longs and shiny black boots and standing easy, their packs and webbing stacked in neat piles, rifles close to hand, and by their appearance displaying an air of supreme confidence and discipline.

As they talked among themselves, I saw them look askance at the group of unkempt PATU sticks lounging beside misshapen piles of packs, wearing combat caps or floppy hats and dressed in many types of civilian and military clothing—frayed green and navy-blue gym shorts or tattered combat trousers matched with short or long-sleeved camouflage shirts. But like the soldiers, their rifles were close to hand, festooned with an assortment of belts and webbing. To go with the rag-tag clothing was a motley array of footwear that included takkies, sandals, and veldskoene (South African soft leather shoes).

The men who made up these sticks were of indeterminable age. There were many younger than I was and some much older—ex-servicemen who may well have seen action in the Congo or elsewhere around the world. Having had their share of discipline, perhaps they now sought to share a more personal conflict with those who came after? Perhaps theirs was a proving of past battles won or lost, or simply a yearning for companionship without the fetters of maturity. They stood together, these ghosts of the past, with the spirits of the future—a mix of young farmers with farms and families to protect and a sprinkling of directors of strategic companies. Through the secretive or specialized nature of their business, the latter were exempt from Call-up, but they had secret training to take part in emergency situations and chose not to wear the Leopard-pad insignia of PATU.

Aside from these two groups, a platoon of RLI Fire Force were clustered around the trunks of a grove of msasa trees with the remnants of last year's pods still dangling from their branches. What a contrast was revealed in the actions and expressions of these youngsters. Confident, they were loud and brash, barely out of their teens; their fresh young faces alight with the fearlessness of youth and with an exuberance that extolled the virtues of love, death and the raw rich stuff of life. They were men before their time, killing machines, with a language of their own:

Ja, ek se … long gooks footing down the gomo …
long culling with the G gun, ek se … food for the flat dogs …
and four shumbas and a cane for the pain, eh.

Beyond the noisy throng in an open stretch of veldt stood a small fleet of RLs with drop-sides hanging ready to board, their drivers sat smoking in the shade of the cabs. Not far from them, in a circle of red dust surrounded by whitewashed stones, stood an Allouette on toy wheels with a 20mm cannon poking through its perspex shield. It looked overworked with its vanes hanging listless like leaves on a wilting plant. A mechanic with a bottle of beer in one greasy paw, a soiled cloth in the other and a cigarette dangling from his mouth leaned against the transparent bubble. Lazily he wiped the cloth along the barrel of the cannon then walked away to join the Fire Force. I last saw him stretched out on the ground, the bottle glued to his mouth, and I watched in awe as he finished the beer without once moving the bottle from his mouth.

The rest of that day was spent preparing for the night walk.

The planned operation was extensive but simple. A sweep force of 24, drawn from the 2nd battalion under the command of Call-sign Charlie One stationed in the Allouette gunship, were to move into a sweep position, five kilometres east of the suspect kraal in the early hours of Monday morning. A further force of six PATU and four Police Field Reserve Call-signs, that included ourselves, under the command of Charlie One would provide blindfolds (ambush) positions along the west bank of the Hunyani River—quite simple. However, the most difficult part of the operation was the 20-kilometre footslog the PATU and FR Call-signs would carry out from a drop-off point on the Sipolilo road. The orders were to complete the walk over two nights, lying up during the day to avoid compromising the operation, and at all costs to cross the Hunyani River and be in the blindfold positions two hours before sun-up on Monday.

To complete the operation an unknown force of PATU and Police Reserve sticks drawn from the farming and mining communities, under the command of Alpha Base, a relay radio base situated on top of a gomo south of Musikas Kraal (the one I knew as a boy), would provide a series of stops along the Mupingi and in the adjacent white farming areas should the gooks decide to 'bombshell'.

The two trucks moved slowly through the dark glow of moonlight with lights extinguished, hoping not to waken the inhabitants of the kraals along the way. Despite it being summer there was a nip in the air, which was a good thing because it appeared to keep the kraal dogs quiet. Our truck swerved to avoid some cattle lying in the fine sand on the verge. They were spattered with grit and dust yet refused to budge and simply turned their heads to face the other way.

The moon scuttled in and out between patches of wispy cloud. I watched, amused, as the features on the faces of my companions seemed to jerk in strobes of black and silver like some old movie. Every now and then the wheels hit a bump, prompting curses that rose sometimes above the noise of the engine and the rattle of stones against the undercarriage. The journey lasted two hours before we stopped briefly on a bend in the road. With the engine idling the tailboard was lowered and Alpha Lima tumbled off like dung beetles as the truck moved on, showering the stick with grit and dust.

It was less than a kilometre to the Mupingi from the road, but it was hard going. The bush was dense and to make things worse the moon had begun to wane so a barbed-wire fence was not easily seen in the dark. This was perhaps the most harrowing part of the journey. We were passing through white farms crisscrossed with cattle paths that would have made the going easier but had to be avoided for fear of leaving tracks, not only for terrs but also for mujibas. It was with some relief that we reached the Mupingi only to find that the river was mostly dry except for the odd pool of stagnant water that had been turned to mud by the hooves of cattle and game. This necessitated us having to dig into the sand to filter the water in order to fill our water bottles.

For the next nine hours we trudged through the darkness. By then the moon had disappeared which made for hard going through the thick bush and along the rocky river bank. It was a relief when occasionally the riparian bush gave way to open grassland, but this was no time to relax for it was in such places we passed close to habitation and progress slowed to a crawl. After passing such obstacles we moved at such a fast pace that we had to stop for a drink and a chance to catch our breaths.

At around 5 a.m. in the distance we heard the sound of dogs barking and the lowing of cattle. We knew that not far ahead was a kraal or a farm workers' compound so we looked for a suitable thicket to lay up for the day, leaving one of us on guard. As dawn approached and the light improved we found we were close to the edge of a clearing, so we spread out a bit and crawled deeper into a patch of thick bush that gave us more cover from the sun.

I was awakened by Chipo after only a short nap as he crawled to each of us in turn. He was on his stomach that warned us of imminent danger. I raised my head ever so slightly and peering through the bushes I could see a herd of cattle being chased by two irate native children and headed straight for us. There was no time to move. I looked over my shoulder at Jimmy who too, sensing the hopelessness of the situation, motioned with his hand for me to lie flat. I released the safety-catch as stones began to fly, one so close it missed me by inches. Suddenly the beasts must have sensed us because they veered off when only metres from us and crashed past, followed by the two small herders, one so close I could have stretched out a hand and tripped him.

It was time to move. I could see Jimmy was worried.

Neither of us could believe we hadn't been seen, though our two companions assured us that the two children were too young to be mujibas and if they had seen us, they would have screamed so loud the whole village would have been here by now to see what was going on. We moved anyway to a kopje about a kilometre away. As daylight gave way and the moon rose we moved away from the river to avoid the kraal and rejoined the route much further on. From there the closer, we moved towards the confluence the less hilly was the country but the denser it became. However, we had made such good time that we were able to stop a kilometre or two short of the confluence and brew up a cup of tea on our portable gas-stoves. It was close to 4 a.m. when we arrived at the Hunyani and there was enough light before dawn to cross the river just below the confluence and look for the ideal ambush site.

The spot Jimmy chose for the killing ground was in a shallow valley where a footpath led to the Angwa River and the Zambezi valley and was still used by the inhabitants of Masikas. It wound down a steep bank to the river's edge to a point where the rocks in the river had formed a natural causeway that even when the river was in flood provided a possible crossing. I knew the spot, Bob and I had crossed there often. The path leading from the river to our position rose up a steep bank and was overlooked by a rocky outcrop that afforded us the perfect cover. Anyone having crossed the river would have nowhere to hide. "It's perfect," whispered Jimmy.

We took up our positions in the outcrop, lying on our stomachs, rifle barrels resting on our packs, while each man agreed in whispers to his 'arc of fire'. Before giving our night-loc to JOC Darwin, Jimmy indicated to each of us what should be the direction of retreat should the tables be turned. There was not another word or movement as we settled down to wait with the night sounds and the almost inaudible and comforting hiss of the Small Means.

I always found the worse part of war to be the waiting. It gave me the time to think too much. Jimmy and Pfupi were so close I could hear their breathing above the sounds of the night. I might have seemed to them as they seemed to me, to be in control, but the truth was my mind was in turmoil. My thoughts turned from the present to the past and visions of my wife and children.

For a moment there was peace of mind as I imagined them walking up the rise from the river, then as suddenly, the vision faded and my memories soured, to be replaced by reality as guilt played games with my mind and hidden memories best forgotten flooded to the fore to wrack my wretched soul with spasms of self-reproach. Above all else was the fear, not of death itself, but of dying without knowing from whence I came. Names rattled my senses, ghosts from the past, haunting, laughing, weeping... Evelyn... Pat... Michael... Mother and Father. God, I missed them! So much I needed to know... not enough time and should I not survive mine will be a lonely passing. Just at that moment I felt more alone than I had ever felt before. Another world presented itself. I must have dozed, the luminous dial on my watch spelled out the approaching dawn. Beside me Jimmy stirred at the sound of a pair of francolins calling to each other across the killing ground, then he was woken by the raucous cry of a pair of grey loeries, quarrelling and flapping in the branches of a dead acacia with peeling bark that suddenly sprang to life with the golden tinge of dawn. For that splendid moment, the birds were the centre of my universe, a symbol of peace that even at that moment defied the hostile undercurrent.

The cries of the birds disturbed a duiker feeding within my arc of fire. It halted its feeding to sniff the morning air, its dainty body filling the peep sight of the FN. Instinctively my finger tightened on the trigger guard. Suddenly the buck was gone, and then from out of the corner of my eye its flapping ears betrayed its grey form half-hidden between two boulders worn smooth by countless floods and which, even as I stared, began to reflect the warm hues of sunrise and towered above the trembling creature like gilded monoliths. For just a moment, the buck seemed to lose its inherent fear and basked in the glory of its existence before it was spooked by a splash from the river. It leaped from my arc of fire and bounded up the slope towards us, then sensing our presence, veered off and disappeared into the shadows.

Then it came! A rude awakening as the sun broke free from the mantle of trees that lined the riverbank... a single explosion and the crackle of gunfire that echoed and re-echoed from across the river.

Inside his celluloid bubble, Charlie One had initiated the strike.

The explosion, we learned, was an RPG splintering the door of the headman's house and exploding, killing the headman and his wife. It was followed by the rattle of gunfire that killed a ZANLA Section Commander and his aide as they tried to escape through a window. There was a muted return of AK fire from a few gooks hidden amongst the huts as the sweep-line entered the village. This was followed by a spirited response as the soldiers fired tracers into thatch, setting the huts alight and illuminating the forms of villagers too terrified to flee. There was no fight in the villagers and a smattering of gooks hid their weapons and donned the garb of the peasants to seek refuge amongst the fleeing population. Here and there gooks more brave than the rest resisted the advance of the sweep-line. Two gooks holed up in a hut sprayed the advancing troops with an RPD. The fast chatter of lead from the light machinegun had the soldiers scattering for cover, until we heard the leader on the ground call for back up from Charlie One. The Alouette circled the hut once then opened fire, flattening the hut. The sweep-line meanwhile had moved on to the last row of huts as yet untouched by the carnage, leaving behind miserable groups of villagers that could do no more than look up at the hovering vulture. The vroom-vroom-vroom of its wings beating at the heat waves showered everything in a cloud of dust, adding to their misery.

From our position I could see the smoke rising above the treetops. The sound of gunfire had become more sporadic as the sweep-line reached the end of the village. Those that could had fled to the relative safety of the tree line along the river, leaving behind the remains of a village that had become quiet except for the wailing of women and the clack-clack-clack of the chopper hovering above the trees.

It was unreal lying in the shadows listening to the whisper of the Small Means. The voice of Charlie One sounded like a character in a radio drama directing operations in a thriller playing out hardly a kilometre from where I lay.

"Alpha Lima... Alpha Lima... Charlie One"

Jimmy snatched the transmitter and pressed the button in one smooth motion.

"Charlie One, come in, Over."

"Alpha Lima, charlie tangos and mujibas approaching your lock, possible charlie tangos have exchanged uniforms... take them all out... but do not cross the river. I say again do not cross the river. Copy?"

"Roger that, Charlie One."

Jimmy replaced the transmitter and reduced the volume to avoid the sound carrying to the enemy who maybe even then could be lurking in the reeds.

I glanced across to my left at Pfupi who was dead still, his face hidden beneath the brim of his bush hat, the barrel of his FN an extension of his torso like the proboscis of a giant insect. On my left Jimmy settled his body into the soil and wriggled sinuously like a burrowing lizard, leaving nothing to be seen from below but the black eye of his gun's muzzle pointing through the brush and could be mistaken, with mine, for two spots of shadow peering out over the killing ground.

The bloody waiting again! I could feel my trembling, imperceptible to all except me. It came from inside and I could see it through the movement of objects spied through the peep sight, objects in the sphere that spring to life. A shadow became a creeping being, a rock a face, snarling or smiling in the sunlight. I took a deep breath, suddenly the movements ceased and I was in control. I panned the barrel back and forth across my arc of fire, halted at a movement that quickened the senses. In slow motion with the tip of my finger I wiped too late at a bead of sweat that stung my eye. I prayed for a movement, anything, that would betray their presence.

It had already been agreed that we would hold our fire until the enemy had almost crossed the river. That way the bulk of them would be in the killing ground and those that sought to escape by fleeing either up or downstream would become targets for the other Call-signs hidden on the bank to the right and left of us. The K-Car was still circling above the thick bush about a kilometre across the river. We were able to ascertain from the voice of Charlie One, that the sweep-line that was now less than 500 yards from the river had been halted to avoid being fired upon by ourselves and the other sticks along the river that had formed stops to trap those that might flee back when the firing began.

The first to move into the killing ground was a boy carrying a billycan that he dipped into the river. I'll never forget the drops of water sparkling in the sun as he lifted the can to his mouth and when he was finished handed it to another boy. Soon there were at least a dozen children standing amongst the rocks unsure of what to do until somebody from the trees behind them called out and they began moving forward, climbing carefully over the rocks. I could hear clearly the splashes as they waded through the water. They were followed by unarmed mujibas dressed in green overalls.

The children were about halfway across when Chipo opened fire at what he took to be a gook carrying a rifle, but as it turned out was a mujiba carrying an axe. It was a match to a keg! Within seconds we were firing at anything that moved in our arc of fire. Oh Jesus! I lost my humanity! Thank God for the thunder of rifles, it helped block out the screams. I squeezed the trigger at anything that moved in the sight—something pink—I squeezed and it was gone! Oh Christ! What have we done?

Fortunately most that died that day were genuine mujibas, sent ahead with the few children as cannon fodder by twelve 'courageous' ZANLA guerrillas who escaped along the west bank of the Hunyani. Six 'charlie tangos' (communist terrs) were killed in the kraal, eight mujibas, two children and one unidentified female dressed in a pink polka-dot dress died on the river. Part of me died too.

Alpha Lima stayed on the next day carrying out a 360 of the area. Masikas was a mess, the bodies had been removed and most of the villagers were still wandering the bush, afraid to come in. Our patrol took us past the ruins of Bob's and Ina's house.

While the stick were resting, I wandered down to the Mupingi. Nothing had changed much: the wild fig had taken over its host... the path leading to Masikas was still worn... even the metal pump stand, though almost rusted away, was still evident on top of the long flat rock... the pool, though it was September, was still full of water.

Chapter Thirty-Six

To England and the Meeting of the Clan

August 1978

As the war increased in intensity, my experiences and those of others had left me with the realisation that it was not beyond the possibility that I may not survive.

It was this thought, coupled with the fact that I consider myself to be a bit of a coward, which prompted me with the help of Pat to take a more pragmatic approach to my search for family. I began by writing to different British government departments, including Social Welfare, The Fairbridge Society, Warren Farm School, and others I have forgotten. I even wrote to an address that I dreamed of (I don't know how else it came to mind) that had been there since childhood:

                112 Eldred Avenue, Woodingdean, Brighton, Sussex

I got a reply but nobody knew my name. It's one of those undecipherable mysteries.

In each case my efforts drew a blank. Disillusioned and desperate we took the bull by the horns and made a decision to take a trip to England, and once there attempt to retrace my life. But in order to do so, I required a birth certificate to acquire a passport.

Fortunately my friend Maurice, of Whisky Hotel fame, was off on a trip to England and so armed with my meagre information, he obtained my birth certificate from Somerset House. What a day that was when he presented me with it, for now I had the name of my parents and it wasn't long before I had my passport.

Obtaining a passport for Pat presented its own set of problems however, because there was the distinct possibility that our marriage would not be recognised by the British if the Certificate of Marriage had been signed by an appointee of the UDI government rather than an appointee of the British. It turned out we were lucky, for the ceremony had indeed been presided over by the latter. Within a matter of days Pat received her passport, I purchased the air-tickets well in advance and we were all set to go.

As I have mentioned before and therefore at the risk of repeating myself I say again that life is filled with 'meanwhiles' that tend to overlap and therefore upset the chronological turn of events.

For example, somebody meanwhile, a few months earlier had suggested I write to the National Insurance in the search for my father. I'd forgotten all about that until I received a letter from them informing me that they had come across a person who fitted the description I had obtained from my birth certificate. However, they were not at liberty to disclose the address but if I were to write a short note they would ensure it was delivered. At a loss as to what to say, I kept that letter aside for some time then almost as an afterthought, I wrote down my flight number and the time of arrival, posted the letter, and forgot all about it.

I can't remember the exact day we flew, but it was the day before that the postman pitched up on his bicycle bearing a telegram. I was in the garden when I heard Pat scream. I rushed into the house. She was waving the telegram that read quite simply:

MEET YOU AT HEATHROW. LOVE DAD

I didn't sleep much on the flight going over, I rehearsed over and over in my mind what I wanted to say but nothing seemed to make sense. What does a 39-year-old say to a father he hasn't seen before? If only I'd been able to give him a face!

I fell asleep at one stage and dreamed the plane was going down and woke from a nightmare, fighting with Pat as she struggled to subdue me as I threw a cushion across the aisle. While Pat tried to explain my actions to an irate passenger, I remember distinctly having the presence of mind to look surprised and innocent. My nightmare must have had an effect however, because as the plane touched down I remember very well the nervousness that overcame me as I prepared myself for the meeting with my father.

It was my 10-year-old daughter who saw him first amongst the crowd in the passenger hall. She led me by the hand to a little old man with a hat on and a placard around his neck that bore my name. It struck me then how unalike we were and how lonely he looked in the crowd.

He didn't recognise me any more than I did him! We were the proof needed to disprove the theory that an invisible bond and human instinct were all that was needed for a father to recognise his son and vice versa. Had he had a smile on his face or looked less bored, perhaps that might have sparked some form of mutual recognition. But he didn't, so it was more from a sense of duty than anything else that, after it was confirmed by word of mouth that it was indeed him, I acted out the scene I had always dreamed of and flung my arms around him. That was a mistake for there was no reaction from him other than an embarrassed clearing of the throat and a pulling away before he stuck out his hand and murmured "Hello, son." How more fitting, I thought afterwards, would it have been for me to have simply stuck out my hand—like Stanley did when meeting Livingstone—and said, "Mr Bowley I presume."

His wife Rose and he were 'birds of a feather'. I didn't have the urge to hug her, neither she me, so I shook her hand which was like grasping a dead fish.

She was his third wife and I avoided her as much as possible when I learned later that she had been sleeping with my father while his second wife was ill on her deathbed. I didn't feel the least bit sorry for her either, and lost even more respect for my father when I learned from my sister Evelyn that it was his wife who had insisted Father leave us in Warren Farm after he returned to England, rather than bring us home to share her house with her two Down's Syndrome children. But hang on! I'm drifting off-course into the future when I should be sticking to the present, to describe what should have been a momentous occasion, but instead was reduced to a meal at a local hotel (that I paid for) during which Father remained dumb and Rose took the floor. After being questioned by Pat, she proceeded to recount the history of my brothers and sisters who were still only vague memories to me.

Evelyn, she told us, was married with one child and lived in Yorkshire, while Pat, my half-sister, (who Rose said she had never set eyes on) lived (she was told by her husband) only a few miles from them in a suburb of Brighton. She seemed hesitant when I asked about Michael and left it to my Dad to tell me he had been sent to Australia. It wasn't a happy meal as it should have been. In fact, as I recall, it was like eating with strangers— which come to think of it, they were.

Meanwhile, after Pat and I had decided to make this sabbatical in search of my family, we had thought it would take a long time so we had hired a cottage for six weeks on the south coast in a beautiful little village called Selsey Bill. It proved to be a good move in hindsight because we didn't have to stay with Dad and Rose and her two spoilt Corgis.

Now it is said that even in the worst of us there is some good, and this proved to be the case, for despite all the bad things I was to learn about my father, there was a side to him that I was convinced none had ever seen or acknowledged and that was his love for his profession as a sign-writer. I sensed his pride as he drove me around Burgess Hill and Brighton and pointed out his handiwork.

In a cupboard in his garden shed were dozens of unframed canvasses he had painted over the years, including one that I fell in love with, which he framed and gave to me as a present. It became the seed that produced my years as a part-time painter of raptors that, while possibly not achieving my father's standards, were proof that I had inherited at least a portion of his artistic talent. What a contrast it was to meet Pat, my half-sister. For some reason, Dad seemed reluctant at first to take me to see her. In fact, it was Rose who persuaded him to take me to see her. Imagine my surprise when, instead of taking me to her door as I expected he would, he dropped me off in the middle of a road crammed with terraced houses and pointed to an entrance across the street.

I remember knocking on the door and hearing voices, children's voices, before the door was opened and there stood Pat with two children hanging onto her jeans: "Can I help you?" she asked.

"Yes please," I answered, still unsure if in truth it was her, "Is your name Pat?"

"Yes, why?"

"I'm your brother George from Rhodesia," I said, still unsure, "and this is my wife Pat and my daughter Michelle."

"Good God!" she cried, "then you'd better come in!" She led us through to a tiny lounge with a bay window that looked out over the street. I still remember that the curtains were drawn and across the street I could see Dad sitting in his car.

Within a few minutes all the awkwardness and formality fell away as I sat beside her on the settee and took her hand. Suddenly she did the strangest thing. She began to cry, not loud, just a gentle sobbing, and I found myself doing the same.

I can't remember how long we were together that first time. We were both so emotional and confused that I doubt whether she does either. To add to the confusion, she admitted to having met Evelyn fleetingly years before when her children were babies, and was told then that she had brothers and that in fact she was a half-sister.

"It was all so confusing," she said, "because my mother (her adoptive mother) has never spoken of my biological parents, except to say my mother had died and my father had deserted me." This, in essence, was correct. "It's just such a pity" she said, "that after all these years my sister and I have never made contact. In fact if we were to meet tomorrow, I don't think I would recognise her."

To add to the uncertainty, just as I was leaving she grabbed my arm as I stepped from her doorway and pointed to my father, sitting in his purple car. "It that your father?" she asked.

"Yes, do you want to meet him?"

"No," she said, "but I've seen him often."

"Where?" I asked.

"Right there where he is now. I always thought he was a dirty old man staring at me. Now why on earth would he do that?"

"I don't know," I replied, "shall I ask him?"

"No," she said, "at least I know who he is, so just leave it."

I was tempted, when I got back in the car, to question him about his odd behaviour, but I didn't want to embarrass him. I knew inside it had something to do with my mother.

I didn't get the chance to meet Pat's adoptive mother that trip but I did a year later while on a return trip—and what a nice woman she was. I guessed her to be in her late fifties, but I was and still am a poor judge of age, especially of a lady! She described me to my sister as 'your bronzed and handsome young brother'. I liked her, not so much for her flattery but because she was so refreshingly intelligent, kind, and sensitive to the occasion. While Pat made tea in the neat and compact kitchen of her tiny council house, she and I sat making small talk as we got to know each other. The living room was crammed with bookcases and a showcase filled with delicate china and glass ornaments. Everything and everywhere spelt 'Woman'. Even a group of photographs standing on a bookcase that was so close I could have reached out and touched the pictures, were of women, except for one. It was a photo portrait of a young man in uniform who, as it turned out, was her fiancé, who was killed when the war had barely begun.

She told me all of the little she knew of my family and its history leading up to Pat's internment in Warren Farm. I was relieved as well as enlightened to listen to her first-hand accounts of the hardships and difficulties that she and every other woman went through during the war. Without mentioning her by name, I knew somehow that my mother was included in her observations and yet, though I was to learn later that mother had possibly been a prostitute, at this time Pat's mother was kind and sensitive enough not to even hint at that possibility.

I asked her if she knew my father. She nodded her head but shrugged her shoulders in a noncommittal way, the way I did if I wished not to pursue a subject. She then made it even more obvious by changing the subject to 'me'. So I talked about me, my memories and my life in general.

I would have purposely avoided politics and the war if she hadn't drawn me into the subject herself. She surprised me by declaring an admiration for Rhodesians in general and Ian Smith the man, his exploits as a fighter pilot, his injuries, and his time in the resistance. She even agreed, though not entirely, with my perceptions garnered after my previous and current trip to England, that had me believing that the country was split over Rhodesia's UDI into two simple factions—those who backed the move and those who didn't.

To enforce my views, I pointed out to her the scores of advertisements that appeared in upper-class magazines such as The Tatler, The Lady, Country Life and so on, that offered in sympathy, positions of employment expressly to Rhodesians.

These adverts, combined with letters of support published in the Conservative-backed newspapers, had led me to the conclusion that those that supported UDI and a multiracial government were the Upper Class and a section of the Middle Class that still dreamed of the survival of a mighty and glorious, but sadly almost defunct Empire. It was at this point in our discussion that she disagreed with me, even accused me of taking a defeatist attitude. "It's not over yet," she said, "there may still be an agreement should Margaret Thatcher come to power next year."

But she did agree entirely with my opinion of those with the opposing view, when I described them, rather heatedly, as a bunch of dishonest and appeasing politicians, hypocritical churchmen, ignorant trade unionists, woolly-brained students, and immigrants. All of them, bar the latter, suffered in my opinion from a guilt complex that stemmed from the realisation that they, too, were direct descendants of a cruel power that had once ruled half the world.

It had been like 'coming home', despite the 30 years I had been away. I loved England with a passion. Her beauty cured me of bitter hatreds and bitter ignorance. Even the eyes, over-tired from gazing against the sun, were rested in the grey coolness of Autumn. Pat, my wife, loved England most for its surpassing history and recognising this, on the long drive to Yorkshire, we stopped off at every museum and every church on the way as well as the graveyards to look over gravestones in a search for those with the earliest dates.

I met my sister Evelyn at last, in her spacious house in the suburb of a town called Northallerton in the North Yorkshire dales. She had lived in Yorkshire off and on for most of her life after she had been evacuated from Warren Farm to several homes where, in her words, "I didn't fit in," Then, in 1944 she was placed in the foster care of two sisters who lived in the village of Hutton-Le-Hole on the Yorkshire downs, not far from Northallerton.

"They were the happiest years of my life," she told me that evening after everybody had gone to bed and we sat up remembering the past, "and would have remained so had it not been for a stranger, our father, who in 1946 removed me from the family I had grown to love. And now began the worst years of my life, years of persecution and cruelty. I became a slave in his house; a victim to his blind rage and revenge and all because I looked so much like my mother. Then one day in a rage he tried to throttle me and would have done so if it hadn't been for his wife who pulled him away. That same day, at the age of fifteen I left home and never again have I set eyes on our father."

It was clear her loathing ran deep and absolute, and nothing I said then or in the future would assuage that hatred. My father's actions had been like a cancer, for not only had it unsettled Evelyn's mind, but was I believe responsible for her attitude towards our half-sister Pat who she had met about ten years previously while on a holiday in Sussex with her daughter Jane. Unlike Pat, who I had sensed was genuinely sorry that nothing had come of the meeting, Evelyn on the other hand, appeared unconcerned which saddened me considering all that had gone before.

Strange and sad, isn't it, how some things turn out? For years I had prayed for the day when I would find my family and we would be together again. Indeed, my prayers had been answered but not fulfilled, for Michael was still the forgotten one and except for me, the family as a whole were as divided as they had ever been.

But it was Evelyn who fitted what we thought was the last piece of the jigsaw in place, and it was she, too, who unearthed the secret that will appear in my epilogue.

The last two days of our stay with Evelyn and Mick were spent travelling around the dales and I understood Evelyn's love for them, for in all our travels in my country there was nothing to surpass their wild beauty.

We drove out to Hutton-Le-Hole. It was magic in its setting and beckoned with its rustic charm, but try as I might to persuade Evelyn to drive into the village, she declined to show us the house that had been her home and the school where she had shown such promise—and I think I know why.

She drove us instead through the emerald hills to 'her' spot on the narrow winding road. We looked down at the sunlight flowing through the valley, magnifying and mellowing the stone walls that ran across the fields and pastures in full curves. I marvelled at those hand-built walls and imagined the centuries of work that had gone into their construction. Millions of fragments from the limestone hills, each piece handled and fitted in its place, and inside the borders of stone stood farmhouses built with the same stone. On the hillside above them were neat stone sheds where cows were milked and hay was stored for the harsh winters. I looked at all these things and dreaded leaving them.

Before we said our goodbyes, Evelyn gave me a poem she had written for our father but was never posted. These words describe her life with him better than I ever could:

FATHER

My earliest childhood memories are difficult to re-call,
Like sketches played out on a cloudy stage, no reality at all.
A lady crying upon the stairs, I was told 'she is your mother',
Crying as though her heart would break, and by her side my brother.

Going to the shop with sixpence in my hand and never getting there,

Hit by a car and sat on the lap of a lady dressed in fur,
Being held down tight on a hospital bed,
While nurses stitched the gash in my head.

Big brass bed in a cold bare room,
In which I slept with my three brothers
And our mother in the gloom.

Things hadn't always been that way, I can't remember back that far.
We had, it is said, a smart little house, before you went to war.
When you came home the house was sold, mum was dead,
And your children flown.

What happened to our mother, Dad? No kiss before we parted,
No goodbyes, her children gone, leaving her broken hearted.
Did she ever have a say in our future, as your wife?
Or did you take it on yourself to shape our future life?

I later found that she had died when I was nine years old,
But where she had been, what happened to her, I was never told.
Did anybody mourn her, or shed a quiet tear?
How sad she had a family, but none of them were there.

We were put in a children's home, out of sight and out of mind,
Leaving you free to do as you pleased, unfettered, you left us behind.
All that we owned when they took us away were spongebag, toothbrush and flannel, and a gas mask each to

protect us should the Germans
Come over the channel.

The boys all stayed in the home, but I was moved from place to place,
To families who didn't want another child, but must as they had the space.
You didn't know of the things they did, but would you have cared?
Punishment seemed a way of life just because I was there.

Eventually though, I had some luck, when as an evacuee of seven,
A village high up on the Yorkshire moors became my second heaven.
A welfare officer took me there and I stayed for three whole years,
With two sisters who gave me unlimited love, happiness and laughter, no tears.

When the war ended, you arrived on the scene, though I didn't know who you were.
I had always thought I was an orphan, so it came as a shock to know you were there.
Why all those years was I kept in the dark, why was I never told?
All those lonely battles fought till I was eight years old.

My brothers were never talked about, their whereabouts I never knew,
Michael the youngest you left in the home,
But what of the other two?
You sent them to a foreign land.

You couldn't wait to wave them goodbye,
Now on somebody else they would always rely.
Once again you had used all your guile,
To get rid of those who might cramp your style.

It cost you a little money to send them away,
That must have hurt, but you did it anyway,
And hoped you would never see either again.
In your eyes you were guiltless and felt no pain.

For four years I lived at home with you,
Michael stayed in the home, and when birthdays were due
I took him a present, you never did go.
How could you treat your youngest child so?

So we were all strangers, no family togetherness.
You kept us apart with your own cruel selfishness.
With the boys dealt thus, it left me alone,
For what you had planned needed me on my own.

Most of my childhood had gone when you came
Into my life and made your legal claim.
You don't have a mother you told me, she's dead,
But think yourself lucky, you've a step-mum instead.

I had parents at last, I felt so warm inside.
I would now know the love, so long denied.
My own mum and dad. A family at last.
Now I could forget my unhappy past.

But I didn't know that revenge was your aim,
That having me home was all part of a game.
You didn't wait long though, your plans to relate,
When in terms black-and-white you unfolded my fate.

You'll keep your mouth closed lest we speak to you,
And tell nobody else what I say or do.
The rules won't be broken, because if that's so,
There are things I can do and people I know.

You are your mother's daughter and I don't forgive,
Her wrongs you will pay for as long as you live.
You'll pay the price and nobody tell,
And never forget I can make your life hell.

You might as well have used your fists,
For those words hurt me so.
The effect was just as devastating,
Though of course the marks didn't show.

But that was only the start of things.
So much misery, cruelty and strife,
And when that didn't satisfy,
You tried to take my life.

How could you look into the eyes of your child,
The one you abused, detested and defiled?
With eyes full of hatred and words so unkind,
I couldn't imagine what went on in your mind.

I had no comprehension of the things you would do,
Of the rules you would make, how you'd hate me so.
What on earth did I do to cause all that bother,
When the only sin was to look like my mother.

No speaking allowed unless spoken to,
No mixing with guests, the kitchen's for you.
No trips or holidays with us will you share,

You are too ugly, we don't want you there.

You'll do all the housework, you're old enough now.
Her skin can't take cleaners or soap as you know.
You will wash on Mondays straight after school,
The work will come first and I don't bend the rule.

Stopping school sports was a cruel thing to do.
You were a champion runner and footballer too.
You should have been proud of me and understood,
It needs lots of practice to make anyone good.

You just couldn't bear to see me do well
At anything; you wanted me under your spell.
You succeeded in what you set out to do.
You broke my spirit, I'll give credit to you.

I was so pleased when I passed the 11-plus,
You'd promised me a bike if I passed,
But it didn't materialise, another promise not kept.
I was so disappointed but I never wept.

For tears fanned the flames of your temper, and then
I knew what the outcome would be once again.
Thrown into the kitchen where no one could hear,
I would know once again heartbreak, terror and fear.

Was it pure hatred I read in your eyes?
When you screamed and heaved, and pulled on the tie.
Round my neck, till I thought I was going to die.
He's my father, why's he doing this, why, tell me why?

How could you possibly get pleasure at all,
From calling me names and banging my head on the wall?

You'll end up in the gutter you'd constantly say,
Just like your mother, she ended that way.

I forgive my stepmother, for she saved my life,
She didn't have to like me, being his wife,
But she agreed I was ugly and refused to take me out,
And that had an effect on my life without a doubt.

You took away my confidence and tore it into shreds,
And left me full of doubt and fear, and self-consciousness instead.
Although through life I've done my best to show a brave façade,
I may have fooled the world at large, but it's only a charade.

Father, you terrified me when you were still alive,
Now you are dead, I hate and loathe you, detest you and despise.
Even at this moment though I am sixty-three,
I still remember the smell of fear when you were close to me.

And now the big decision, do I actually put into print
Those secrets I've kept hidden, or merely give a hint?
How I used to watch your shadow beneath my bedroom door.
No, they stay locked up inside me and I shall say no more.

I had then to make my mind up, what my job in life would be.
I want to work with children and take a suitable degree.
But you just wouldn't hear of it and refused to back my dream.
You could have broken it gently, you didn't have to scream.

Get yourself down to the Labour Exchange, a job as a
nanny will do,
You can look after children and do the work, that's good
enough for you.
I found one down in Dorset, and you actually smiled at
me,
But only because it was far from home, and you would be
free of me.

You never wrote or came to see,
For you had washed your hands of me.
I was told that when I came away,
You then had Michael home to stay.

He really must have wondered why
He was wanted home, but by and by,
He found the reason, he would be
Doing the work instead of me.

It didn't last long though, he didn't stay.
To Australia he went, couldn't be further away.
So how did you manage with no skivvy around?
She wouldn't work. Was a 'daily' found?

I suppose she had to do the work.
All the jobs she had chosen to shirk,
Because of course you wouldn't pay for help.
That never was your way.

My work was hard, the hours long,
The money poor in comparison.
But at least I had food and warmth and a bed,
And a decent roof above my head.

> But I did my best to do everything right,
> And worked hard for my money, from morning till night.
> I still felt your presence enveloping me,
> But from physical contact I was now FREE.

I was sad to leave England and the family I had been deprived of for so long. But at least it had been a reunification of sorts and I was able to realise that my memories had not been a figment of the imagination. How fulfilling it would have been, if I had through my presence been able to bring the family together. Instead, I left behind a brother—still missing—and a family in tatters.

Chapter Thirty-Seven

Towards The End 1979

The situation in Rhodesia was dire. There was talk of an invasion by ZIPRA using conventional weapons, the result of which saw the Security Forces visit Lusaka again, and again and again, and each time the chance of a settlement drifted further and further away. Elections were held to form a new acceptable government. The hopes of the nation rested in the hands of Bishop Muzorewa. He won, and hopes soared when as Prime Minister-designate he appealed to the United States for recognition as the bush war entered its final conventional stage.

Elections were held and a black dominated government was formed. Yet still the British remained intransigent.

European men aged 50-59 were called up for duties in the urban areas while Africans in the 18-25 age group became liable for call-up, followed by African apprentices.

In a last-ditch attempt to thwart the invasion of Zimbabwe (Rhodesia) from Zambia, the security forces crossed the border and destroyed ten major bridges. In Mozambique, our army joined forces with the MNR (Mozambique National Resistance) in an attempt to overthrow Frelimo. But it was all too little, too late.

To prove conclusively the futility, sorrow, and pain of war, my former employer of Farraline days, Mr Palmer and his wife were gunned down in their farmhouse a few months before peace was declared. She, a well-known champion of the African cause, died instantly. He survived a wound in the throat but died anyway, it is said, from a broken heart.

I returned alone the following year to England to seek

employment, and at the same time salt away my savings in the Northern Rock Building Society. It was heartening to see my family again, but the job-hunting proved fruitless. I must confess that my heart wasn't really in it because I missed my family too much. Perhaps if Pat had accompanied me on that trip it might have turned out differently.

I returned as Mugabe's Red Brigade ran amok in Matabeleland, slaughtering thousands of N'debele tribes people. Mugabe, now the elected Prime Minister, had feared they might revolt under the leadership of Joshua Nkomo.

I stuck it out, like a fool, for another two years as my friends and family deserted 'the sinking ship'. I waited in the hope that the situation might change. But it didn't and it grew steadily worse as Mugabe continued with a witch-hunt, despite his assurances made in his sickeningly duplicitous acceptance speech.

A work colleague, who back in the war years had perfected a mine-detecting robot that was to be used to detect and destroy mines in a civilian environment, was held and questioned for weeks. He was subsequently forced to leave the country. Another close friend of the family employed by Posts and Telecommunications, had his house searched and was found to be in possession of old maps and documents relating to the bush war. He narrowly escaped a life sentence in Chikarubi prison.

It was incidents like this that unsettled me and hastened my decision to 'take the gap'.

The opportunity came when my friend Ugo, having heard of my predicament, offered me employment in a glass-bottle factory he had recently commissioned in Johannesburg. Within a matter of days I accepted the position, and a month later on the 8th June 1983 we said goodbye to what for us had been 'God's own country'.

Chapter Thirty-Eight

South Africa

The first year in South Africa was indisputably the worst of my life. Not only was I out of my depth in the workplace and with those I worked with, I suffered immensely from homesickness.

In fact, it was so bad that on more than one occasion I nearly packed my bags. I would indeed have done so if it hadn't been for my wife's determination, and Ugo's placating influence when it came to dealing with a bunch of UK expatriates who were intent on having me removed and replaced by one of their kind. God! We even had to live amongst them in a huge block of flats named Jenn Place. Except for a few, what a bunch of savages they were, with nothing better to do than beat each other up, sleep with each others' wives, and hold wild parties to all hours while I was trying to get some sleep between shifts.

To this day, I don't know how I lasted the two years before the seeds of the mind fell and I explored and devised a plan that would enrich not only the company but myself as well. I worried because it had to pass Ugo's scrutiny first, but I needn't have, because just as I was about to present it Ugo left the factory. His replacement, realising its potential, accepted it!

Shortly after Ugo left, I left too, and started out on my own as Bowley Resorts— official re-sorter to Metal Box Glass. I was tasked with the re-sorting of a vast stock of bottles that had been condemned during the commissioning of the factory. Enough, as it turned out, to last for five full years during which fortune and a fair amount of hard work made it possible for us to retreat to East London on the east coast of South Africa, ostensibly to semi-retire.

But sometimes life has other plans, and rather than sit

at home or fish all day in the lagoon below my house, we purchased and ran a little country stall that ended up akin to a mini-supermarket. For close on two years we worked our butts off, seven days a week, until I had had enough of life at the coast.

Although sad to turn my back on the sea, we sold up and returned to what we thought would be a more quiet and sedate life on a small farm on the outskirts of a small bushveld town called Brits. The only good thing that happened there, besides the most pleasant of pastimes raising calves and a flock of sheep, was a visit from my sister Pat who thought our place was heaven. It was for a while, until she returned home and everything changed overnight.

Our sheep died of a disease called Heart Water, and a thousand broilers we had purchased as an investment died very quickly of Newcastle Disease. The final straw happened when our borehole pumps (both of them) were pulled up and stolen overnight, leaving us without water until I could have them replaced.

To put it mildly, we'd had enough! We returned full-circle to the house we had built for us two years after emigrating to South Africa and which we'd left in the care of tenants 14 years previously. So in a suburb on the East Rand—east of Joburg, I began to write this book.

EPILOGUE

Should you read to the end of this book perhaps you will ask, as many do I think, "And what happened next?" As briefly as I can, I will try to tell you.

You have read as much as I wish to tell of my life and the events leading up to and after the discovery of my family, but quite by accident and quite unintentionally, what follows must surely be one of the highlights of my story.

It began one afternoon with a phone call from England. A very excited Evelyn told me to sit down, before she told me of the discovery she had made of a brother nobody knew we had. She had found him, she said, while trying to trace possible relatives through our mother's maiden name, and had come across a Tony Brockbank. She had met him and without any doubt could confirm he was indeed our blood brother!

It took a while for it to sink in, and even longer for me to pluck up the courage to write to him. I started very hesitantly, but no sooner had I begun to write that I couldn't stop. I didn't measure the words, I wrote them down without thinking as fast as I could until I had filled three pages. Without re-reading it, I posted the letter. I received a reply and after the first few paragraphs I knew for sure it wasn't a dream. We wrote to each other at least once a week for a year and exchanged photographs that were proof perfect of brotherhood. In fact, if it hadn't been for our six-year age difference we could have passed as twins.

With each letter came the desire to meet and I promised him we would before the year was out. We did, through the kindness of family.

Our meeting took place at the door of his house. The media were there to capture the moment, but I didn't even notice them as we hugged and cried like children. I felt as if I had known him all my life!

Later the tears flowed again during an interview with the BBC. Memories appeared in print and were serialised on radio. It was a very emotional time that drew more on Tony's reserves than mine, for unbeknown to me, he and his wife Margaret had both been ill for some time. She had a lung disease, and Tony had prostate cancer that had been in remission for years but had now returned.

However, such was his resilience that it didn't stop him from driving us around to meet his family. They included his foster sister Joyce, a warm loving person, and a son Adrian who for one reason or another hadn't spoken to his father for ten years. It had something to do with Adrian's wife apparently, but whatever it was didn't matter, it was a time of miracles. We sat down, I started a conversation, and soon they were chatting the hind legs off a donkey. When we got home and I told Margaret, she said, "It's bloody impossible!" but sure enough, Adrian went around to her the next day and apologised. Since then I am told, despite the distance he has to travel, he visits at least once a week.

You know, Tony was quite amazing, he never lost his rag! I went with him to the hospital so he could have a new bag fitted to catch his urine and after having waited for hours, the nurse fitted the wrong size bag that leaked so much we were house bound for the next day or two. I was angry—really angry—but he never complained and made me promise on our way back to have it refitted, not to stir it with the staff at the hospital, and even made excuses for them. He never let me think his affliction was getting him down, but I knew it was. We visited him one morning and he was still in bed. Margaret whispered to me that she had found him downstairs, sobbing with pain. Then, would you believe it, that same afternoon despite our protestations he drove us to Gravetye Manor, a huge and grand private hotel where once he had plied his trade as a cabinetmaker. There were few homes or hotels around East Grinstead that didn't carry his trademark.

There were days, of course, when Tony and Margaret needed their rest, days when instead Pat and I both trod the paths of my childhood.

Warren Farm had been torn down in the early sixties to be replaced by the Nuffield Hospital, but wonder of wonders, the flint stone walls were still there! As I stood in their shadow, fighting back the tears that seemed to come without warning, I pointed out the section where the green railings had once stood and the V of the sea between the hills.

Later that same day we visited St Wulfrans Church. It hadn't changed in the slightest, and because of that I was able to sit in the same spot that had been mine a lifetime ago. Together we stood amongst the gravestones, before I was left to ponder and remember as I climbed the same stile and sat for a while to look over Happy Valley and a path that was being used at that moment by people exercising their dogs. I wondered if it was the selfsame path that had once led to the doors of Warren Farm. It was strange—as I stepped down from the stile, I stopped for a moment and imagined I heard the voice of my friend Irene. But it wasn't, it was Pat calling to me from the car.

A day or two before we were due to fly home, Tony organised a dinner at a local restaurant to which all of his family were invited. I met and said goodbye to each and every one of them. I could not believe that the family, who I had once believed numbered perhaps a dozen, that night numbered 32!

It was a year before I saw Tony again but then it wasn't a time for rejoicing. Over the year his condition had deteriorated. One day the news was good, the next bad, and while Tony was fighting the odds something else was happening.

In Australia, their Prime Minister had apologised to the surviving child migrants for the misrepresentation and abuse they had suffered. The UK government had been strangely silent until then but there was growing pressure for an 'apology' after stories of abuse resurfaced in the media. That encouraged Gordon Brown, the British Prime Minister, to set a date of February 24, 2010 for a formal apology to be issued.

While this was going on there was somebody else who had witnessed our meeting and who then took up the cudgels on my behalf—the Reverend John Watson. John's brother Ronny and Grace (Ronny's wife) between them had donated the fares for the reunion. John fought tenaciously and tirelessly in his inimitable way with the Department of Health (UK) that controlled the affairs of migrants, and made them aware of my brother's ailing health. In particular, the Secretary of State for Health, Andy Burnham showed compassion a year later, by granting the airfare that enabled me to be at Tony's beside before he fell into a coma and died on the 13th February 2010.

His death coincided with the death of my half-sister Pat the month before in Spain of a brain tumour. The youngest and the eldest gone in the space of a month! So I rushed down to Brighton to be with Kerry and Darryl, her children, and spent the weekend with them. We visited the crematorium on the Sunday and I saw where they had spread Pat's ashes beside a rose bed. Some of them were still evident so I scooped them up and held them in my hand, then spread them again and wept.

When I got back to the house, there was an invitation from Andy Burnham requesting my attendance at the Official Apology to be held in the Palace of Westminster on the 24th— a little more than a week from then. It was just too much, I couldn't handle it, so I declined.

But that all changed when Evelyn phoned to say she was going to spend a week with us to help us get over our grief. Despite the circumstances, it became a week of joy when I really got to know her and some of the secrets of our troubled past—they will remain a secret!

Just before Evelyn left, I received a call from Dame Margaret Humphreys of Empty Cradles, a champion of the Child Migrant cause. Having commiserated with me over Tony's death she persuaded me, very gently, that it would benefit my circumstances to attend the Apology as a representative of the Rhodesian children.

The night before the ceremony, I slept in a hotel in London that was also occupied by a contingent of the children of migrants who had been sent to Canada. I was touched when the head of the party presented me with a badge of the Canadian Migrant Society.

I was the only one out of the 70-odd people who attended the Apology that was from Rhodesia. The rest, bar a few from New Zealand, were from Australia.

It was a very moving ceremony with few dry eyes when Gordon Brown, Margaret Humphreys, and the head of the Australian Child Migrant Society gave their speeches. It was only after the cocktail party that followed when I had a chance to mingle and meet others, that it was brought home to me just what the Apology signified. I spoke to two fellow migrants about my age. One of them was carrying a framed photograph of the mother he had never known, the other was holding a moth-eaten teddy bear that he told me he had carried with him on the ship from England in 1947. When I think back at those two old men, I can't help thinking, "There, but for the grace of God, go I!"

 George Bowley's was born in 1939 on the eve of the Second world war. When he was five years old, his mother was imprisoned for petty theft and he and his four siblings were sent to an institution for orphaned and destitute children. In March 1948 George and his brother became victims of the British policy to encourage child migration to the colonies and became wards of the Fairbridge Society on a journey to Southern Rhodesia. There followed eight years of unimaginable excitement and abject cruelty.

At the age of sixteen, armed with a G.C.E, he was considered suitable to help fulfill the Fairbridge vision. For nearly ten years he was passed from farmer to farmer to do with as they pleased. For a pittance he weathered a storm of hard slogging, abuse, racism, brutality and deceit.

His luck changed when he found love in 1967 and married the woman of his dreams, turned his back on the soil and entered the Corporate world. After two years of study and hard work he became manager of the pulp plant. Alas the euphoric life was to be short lived as the bush war intensified and he became embroiled in a conflict he believed was a lost cause. As the situation grew worse, he like many of his fellow migrants had that yearning for identity and one day after having survived an ambush, memories flooded back. This brush with death was a catalyst that led him that led him on a search for the family of his memories and the father he had never known.

In 2010 George was invited to represent the Rhodesian migrants at the Palace of Westminster to receive an apology given by the Prime Minister Gordon Brown. There were migrants from Australia, Canada and New Zealand.

George has one daughter, a step-daughter and step-son. He lives with his wife and daughter in Johannesburg. South Africa.

Available in English, Paperback, Kindle, Kobo and PDF formats

See our website: www.penrose-publishing.co.uk

See also books from our other authors:
Grace Harding
Devon Volkel
JR Smith
Aaron Smith
Les Bill Gates
David Palmer
Joshua Mercott
Susan Mehra
Richard Lyon

www.ingramcontent.com/pod-product-compliance
Lightning Source LLC
LaVergne TN
LVHW051110080426
835510LV00018B/1976